Horror Films
Current Research on Audience Preferences and Reactions

edited by

James B. Weaver, III
Auburn University

Ron Tamborini
Michigan State University

Routledge
Taylor & Francis Group

NEW YORK AND LONDON

First Published by

Lawrence Erlbaum Associates, Inc., Publishers
10 Industrial Avenue
Mahwah, New Jersey 07430

Transferred to Digital Printing 2009 by Routledge
270 Madison Ave, New York NY 10016
2 Park Square, Milton Park, Abingdon, Oxon, OX14 4RN

cover design by Gail Silverman

Library of Congress Cataloging-in-Publication Data

Horror Films : current research on audience preferences and reactions
    / edited by James B. Weaver, III & Ron Tamborini
            p.   cm.
        Includes bibliographical references and index.
        ISBN 0-8058-1173-7 (c : alk. paper). — ISBN 0-8058-1174-5 (p.
    : alk. paper)
        1. Horror films—History and criticism. I. Weaver, James B. II.
    Tamborini, Ronald C., 1952– .
    PN1995.9.H6H72 1995
    791.43'616—dc20   95-19040
                                                              CIP

Publisher's Note
The publisher has gone to great lengths to ensure the quality of this
reprint but points out that some imperfections in the original may be apparent.

Contents

Contributors

Joanne Cantor, Center for Communication Research, University of Wisconsin-Madison, Madison, WI 53706

Rhonda Gibson, College of Communication, University of Alabama, Tuscaloosa, AL 35487-0172

Douglas Gomery, College of Journalism, University of Maryland, College Park, MD 20742-7111

Patricia A. Lawrence, Department of Communication, University of Texas-at El Paso, El Paso, TX 79968-0550

Fred Molitor, Sacramento AIDS Foundation, Sacramento, CA 95814

Mary Beth Oliver, Department of Communication Studies, Virginia Polytechnic Institute and State University, Blacksburg, VA 24061-7163

Philip Palmgreen, Department of Communication, University of Kentucky, Lexington, KY 40506-0045

Barry Sapolsky, Department of Communication, Florida State University, Tallahasee, FL 32306-2064

Glenn Sparks, Department of Communication, Purdue University, West Lafayette, IN 47907

Ron Tamborini, Department of Communication, Michigan State University, East Lansing, MI 48824-1212

James B. Weaver, III, Department of Communication, Auburn University, Auburn, AL 36849-5211

Dolf Zillmann, College of Communication, University of Alabama, Tuscaloosa, AL 35487-0172

Marvin Zuckerman, Department of Psychology, University of Delaware, Newark, DE 19716

Preface

Why do so many of us enjoy being told frightening stories? What are some of the consequences that result from such exposure? In light of the considerable popularity of horror films over the last three decades these questions have become the focus of growing attention for many scholars. However, research on audience preferences for and reactions to horror films has been done eclectically by investigators from varied theoretical and methodological backgrounds. Although considerable insights have been uncovered by different parties, efforts to integrate such findings have been limited. To our knowledge, there has never been a book published that has brought together the most recent research in this area. This volume was organized in an effort to end this dilemma and to put the study of audience responses to frightening fiction on the map as a significant research venture.

The first chapter of this volume offers a brief historical account of fictional horror. From fireside fables to pulp fiction to the modern horror film, Tamborini and Weaver trace the development of frightening fiction as an entertainment enterprise.

Zillmann and Gibson also examine the history of horrifying story telling, but from a different perspective. In chapter 2 they explore the socialization function of such tales noting, in particular, that the modern horror film may be a last vestige of ancient rites of passage.

Considerable debate has emerged over the last decade concerning the content of modern horror films. In chapter 3 Sapolsky and Molitor provide a review of several content analyses of horror films. They conclude that some basic assumptions regarding the content of these films are unfounded.

In chapter 4, Gomery points out that the horror film ranks as one of the most popular and profitable of film genres. He then provides a detailed analysis of the economics of the horror film industry. Gomery concludes that the horror film should continue to enjoy a stable position in the repertoire of Hollywood.

Cantor and Oliver examine the issue of how children and adolescents respond to horror films. In their exploration of developmental differences in responses to horror, Cantor and Oliver offer an illustrative and informative presentation of young adults' retrospective reports of intense emotional reactions to horror. They conclude chapter 5 with a discussion of how parental involvement is the key to helping children cope with media-induced fright.

In chapter 6, Zillmann and Weaver advance a theory of gender socialization of affective behaviors and displays. Specifically, they propose that, through consumption of horror films, adolescents and young adults are provided a safe environment where they can engage in societally prescribed displays of affect and emotion. Further, they propose that such displays during the consumption of cinematic horror have significant consequences for interpersonal attraction and interaction.

Tamborini, in chapter 7, also examines emotional reactions to horror films. Specifically, he outlines a model that illustrates the processes by which the aesthetic emotions are elicited by imaginative involvement with environments created by horror films. He concludes that empathic processes are critically important in determining how we respond to graphic horror.

In chapters 8 and 9 Sparks and Zuckerman each tackle the issue of why some of us enjoy graphic horror whereas others do not. These authors argue that consideration of viewers' personality characteristics offers an informative avenue for untangling this puzzle. Both of these scholars offer psychophysiological evidence suggesting a link between personality and responding to horror films.

Lawrence and Palmgreen, in chapter 10, also explore some of the reasons why many individuals are enticed by horror films. Utilizing data from an extensive survey, these authors concluded that an "arousal need" is a key factor underlying most individuals' preference for horror films.

Finally, in chapter 11 Tamborini and Salomonson turn to the issue of how exposure to horror films may influence our social perceptions and behaviors. Although undesirable effects for the individual viewer or society at large are probably not intended by the producers of horror films, the review of research findings provided by Tamborini and Salomonson suggests that such consequences do occur.

The principal acknowledgment in a collective work such as this goes to the contributors. We are most grateful for all they have done to make this volume possible. A special thanks to our graduate students who, in one capacity or another, helped us complete this work. We are both indebted to Dolf Zillmann who has patiently guided, stimulated, and encouraged us. Finally, we owe a debt of gratitude to our families for both their support and tolerance in granting us the time needed to complete this task.

James B. Weaver, III
Ron Tamborini

Chapter
1

Frightening Entertainment: A Historical Perspective of Fictional Horror

Ron Tamborini
Michigan State University
James B. Weaver, III
Auburn University

It can be hard to understand the "nature of the beast" when we are always running away from it. So it seems as we attempt to define the modern horror genre. Indeed, as we looked for a clear, precise definition of the horror genre, we discovered instead a deeply entangled and controversial concept. It is not uncommon, for instance, for scholars to be centuries apart when identifying the genre's inception. Some trace the ancestry of horror to early cave drawings and primitive rituals (see Zillmann & Gibson, chap.2, this volume). Others put its roots in the mid-18th century beginning with the "Age of Reason" (Edwards, 1984; Twitchell, 1989), and mock those who would describe horrid fiction "in mythic, legendary terms, as if there were any resemblance between a postindustrial American teenager, screaming in delight at a monster movie, and some medieval peasant who trembled in the dark for fear a ghost would get him" (Kendrick, 1991, p. xxii). Still others suggest that the modern horror genre originated only in the early part of this century when scholars first began to write anthologies on horrid fiction, or, perhaps when critics affirmed it by decree (Joshi, 1990).

There is some merit in each of these perspectives depending on the facet of horror considered. If one begins with an interest in the functions served by horror (such as Zillmann & Gibson, chap.2, this volume) we might assume that certain needs associated with these stories have not changed since prehistoric times, whereas other needs may be associated with much more recent developments. In the same manner, interest in the genre's form might focus on characteristics of horror that have been a part of frightening *narratives* since preliterate times, or focus on characteristics of frightening *fiction* that have distinguished modern horror from other related genres since the middle of the 18th century.

Whichever perspective is embraced, little appears to have changed as the telling of horrific tales has moved from campfire fables to pulp fiction to the modern film. This chapter offers a brief historical overview of the development of frightening entertainment.

DEFINING HORROR

One problem associated with defining horror is confusion about the nature of the threat implied. Separate examinations have made similar attempts to distinguish the sensation experienced in the face of physical danger from that experienced as a form of supernatural threat (Barclay, 1978; Derry, 1977; Prawer, 1980). Lovecraft (1923/1973) suggested that horror found in weird tales of this type:

> Has something more than secret murder, bloody bones, or a sheeted form clanking chains according to rule. A certain atmosphere of breathless and unexplainable dread of outer, unknown forces must be present; and there must be a hint, expressed with seriousness and portentousness becoming its subject, of that most terrible conception of the human brain—a malign and particular suspension or defeat of those fixed laws of Nature which are our only safeguard against the assaults of chaos and the demons of unplumbed space. (p. 15)

Edwards (1984) suggested that the clear separation between horror and fear lies in the distinction between external threat and the idea of threat, but to this she added that terror is associated with extreme fear, whereas horror couples extreme fear with disgust. Thus, one may feel terrified by the impending danger that could result in death, but horrified by the thought of being dead and the disgust of corruption and decay. This designation of horror is similar to that found in literature on emotion (Lazarus, 1991) and used elsewhere in this volume (see Tamborini, chap. 7, this volume). It implies that horror is characterized by fear of some uncertain threat to existential nature and by disgust over its potential aftermath, and that perhaps the source of threat is supernatural in its composition.

Defining horror in this manner provides a starting point for understanding the complexities of the phenomenon. A more detailed conception might be gained by examining the typologies consistent with this definition that have been developed to distinguish the concept. Penzoldt (1965) suggested that horrid fiction can be categorized as a Gothic tale, science fiction, or psychological horror; Derry's (1977) typology includes horror of the demonic, the horror of Armageddon, and the horror of personality; and Joshi (1990) proposed classes including supernatural horror, quasi-science fiction, and nonsupernatural horror. Although the typologies were created for various purposes and the nomenclature seems to differ, much in common can be found in three dimensions that are shared by each typology. The terminology of Joshi (1990) is employed here for its more broadly inclusive features.

Supernatural, Gothic, or horror of the demonic all begin with the assumption that the real world is governed by "natural law" and we live our lives according to this belief. Lovecraft (1923/1973) suggested that horror is created when some "natural law" is violated. When this occurs, life as we once knew it starts to function according to laws we do not understand and over which we have no control. We are at the mercy of supernatural forces that appear to have malicious intent.

Quasi-science fiction, science fiction, or the horror of Armageddon once again begins with the assumption that the real world is governed by forces that are well understood, even though the impossible seems to have occurred. In this case, however, the violations are accounted for in some rational manner. Quasi-science fiction presupposes that the impossible is an issue of epistemology, and not an issue of ontology. The impossible is accounted for not as a function of reality being violated, but as a function of our inability to yet understand the reality that we know to exist. As such, although the violation may appear supernatural at present, it is implied that we will be able to explain the phenomenon in the future. Nonetheless, again we are confronted by malevolent powers beyond our understanding or control, and the threat it presents is horrifying.

Nonsupernatural, psychological, or horror of the personality has been the most difficult to classify as part of the genre. Joshi (1990) suggested that nonsupernatural horror has two autonomous divisions: *pseudonatural*, in which events that appeared to violate natural law are later shown to be the account of an abnormal state of mind; and *conte cruel*, a tale of inhuman brutality. Lovecraft (1923/1973) and others believed that attempts to integrate the nonsupernatural, particularly conte cruel, confuse understanding of fictional horror; however, denying its inclusion would eliminate materials central to many audience conceptions of the genre. Classics like *Psycho* and other nonsupernatural horrors would have to be left out. In order to avoid limiting our concept to one unrelated with these audience experiences, a broader meaning that incorporates nonsupernatural horror seems appropriate in this situation. Although the divisions may appear somewhat blurred, this inclusion seems appropriate if psychological horrors can be considered part of the supernatural. For example, in *Psycho*, Norman Bates is classified as schizoid. If this diagnosis is taken to mean that as yet we really do not understand what is going on in the person's mind, these stories of unexplainable forces with malicious intent fit more easily within the genre (Twitchell, 1989). In either account, when stories of this type center on the provision of extremely loathsome images they seem more compatible with horror than with affiliated genres predominantly owing to their attempt to disgust.

Exploring these typologies helps us clarify different meanings of horror employed by audiences today, but viewing archaic thoughts on horror according to this conceptualization is unlikely to give us an accurate account. Clearly, these categories are inappropriate for understanding the phenomena prior to the 18th century when prevailing ontological assumptions would have provided no meaning for categories like supernatural, psychological, and science fiction. Perhaps today it is still the case that each of these is just a function of uncontrollable fear from an unknown existential threat, and that this understanding has not changed across time.

Nevertheless, in order to comprehend modern horror, it is important to understand something of its origins. As such, when considering the development of entertaining horror as we know it today, there is good reason to look back as far as recorded history. The horrific images we find in today's graphic films can be traced to their origins in visual and verbal media. Although the form differs somewhat, the context is essentially unchanged. We are frightened by forces we do not completely understand and by things that go bump in the night.

THE FABLED PAST

Stories of preposterous violence are apparent in the earliest cave paintings, and are likely to have been in existence for much longer. Frightening fiction has a legacy as old as recorded time, and its genealogy can tell us much about the role it plays in our daily lives. Historians like to trace horrid fiction to a tradition so primordial that it might be considered a part of human nature. Throughout the ages, they suggest, people have gathered in circles to frighten each other with horrifying tales. This image is not a hard one to accept based on available evidence. For centuries, archaeologists have collected antiquated fables and primitive tales from all cultures and corners of the earth. The stories are enough to raise goose flesh on those who listen to them without disbelieving ears.

The monsters, demons, and maniac killers of the modern horror genre have clear-cut predecessors. These legends and fables from centuries ago may provide us with clues to their attraction. Lovecraft (1923/1973) traced the heritage of what he termed "the weird tale" to archaic ballads, chronicles, and sacred writings. The similarity between the themes found in these ancient artifacts and those found in modern weird tales provides a clear indication that the form and functions of today's horrid fiction have been with us since an earlier time.

Support for this notion can be seen in the recurrent themes found in myths. Kluckhorn (1960) maintained that universal themes are contained in the legends of widely diverse cultures, and it is apparent that many of these themes are standard in the subject matter of today's horrid fiction. Fables of witchcraft and tales of hideous monsters can be found in most if not all cultures studied. The appearance of these forms across time and cultural divisions suggests functional equivalence in the motives that lead to their popularity.

The functions served by frightening myths and scary stories have been the focus of much scholarly speculation. It has been suggested that fables are often employed as a substitute for fact when people are attempting to explain mysteries beyond their understanding (Levin, 1960). The legends and fables provide an acceptable explanation for the events they are attempting to understand. The telling of fairy tales, even repulsive stories about hideous demons and fiendish killers, functions to provide children with the opportunity to confront their fears through ritualized exposure in a protected environment (Bettelheim, 1976).

Learning to master our fears is an important part of development, and rituals can play a big role in this learning process. Perhaps that is why ritual has always been such an important part of horror and the fear that we associate with this genre. For centuries, the conquest of fear has been accomplished by rituals and rites that require the direct confrontation of the threat (see Zillmann & Gibson, chap. 2, this volume). At the same time, however, many rituals confront threats using a symbol to represent the source of fear. From simple representations of early cave drawings to graphic depictions of 18th-century intaglio engravings, symbolic representations have allowed us to face our fears in rituals that help us cope with different threats. Myriad examples of graphic violence and horror can be found in classic literature from Homer to Shakespeare as small segments inserted in larger stories. Although feature-length horrid novels did not emerge until the 19th century, the attraction to such themes appears to be very old (Kendrick, 1991).

FACT OR FICTION

Certain aspects of horror as we know it today are generally accepted as descending from early legends and fables, but changed attitudes about death in the mid-18th century altered the nature of how these stories were perceived. When we consider the genre along divisions of supernatural, nonsupernatural, and quasi-science fiction, we are dealing with an understanding of horror that did not develop until the concept of fiction began to acquire its present form (Daniels, 1975).

The change that occurred in perception of horrid stories during the 18th century can be identified by a growing disbelief in things that could not be observed.   Although many features of these stories remained relatively unchanged from ancient legends and fables, the audience attitude toward them was different. The 18th century "Age of Reason" brought a skepticism toward the supernatural that before had not been seen. Because the supernatural was accepted as a part of reality, there was no "violation" of natural law before the 18th century.   With the incursion of empiricism, the fantastic was now curtailed or accounted for in most narratives.   Tales in literature were introduced as stories related to the author by a source claiming the report to be true (Brockett, 1964). The crumbling settings and loathsome violence were still present and frightening, but increasingly were looked on with disbelief.

Whereas change in 18th-century attitudes toward horror are characterized by disbelief, change in the format of horror came as result of technological advances. Twitchell (1989) suggested that attitudes toward violent death were influenced by developments in printing that provided a thrilling new form of "mimic" aggression. Much has been said about advances in stereography that made typesetting more efficient and inexpensive. These advances, no doubt, had an impact on the availability of literature for those who knew how to read. At the same time, however, other developments in print technology may have been more influential on illiterate audiences.   When the labor-intensive techniques of early relief printing methods were replaced by intaglio engraving, the inexpensive production of illustrated copies became a possibility. Many early attempts to profit from this technology came in the form of gruesome images.

One of the first attempts to find a mass audience for this type of graphic imagery can be found in the work of Horgarth during the latter half of the 18th century (Paulson, 1970).   Horgarth created a strong impact by connecting illustrations to relate a short story in pictures. Because verbal literacy was limited to the educated upper class, a larger audience could be reached by telling the tale through his drawings. Although the story lines were often simple morality tales, they provided a forum for explicit images of sadistic brutality and gruesome retaliation. His illustrations were so popular, that soon he started to hire other artists to help produce illustrations for his tales. Some, like *The Four Stages of Cruelty*, which featured the savagery of a fiend named Tom Nero, were so successful that they were followed by sequels (Twitchell, 1989).   In much the same manner that monstrous killers now return until audience members lose interest, Tom Nero appears a forerunner of today's film demons. He was a nonsupernatural sociopath, a Mr. Hyde without a Dr. Jekyll.

The rigid curtailment of the supernatural in literature was swept away in the late 18th century and replaced by a style that would have a lasting impression on traditional supernatural horror. As the romantic movement began to take root, the drive toward rationality was supplanted by reliance on intuition. The fantastic was once again a topic accepted in polite circles, and in demand by the general public. With a middle class growing in number and economic strength, it was not long before the supernatural was back in full swing. This time, however, the stories were listened to quite differently than they had been by audiences for early myths and fables. Although tales of the supernatural were fascinating to many, they were taken now as a form of fiction. The eerie tales filled with crumbling buildings or decaying graveyards still put a chill into their patrons, but the patrons now had their doubts (Barclay, 1978).

Castle of Otranto (Walpole, 1764/1840) is believed to be one of the first examples of modern supernatural horror (Lundwall, 1977). *Otranto*, subtitled *A Gothic Story*, is often acknowledged for founding the Gothic genre, yet no imitators came soon on its heels. Nonetheless, it provided a prototype of the features that would come to represent Gothic horror at the turn of the century. During the end of the 18th century and early into the 19th century, Gothic novels had achieved great public favor. Hundreds of novels were written in an easily duplicated style for which publishers could predict a demand. Soon after reaching its peak, however, the craze began to dwindle, and Gothic novels eventually faded into the broadly encompassing movement of Romanticism.

Although the initial popularity of Gothic fiction was short lived, the appeal of horrid entertainment did not seem to vanish. Instead, horrid entertainment materialized in a different form on the early 19th century stage. At a time when it appeared that frightening novels were starting to lose their thrill, the theater seemed able to reproduce these effects with a new and even greater intensity. The theme of the plays did not stray far from novels, but the manner of presentation was extraordinary. Even with the limitations of archaic stage technology, the effects achieved on stage were electrifying for 19th-century audiences. Startling lighting, smoke and mirrors, and the use of eerie music could shock the audience or chill their bones in a fashion not achievable in print.

The stage of the early 19th century was captured by a new style that would have a strong impact on the evolution of horrid fiction. The melodrama had a thematic structure very similar to contemporary frightening entertainment, but it introduced a new use of stage music. Music was used to express the sensation of various emotions like joy, anger, fear, and alarm. The music played before, during, and after actors' dialogue. Sometimes the performer would just stand and hold a pose while the music voiced the passion of the moment. Soon certain musical forms became standards associated with the experience of different emotions. The screeching violins in the film *Psycho*, which penetrate the darkness to warn us of fiendish terror, repeat sounds first heard almost 200 years ago on the early 19th century stage.

In the late 18th and early 19th centuries, fear was only one among many powerful emotions that horrid novels and melodramas tried to induce (Kendrick, 1991). No horror, comedy, or tragedy as we think of them today existed in its pure form at that time. Most episodes of horror in conventional fiction were merely a brief interlude or parts of more complete works. In classical literature, the short story is the first form of fiction to focus entirely on horror. The development of the magazine in the 19th century provided the perfect location for horrid short stories. One of the first examples of this type of writing is found in the short ghost stories of Sir Walter Scott (Kendrick, 1991).

Along with developments in the short story format of horrid fiction came changes in its content. Some of the same appeal of early fables and myths that was based on the belief that they were true can be seen in the popularity of authentic stories about real-life atrocities and crime. Although there were few crime stories written in feature length during the mid-19th century, enthusiasts had to go little further than newspapers and pamphlets whose only intent was to shock. It is difficult to tell what type of person was attracted to these stories, but millions of such items were sold. Based on sales and evidence suggesting their popularity with all classes, however, it appears they were able to attain a broad-based appeal that earlier horror could never attain (Kendrick, 1991).

The early 19th century's focus on real-life crime had an important impact on the development of horrid fiction. When the lunatics who committed savage atrocities in real-life crime found their way into fictional short stories, a new frightening convention was established. In the mid-19th century, this pivotal change in the focus of horrid fiction was initiated by the writings of Edgar Allen Poe (Lovecraft, 1923/1973). Poe led the change in the popular form for fictional horror from episodes in novels to short stories of pure terror, and from the supernatural to a focus on psychological horror. Poe's stories laid the groundwork necessary to move the frightening fiction of early magazines to the next generation of horrid entertainment.

In the latter half of the 19th century, Darwin's (1859) *Origin of the Species* raised questions about the existence of God and his role in explaining natural events. Historians have suggested that Darwin's work had a strong influence on scary stories. With skepticism toward the spiritual and an understanding of nature as the real determinant of ferocious violence, those so inclined could use horrid fiction as a form of diversion to ponder a supernatural that was beyond scientific reason (Edwards, 1984). Although beliefs now dictated doubt in the possibility of such events, it did not stop people's impulse to dabble in the macabre: "Sometimes a curious streak of fancy invades the hardest head; so that no amount of rationalism, reform, or Freudian analysis can quite annul the thrill of the chimneycorner whisper or the lonely wood" (Lovecraft, 1923/1973, p. 13).

Ghost stories and the supernatural made a small comeback in English literature. A fashion of ghost stories at Christmas started with Dickens' (1843) *A Christmas Carol* and comprised a major outlet for scary fiction in England through the end of the 19th century. These ghost stories were not very loathsome in general, much like the Gothic novels they followed (Kendrick, 1991), but the gentility found in these stories was not maintained in other forums of the day. Horror came back to the stage at this point, and took on a vivid new image.

In 1897, the Grand Guignol opened with one goal in mind—to shock its patrons and give them a thrill. The theater put on several different plays each evening, but the emphasis was always on horror. The producers intended to make the Grand Guignol "a place where every social taboo of good taste was cracked and shattered" (Gordon, 1988, p. 18). The actors and stage technicians were masterful in their efforts to create horrifying spectacles that looked remarkably authentic. The sight of blood spurting from real people on stage, hacked with sabres right in front of the audience's eyes, must have been more shocking than any special effect ever created on film. Throughout the history of fictional horror no episode approaches the Grand Guignol in depravity, not even the new horrors that came after the turn of the 20th century.

THE MODERN HORROR GENRE

Joshi (1990) suggested that the horror genre did not exist prior to the early part of the 20th century, but developed as a result of professionals and academics scrutinizing the works of certain writers. Until this time, these authors had always been considered as essentially no different from other novel and short-story writers. In the early part of the 20th century, nonacademic anthologies of frightening fiction and scholarly reviews of Gothic and supernatural fiction separated these authors and originated the modern genre in the form that we now think of today. Although most horrid fiction gets excluded from broad anthologies of literature, the research devoted to horror specifically has had a significant impact on forms of horror in this century.

The first academic investigation of fictional horror was by Scarborough (1917). Later anthologies have made additions and alterations, but the general outline offered by Scarborough has stayed mostly intact; starting with the early Gothic novels; through Poe, Dickens, and other mid-19th-century writers; to late-century authors like Algernon Blackwood and H. G. Wells. Along these lines other anthologies have focused on early 20th-century writers like Bram Stoker, Henry James, Arthur Machen, and M. R. James, who added gruesome images, elements of the macabre, and a return to the graveyard chill. Although the anthologies differed, the fact that they archived this collection of works added respectability to horrid fictional writing. When scholars and critics called these classic works of literature, horror became legitimate. By the mid-1930s, the genre was well established (Kendrick, 1991).

With the success of the developments in other entertainment forms, it is surprising that it took so long for popular trends in horror to make their way into film. On stage and in print, grotesque physical horror showed its widespread popular appeal. Yet in early motion pictures, the industry did not capitalize on film's ability to shock its audience with ghastly scenes. Although it is clear that, since the first black-and-white films, horror has always had great box office appeal and been profitable (Huss & Ross, 1972), attempts in this area during the early 20th century were tame by the standards of other media.

Many initial horror films created a sense of eeriness with tilted cameras, strange buildings, and shadowy figures. *The Cabinet of Dr. Caligari* (1919) and *Nosferatu* (1921) are good examples of expressionism in early silent movies. Vampire stories seemed particularly well suited for expressionism, and provided the setting for one of the first talking films as well. In 1927, *Dracula: The Vampire Play* was a hit on the London and New York stage. The success of the play led to the film version *Dracula* (1931), and launched a new career for its stage star, Bela Lugosi. With the film a commercial hit, Universal Pictures looked for a successor and quickly found its heir in *Frankenstein* (1931). Boris Karloff, the Frankenstein monster, joined Lugosi and others in a wave of films during the 1930s that recycled their stories and the subdued conventions of the late 18th-century and early 19th-century horror. Mummies, werewolves, and decaying old castles held their appeal for a while, but within a decade the novelty wore off and the popularity of tepid horror films declined.

The mild nature of these films was largely determined by the Production Code of 1930. Films generally curtailed loathsome images on camera in compliance with the standards of the code, but what horror fans could not get on the motion picture screen they could find in a new horrid medium. The extremes of the pulp magazines, which originated during the 1920s and developed in the 1930s, drove scary fiction out of legitimate publications.

After the pulp magazine *Weird Tales* first appeared in 1924 with morbid stories of bloodshed and the macabre, horrid fiction was no longer published in traditional "slick" magazines, but only in the "bloody pulps." Whereas restraint was the rule for film at this time, indulgence better describes stories in these issues. In 1939, when Arkham House was founded specifically to publish scary fiction in volumes by writers like H. P. Lovecraft, horrid fiction almost stopped appearing in all other book forms. As horror was pushed underground, the popularity of the bloody pulps grew to cult levels within a limited audience, but the audience limits changed when the pulps' horrid stories came together with a new type of carrier. In the 1940s, when the comic book put horror in a form written for juvenile readers, scary fiction found the audience of adolescent boys, and the match between them became profitable.

Comic-book horror made a brief first appearance with *Eerie* in 1946, but its popularity exploded with issues like *Tales from the Crypt* released by EC comics in 1950. Horrid comics far exceeded the pulp magazines' indulgence in the macabre. The bright colors added a vividness to the gore that black-and-white film could not match. Although they often revived the old graveyard motifs, they went beyond a sense of unearthly fear to images of disgusting depravity. Disembowelment, festering wounds, rot, and putrefication were the ghastly images that appeared in full color. It was not long before many were concerned about the harm they might create.

By 1954, it is estimated that 150 million comics were being bought each month in the United States (Benton, 1989). That same year, *Seduction of the Innocent*, Fredric Wertham's bestseller, attacked what he considered the blight caused by comics, and horrid comics in particular. Wertham was not alone in his view that social ruin was attributable to juvenile corruption (cf. Twitchell, 1989). Following Senate hearings, and fearing legislation, the comic industry developed guidelines including a ban on the walking dead and "scenes of horror, excessive bloodshed, gory or gruesome crimes, depravity, lust, sadism, masochism" (Goulart, 1986, p. 266). Instead of *Night of the Living Dead*, we now had the dawn of *Jughead*.

About the same time, change in the marketing of films would have implications for horror. When television put an end to film as a medium of universal appeal, producers discovered they could profit from films aimed at a limited audience (Doherty, 1988). One audience with both enough time and money to spend included the same juveniles who had been reading comics. This market for limited appeal horror first became apparent with a series of films from Hammer that starred Peter Cushing and Christopher Lee. Starting in 1957 with *The Curse of Frankenstein*, Hammer films got serious about horror by using Technicolor and close-ups of the bloodshed. The modest success of these and similar low-budget U.S. films caught the eye of film makers like Alfred Hitchcock. The outcome was *Psycho* (1960), a watershed in film horror. *Psycho's* huge success led to a flood of imitators, and Hitchcock's stature added legitimacy to gruesome films of bloody murder.

From 1960 to the 1990s, the enormous number of films produced makes detecting major trends virtually hopeless. Although *Psycho* seems to culminate a general shift in scary fiction from the supernatural of the mid-18th century to the nonsupernatural and quasi-science fiction, the most apparent development since the 1960s is the drive toward more graphic horror. Over the genre's brief history, special effects have played a key role in determining frightening fiction's success. From smoke and mirrors on stage, to camera angles and mood lighting, to special make-up, hydraulic apparatus, and computer technology, with each advance we got a better view of the bloodshed and destruction whenever the violence began. The future may offer even more realism with the clarity of 70-mm high-speed film and imagery of virtual reality.

In large part, special effects have been responsible for the popularity found in current descendants of *Psycho*: the maniacal killers from *Texas Chainsaw Massacre* (1974), *Halloween* (1978), *Friday the 13th* (1980), *Nightmare on Elm Street* (1985), and the myriad of less successful imitators. The special effects used to create the maniacs and their uncanny behaviors have led some of us to be more interested in these demons than in their victims. In fact, a recent form of "slasher" horror films delivers endings in which the fiend turns out to be the victor. This change in the prominence of fiend retribution raises questions about trends in horrid storylines. Twitchell (1989) claimed that the revenge motive of EC comics is not gone but simply moved to another medium. He suggests that it is now carried in the prose of Stephen King, the most popular writer alive.

The vast popularity of King's books and their adaptations suggests that his work offers one of the best pictures of the genre's broad appeal today. King's writing contains the same extreme forms of violence found in the most graphic comics and films. He uses retribution to exploit adolescent anxieties dealing with preposterous forms of violence like those found in old horrid comics, modern splatter-film technology, and his own bizarre mind (Twitchell, 1989). King (1981) stated, "I recognize terror as the finest emotion, and so I will try to terrorize the reader. But if I find I cannot terrify him/her, I will try to horrify; and if I find I cannot horrify, I'll go for the gross-out. I'm not proud" (p. 37).

Grotesque bloodshed and repulsive images are often said to epitomize the last two decades of horrid fiction. Although not essential to horror, these images likely play a prominent role in their function. They can be traced to ancient origins in visual and verbal media from oral cultures long before reproducible print. The form has evolved as conventions have changed, but its nature seems greatly preserved. Although we remain fearful of aging and death and disease, we are absorbed by its fictional accounts. It seems to help reassure us that no matter how dreadful things look, there really is nothing to fear.

From fables to pulp fiction to the modern horror film, a common theme crosses the history of frightening fiction. Through these rituals we confront and learn to deal with our fear of death and our thoughts of what might lie beyond. However, it is hard to understand the "nature of the beast" without acknowledging its presence and centrality. We are frightened by death, by things we do not completely understand, and by things that go bump in the night.

REFERENCES

Barclay, G. (1978). *Anatomy of horror: The masters of occult fiction.* London: Weidenfeild & Nicolsm.

Benton, M. (1989). *The comic book in America: An illustrated history.* Dallas: Taylor Publishing.

Bettelheim, B. (1976). *The uses of enchantment: The meaning and importance of fairy tales.* New York: Knopf.

Brockett, O. (1964). *The theatre: An introduction* (3rd ed.). New York: Holt, Rinehart & Winston.

Daniels, L. (1975). *Living in fear: A history of horror in the mass media.* New York: Scribner & Sons.

Darwin, C. (1859). *Origin of the species.* London: John Murray.

Derry, C. (1977). *Dark dreams: A psychological history of the modern horror film.* London: Thomas Yoseloff.

Dickens, C. (1843). *A Christmas carol.* London: Chapman & Hall.

Doherty, T. (1988). *Teenagers and teenpics: The juvenilization of American movies of the 1950s.* Boston: Unwin Hyman.

Edwards, E. (1984). *The relationship between sensation-seeking and horror movie interest and attendance.* Unpublished doctoral dissertation, University of Tennessee, Knoxville.

Gordon, M. (1988). *The Grand Guignol: Theatre of fear and terror.* New York: Amok Press.

Goulart, R. (1986). *Ron Goulart's great history of comic books.* Chicago: Contemporary Books.

Huss, R., & Ross, J. (1972). *Focus of the horror film.* Englewood Cliffs, NJ: Prentice-Hall.

Joshi, S. T. (1990). *The weird tale.* Austin, TX: The University of Austin Press.

Kendrick, W. (1991). *The thrill of fear.* New York: Grove Press.

King, S. (1981). *Danse macabre.* New York: Everest House.

Kluckhorn, C. (1960). Recurrent themes in myths and myth making. In H. A. Murray (Ed.), *Myth and myth making* (pp. 46-59). New York: George Braziller.

Lazarus, R. S. (1991). *Emotion and adaptation.* New York: Oxford University Press.

Levin, H. (1960). Some meanings of myth. In H. A. Murray (Ed.), *Myth and myth making* (pp. 103-114). New York: George Braziller.

Lovecraft, H. P. (1973). *Supernatural horror in literature.* New York: Dover. (Original work published 1923)

Lundwall, S. (1977). *Science fiction: Illustrated history.* New York: Grosset & Dunlap.

Paulson, R. (1970). *Horgarth's graphic works* (Vol. 1). New Haven, CT: Yale University Press.

Penzoldt, P. (1965). *The supernatural in fiction.* New York: Columbia University Press.

Prawer, S. (1980). *Calgari's children: The film as tale of terror.* Oxford, UK: Oxford University Press.

Scarborough, D. (1917). *The supernatural in modern English fiction.* New York: G. P. Putnam.

Twitchell, J. P. (1989). *Preposterous violence: Fables of aggression in modern violence.* New York: Oxford University Press.

Walpole, H. (1840). *The castle of Otranto: A gothic story.* London: Joseph Thomas. (original work published 1764)

Chapter 2

Evolution of the Horror Genre

Dolf Zillmann
Rhonda Gibson
University of Alabama

The telling of horrifying tales is as old as the human capacity to tell tales. The modern horror film is merely the latest form of such story telling.

On this premise, we attempt to trace the evolution of the horror film from its roots in ancient, preliterate societies. Our venture leads us to stories told by hunters, reports from those who survived warfare, fairy tales, rites of passage, blood sports, horrifying staged happenings, and lastly, films from *The Cabinet of Dr. Caligari* to *Halloween, Friday the 13th,* and *The Texas Chainsaw Massacre.*

A new model of the social uses of horror and of the enjoyment of horrifying tales emerges at the end of our journey. This model is based on gender socialization differences that reach back to the division of labor in hunter-gatherer societies, a division that prescribed agonistic roles for men and nurturant ones for women. Although the utility of such gender roles has been severely compromised by societal changes, these roles seem to persist in modification and rudimentary manifestations. For better or worse, critical aspects of the ancient gender-specific socialization have survived and turn out to play a significant part in the enjoyment of horror films, their social uses, and in contemporary gender socialization itself.

IN THE BEGINNING THERE WAS EXAGGERATION

Those ancient ancestors of ours who confronted ferocious animals on their hunt and who survived the ordeal to tell their story were probably the first to relate horrifying happenings. As they relived their anxieties and their actions, they must have succumbed to what we now talk about as impression or image management (Cialdini, 1985; Schlenker, 1980; Snyder, 1981). In the eyes of their peers, these hunters could only benefit from exaggerating the dangers they had faced. Who would admit to having been chased by a wild boar, when the animal could be described as a creature with seven heads? Who would detail a scary encounter with two men from a rival tribe, when the incident could be conveyed as a violent clash with a dozen of them, a clash that resulted in their panic-stricken flight? And who would report to have escaped a minor brush fire, when it could be presented as a towering inferno? With fewer checks on the veridicality of heroic accounts than are imposed on us nowadays, our ancestors were quick to invent fire-breathing dragons, girl-snatching megabirds, enemies with impenetrable skin, man-swallowing reptiles, acid pits from which there was no return, horned men with saber teeth, and hell itself. The mythologies of all known cultures are laden with such products of the human imagination driven by fear and narcissism (Lang, 1968; Mercatante, 1978; Puhvel, 1987).

But bragging, if it did not escalate into the obviously incredulous, not only proved to be good for the teller, it placed listeners in awe and potentially intimidated them. Tales of exaggerated dangers, of threatening bigger-than-reality conditions and supernatural forces, proved useful in controlling believers. Children could be prevented from wandering off into the woods by stories of fierce creatures roaming there, and perhaps women could be tied to the homestead by reports of cannibalistic ogres in the forest.

THE SCARERS LEADING THE SCARED

Most fairy tales feature a good deal of material designed to frighten children and, hence, may be considered bona fide horror stories. The teller, not by accident, is emotionally unaffected by these materials. Listeners, in contrast, are tormented, initially by empathetic distress (Zillmann, 1991a) and later by apprehensions about their own possible victimization by forces and events similar to those described to them (Cantor, 1991). The characteristically happy turn of events presented in the tale's resolution not only terminates the acute torment, but it converts distress to enjoyment and intensifies this experience (Zillmann, 1991b). Having been scared actually paid off. Or so it must seem in the listener's retrospective assessment.

Oddly, whereas the contents of fairy tales and the emotions they liberate have received considerable attention from scholars (Bettelheim, 1975; Yearsley, 1968), the consequences of the social use of such tales have gone largely unnoticed. Their social usage is most intriguing, however, in that it constitutes a model for the social use of all horror tales.

The fact that in the conveyance of horror by a fairy tale the teller is fearless and the told is scared is significant because it provides the teller with opportunities to comfort the disturbed listener. The child, when scared, can cling to fearless mom or dad and be reassured of protection. Caretakers are there to ward off the bogeyman, should he ever come. In principle, tellers of fairy tales create anxieties in the child and then promptly relieve these anxieties by their show of fearlessness. The disturbed seeks and finds comfort from the unperturbed. In terms of operant conditioning, this amounts to the tellers' potentially frequent provision of negative reinforcement to the child (Nevin, 1973; Skinner, 1969)—analogous to diapering, which also terminates a noxious experience. Over time, then, the tellers of scary fairy tales become masters of children's anxieties, and the children learn to turn to their masters for protection. In other words, the children grow dependent on their caretakers, and when disturbed, seek their support.

The process can be seen as another element of parent-child bonding, supplementing the positive reinforcement from feeding and the indicated negative reinforcement from the removal of any bodily discomfort. Alternatively, it may be viewed more negatively as the creation of a dependence by arbitrary, communicative means.

Such creation of dependence has never been limited to children. Through the ages, countless demons have been invoked to elicit anxieties and foster obedience in the mature, the aging, and the old, as well as in the young and inexperienced. Across cultures, rituals have been saturated with devilish creatures (Mercatante, 1978). Hieronymus Bosch painted them in more recent times to instill a shudder in those with wanting imagination and to force these people in line with expectations from prevailing doctrines. And enemies have always been depicted as brutal rapists, ready to kill off all men and children and to lay their hands on the women, in order to prepare and entice kind hearts to maim and kill other humans.

The emerging power relationship is this: Those who are not perturbed by fears and who manage to evoke fears in others attain a degree of control over these others. They do so by their show of fearlessness, presumably because it projects superior ability to cope with fear-inducing conditions. Even if others' fear is not manipulated by the fearless, the show of fearlessness has this consequence. The fearless seem to have the answers, at least as far as dealing with the threatening happenings is concerned. The fearful, in contrast, are lacking the answers and should seek protection from those in the know. Stated more drastically, the fearless, by projecting the ability to cope and protect, define themselves as leaders, whereas the fearful, by turning to the fearless for help and comfort, place themselves in the role of followers.

BRINGING UP BABY

The fearless-fearful dichotomy manifests itself in social situations generally. Nowhere is it more obtrusive, however, than in the socialization of boys and girls, ultimately in that of men and women (Brody, 1985; Maccoby & Jacklin, 1974). In more or less all contemporary societies, boys are placed under enormous pressures to inhibit any show of fear and to project the characteristics of a leader. Girls, on the other hand, are encouraged to exhibit their distress, their fear, and their need for support. Whereas initiative and assertiveness are expected of boys, girls are trained into acquiescence and dependence.

The utility of such gender-role socialization for modern society is very much in doubt and has been severely challenged (Chodorow, 1971; Frisbie, 1990; Weitzman, 1984). Gender-specific socialization persists, nonetheless, as the likely residue of gender socialization of earlier times in which gender-segregated roles did have utility—in fact, in which these roles were essential for survival.

The origins of functional gender-role segregation are to be found in hunter-gatherer societies (Dahlberg, 1981; Friedl, 1975). At the heart of such segregation was the physically limiting condition of pregnancy. Women of childbearing age were pregnant or nursing much of the time and, in the face of continual danger from a hostile environment, truly handicapped. They were less than optimally fit for hunting and warfare, forcing them into the comparatively sedentary roles of child care and of nurturance in a broader sense. The physical handicap of frequent pregnancies forced a need for protection on women. Men, in contrast, were not tied down by childbirth. They were free to roam the territory for vital goods and conditions. Their bodies were generally stronger, too, giving them further mobility advantage. Men were thus prone to grow into hunter and warrior roles. They became suppliers and protectors, roles they have assumed for centuries since.

The necessary preparation of men for hunting and warfare pertains most directly to fear and coping with threat and danger. If men were to be effective in these roles, boys had to be trained to be fearless and brave. And they were (Daly & Wilson, 1978; Lewis, 1976).

Anthropologists who conducted cross-cultural studies (Barry, Bacon, & Child, 1957; Erikson, 1963; Hammond & Jablow, 1976; Mead, 1949; Miller, 1928) report that men and women in virtually all known ancient and modern societies have been socialized from an early age into markedly different gender roles. Men are trained to be fearless, self-reliant, and aggressive, whereas women are socialized into fearfulness, dependency, and submission (Barry, Bacon, & Child, 1957; Bem, 1981; Feather, 1984; Mischel, 1970; Spence & Helmreich, 1978). So-called rites of passage or initiation rites emerged as a cultural universal. In them, young boys were expected to demonstrate the learned mastery of fear and physical hardship (Gennep, 1960). Once such mastery could be shown, boys were rewarded for their bravery and strength, but if they failed the tests of endurance and fright-mastery, they were ridiculed and denied inclusion in adult activities (Miller, 1928). Women, on the other hand, were trained to be submissive and nurturing in preparation for the practices of childbirth and childrearing. Accordingly, their initiation rites involved acts of self-denial, submission, and recognition of the dominance of and dependence on men (Gennep, 1960).

THE HOME OF THE BRAVE

We briefly review typical practices in the discussed rites of passage.

Generally speaking, initiation rites for prepubescent males were severe. They commonly involved the infliction of pain and humiliation. Such infliction was characteristic in nomadic societies. Men's roles as warriors, hunters, and herders could lead them into isolation and danger, situations in which any type of fear or timidity might be fatal (Barry, Bacon, & Child, 1959). Rites tended to be less severe in societies whose economies were based on animal husbandry or agriculture. Men's roles involved fewer isolated activities and dangerous confrontations.

Hunting tribes, such as the Stseelis of British Columbia, developed initiation rites that involved daily whippings for young boys and exposure of their bodies to the elements for days at a time (Miller, 1928). Other so-called primitive societies, such as the Borneo headhunters and the Fijians, urged young boys to torture and mutilate old slaves or prisoners taken in battle in order to instill in the boys a ferocity and callousness toward bloodshed (Miller, 1928). Other societies used various forms of flagellation, mutilation, and humiliation in their rites of passage (Gennep, 1960).

An important similarity identified in the various initiation rites of these warlike hunting societies was the public display by males of fearlessness and physical endurance (Schlegel & Barry, 1979). The Wagenia of Kisangani in Zaire, for instance, conducted a public circumcision of young boys, allowing the initiates to exhibit their bravery and toughness to the women and elder men of the tribe. Any boy who showed fear or pain was ridiculed by other members of the group and denied adult status (Droogers, 1980). The Gisu of Uganda performed the same type of public circumcision on "boys" as old as 25. Those who exhibited signs of weakness were denied full manhood, regardless of age (Heald, 1986). Young boys from the Sambia of Papua New Guinea took part in a ceremony in which each initiate was tied to the back of a male relative and severely beaten by other males of the tribe. The ceremony was witnessed by female adults and children whose role it was to honor those initiates who quietly and courageously withstood the beatings and to acknowledge their induction into manhood (Lidz & Lidz, 1989).

In the great majority of preliterate societies whose very survival depended on the bravery and stamina of men, there could be little tolerance for young males who were fearful of pain or violence. In many of these tribes, such as the Bushmen of Australia, "should a boy show signs of fear, he would be so scorned and mocked that he would, unless restrained, commit suicide" (Miller, 1928, p. 203).

THE WOMEN'S PLACE

In contrast to the violent rites of passage for males, initiation rites for young females involved mostly private ceremonies designed to establish and reinforce nurturance, submission, and dependence.   For instance, the Stseelis, who publicly whipped and tortured young boys, isolated pubescent girls and forbid them to eat fresh meat and fish in attempts to prevent them from becoming greedy (Miller, 1928).   In the Sioux tribes of North America, a girl was "educated to be a hunter's helper and a future hunter's mother.   At the same time she was subjected to a rigorous training toward bashfulness and outright fear of men" (Erikson, 1963, p. 144).   Other initiation rites for young girls, such as those practiced by the Borneo headhunters, involved the teaching of medicinal arts and birth control (Miller, 1928).

Table 2.1 summarizes exemplifying gender-segregating practices in various cultures.

GAMES, SPORTS, AND THE THEATER

As preliterate societies became more efficient in managing their resources and no longer had to focus all efforts on sheer survival, less emphasis was placed on preparatory rites of passage or initiations (Bernstein, 1987).   Gender-role socialization continued, however, despite its lack of adaptive utility.   In many cases, public displays of masculinity previously associated with initiation rites were combined with games, sports, and other forms of entertainment, such as the theater (Kernodle, 1989).   The entertainment was generally violent and gory, giving men ample opportunity to publicly display their mastery of fright, their bravery, and their superior agonistic skills.   Pastimes included bull and bear baiting, violently competitive chariot races, gladiatorial games, and battles between humans and wild animals.   The original Olympic Games, begun in 776 B.C., included the sport of caestus, an extremely dangerous form of boxing involving the use of gauntlets loaded with lead and iron.   The ancient Greeks and Romans, who believed the souls of deceased warriors thrived on earthly bloodshed, delighted in conducting sacrificial funeral games with prisoners captured in battle (Smith, 1831).

Greek culture is usually considered the cradle of enlightened sports spectatorship (Harris, 1972; Sansone, 1988).   The Greeks have been credited with a reverence for grace, graceful physical exercise in particular.   In an uncontrived fashion, athletic performances were aligned with poetic and musical expositions. However, even the Greeks could not resist adding various forms of wrestling and boxing, as well as chariot racing, to civic and religious ceremonies, thereby paving the way for so-called blood sports as mass entertainment (Guttmann, 1978, 1986; Harris, 1972).

Roman urbanization is said to have created and nourished an appetite for sports spectacles laden with mayhem (Midwinter, 1986). In the interest of controlling social upheaval, extravagant entertainment programs were put in place. The centerpieces of these programs were the blood sports, mainly gladiatorial combat and violent chariot races. Rome's Colosseum accommodated more than 40,000 spectators for gladiatorial combat, and Rome's largest race track had crowds of approximately 250,000 spectators in attendance for chariot races (Harris, 1972). Such dimensions of spectatorship are unsurpassed in antiquity. Horror-laden athletic entertainments proved to be far more attractive than nonviolent sports. Footballing in early China, for instance, drew crowds of only comparatively modest size (Midwinter, 1986).

Most of the discussed forms of entertainment were carried out in the presence of women, whose role it was to acknowledge the fearlessness and strength of the men involved. Tournaments, a type of game developed in ancient Rome and continued in Western Europe during the Middle Ages, combined the training of fighters and knights for warfare with an important public display of their strength and agility. A significant part of these tournaments was to duly impress the delicate and noble ladies (Brockett, 1982; Wickham, 1985). Other violent pastimes, such as bullfighting, became extremely popular during the late Middle Ages and provided an arena for men to prove their masculinity. A successful matador was "regarded as the epitome of masculinity" (Marvin, 1986, p. 126). "If the matador is able to meet the challenge successfully, he gains prestige and status, and vindicates his claim to be a true man. Failure brings insult, ridicule and a loss of reputation" (p. 126).

In his acclaimed *Artis amatoriae*, the first Western manual of the joy of sex, the Roman philosopher Ovid reported keen observations about the social function of horror. He described the arena of gladiatorial combat as the most productive dating grounds. The more the mayhem on the field terrified the women in attendance, he surmised, the more likely they would seek comfort from their male companions. They would quiver of excitement, be "struck dumb" (his words), and cling to men in total dependence, a dependence that he thought to yield an appreciation that would express itself in romantic attraction and sexual privileges. Ovid may well have been the first proponent of what has become known as the *snuggle theory of horror* (see Zillmann & Weaver, chap. 6, this volume; also Zillmann, Weaver, Mundorf, & Aust, 1986).

The theater also became a showcase of masculinity and male supremacy in coping with threats and dangers. Much has been written about the 5th-century B.C. Greek playwright Aeschylus, whose works featured special effects and demonic characters so frightening that pregnant women in the audiences

TABLE 2.1
Gender Socialization of Agonistic Emotions and Nurturant Dispositions in Various Tribal Societies

Sioux Indians of North America

Males. Beginning around age 5, males were trained to play violent games that simulated hunting and war. If reluctant to participate, they were "shamed" into being brave. "Every educational device was used to develop in the boy a maximum of self-confidence" (Erikson, 1963, p.143).

Females. By age 5, females played games that taught them to be supportive, nurturing, and domestic. "The Sioux girl was educated to be a hunter's helper and a future hunter's mother. At the same time she was subjected to a rigorous training toward bashfulness" (Erickson, 1963, p. 144).

New Jersey Indians

Males. The men of the tribe would often holler war whoops over the young boys (age 4 and older) to accustom them to threat (Miller, 1928).

Mandan Indians of North America

Males. Beginning around age 7, boys were regularly sent naked into the wilderness, armed only with bows, to participate in realistic maneuvers of Indian warfare (Catlin, 1848).

Borneo Headhunters

Males. As early as age 8, boys were forced to mutilate the bodies of the dead, enemies taken in war, or old slaves to accustom themselves to violence and bloodshed. The most ferocious and merciless boys were the most respected (Miller, 1928).

Females. When a girl began menstruation, she was taught medicinal arts and fertility dances (Miller, 1928).

Bushmen of Australia

Males. Prior to puberty, boys underwent years of torture to make them hardened and fearless. "Should a boy show signs of fear, he would be so scorned and mocked that he would, unless restrained, commit suicide" (Miller, 1928, p. 203).

Mountain Arapesh of New Guinea

Males. At the first signs of puberty, boys were involved in initiation ceremonies during which the adult males cut their own arms and mixed the blood with coconut milk, which was fed to the boys, who were then beaten to make them fierce (Mead, 1949).

Females. At the onset of menstruation, girls entered into a series of fastings that were thought to enhance fertility (Mead, 1949).

Stseelis of British Columbia

Males. Beginning with signs of physical sexual development, boys were whipped regularly and their bodies were exposed to the elements to accustom them to pain and deprivation (Miller, 1928).

Females. At the beginning of puberty (menstruation), women were not allowed to eat fresh meat or fish. This was designed to teach the girls not to be greedy and to save the best for the men (Miller, 1928).

Kurnai Tribe of Australia

Males. Boys age 10-13 were initiated into totem groups through ceremonies that involved mutilations and a violent separation from their mothers. The ceremonies stressed a total break with the women and other children of the tribe and induction into the separate world of manhood (Gennep, 1960).

continued on facing page

TABLE 2.1 (continued)

Tribes of the lower Congo

Males. Initiation ceremonies for boys age 10-15 involved several days of flagellation and mutilation (Gennep, 1960).

Masai of Australia

Males. Boys age 12 were circumcised in an elaborate ceremony that involved washing the boys in freezing water to toughen them and placing blood on their heads to accustom them to bloodshed (Gennep, 1960).

Zuni of New Mexico

Males. Boys age 12-13 underwent a voluntary initiation ceremony during which an adult male of the same tribe, serving as the boy's sponsor, beat the initiate continually with branches until the boy was hardened and brave enough to become a man (Gennep, 1960).

Thomson Indians of British Columbia

Males. Boys age 12-16 participated in ceremonies to teach them how to be hunters and warriors. To be considered "men," the boys had to prove their fearlessness and ability to use weapons in battle (Gennep, 1960).

Females. Girls age 17-18 participated in menstruation-related ceremonies that involved symbolic washings and fastings (Gennep, 1960).

Arunta of central Australia

Males. At the first signs of puberty, boys were stolen from their mothers and forced to participate in a ceremony during which they were "reborn" from a symbolic baby pouch strapped to an adult male sponsor. The adult males of the tribe then cut their own arms and allowed the blood to run over the reborn boys (Benedict, 1955).

Gilbert Islands

Females. At puberty, girls were sent into isolation with only their parents and grandparents. The girls were taught healing and culinary skills to prepare them for marriage (Miller, 1928).

Fijians

Males. Beginning with puberty, boys were taken at night to an area where the adult men had placed a group of bloody supposedly dead and decaying bodies covered with animal intestines. The boys were forced to crawl through the "dead" bodies, which suddenly "came to life." Boys who showed fear were denied manhood (Miller, 1928).

---

actually experienced miscarriages (Brockett, 1982; Smith, 1831). Ancient Greek and Roman theater routinely presented demonic characters in terrifying masks and depictions of evil spirits rising from the dead. Scenes often involved the sacrificing of live animals. Drama in the ancient Orient and in India also featured horrific characters and violent action. Again, these forms of entertainment were analogous to earlier initiation rites and afforded men an opportunity to publicly exhibit their fearlessness, their bravery, and their capacity for protection. Women, in contrast, were consistently portrayed as fearful and in need of protection.

NO FURTHER CALL FOR BRAVERY

The need for gender-specific mastery of threat and danger has vanished in contemporary industrial societies. Technological advances in warfare, in particular, have made physical strength, agility, and stamina expendable. Male bravery is reduced to operating war machines by pushing buttons and fingering joysticks, activities for which women show no handicap. With the virtual elimination of man-to-man combat from the books of military strategy, the last male institution for the show of masculinity and combat supremacy fell by the wayside (Bernstein, 1987).

The vast majority of young men and women continue, however, to be socialized along "traditional" gender roles (Burton & Whiting, 1971). Just as in the so-called Dark Ages, pressures are still brought to bear on boys to exhibit fearlessness and radiate self-reliance, whereas girls are allowed to express their fears and are encouraged to signal a need for protection.

Men who want to exhibit their machismo are hard pressed. They have to resort to daring ventures devoid of all social utility. They can show a disregard for their own safety and contempt for their own life in activities such as racing cars, riding ever-scarier roller coasters, climbing cliffs with bare fingers, bungee jumping, or diving in shark-infested waters. In so-called contact sports, men can level others and "knock their brains out." In football, for example, the bone-crashing tackle leaves little doubt about the player's masculinity. The parallel exhibition of femininity by approving, admiring, and applauding cheerleaders completes the picture and underscores prevalent socialization.

The martial arts may be considered the last vestige of the exhibition of true fighting skills. As in the ancient combative sports, fighters can determine the best, the good, and the wanting among them (Zillmann, 1990). Those demonstrating good fighting skills may indeed have acquired protective capacity. Its utility should be limited, however, to brawls in bars and dark alleys. The good fighter may radiate protection, but hardly can be considered to be of much use in preventing the major dangers of modern life, such as harm from gunshots or car crashes. Even when honing actual fighting skills, then, "protective man" is a facade that offers little protection.

Another consideration weighs just as heavily. The determination of able fighters can produce only a few of superior skill. The majority of men are likely to look bad, mediocre at best, by contrast. If fighting skills were a prerequisite for the protector image, most men would probably fail to impress the ladies who look for a shoulder to lean on. Thus, in order for the large majority of men to be able to meet their societally prescribed macho role and succeed in acquiring the traditional role image of male protector, there must be procedures for the demonstration of machismo that are significantly easier than the achievement of superior skills in a martial art.

Societies that continue to adhere to the traditional gender-role segregation must find ways to provide young men and women with *manageable* opportunities to establish and refine expected dispositions and affections. Surely, sports and especially contact sports offer many such opportunities. By performing essentially useless physical skills, boys can demonstrate machismo and girls can admire them for it. In these terms, high school football might be considered a most productive societal institution. The activities allow boys to display strength, agility, and stamina, and "participating" girls, the cheerleaders, are literally sidelined and forced into adoration and reverence model roles.

On the other hand, many such institutions have compromised their segregating utility by accepting women as equal competitors. In Little League baseball, for example, girls are truly incorporated; and some, with the display of their skills, give boys reason to feel awed and intimidated. Moreover, women have made inroads into daring sports of the greatest macho sanctity, such as parachute jumping and arctic dogsled racing. It remains to be seen, however, to what extent women of great athletic achievement and bravery will inspire awe and adoration in the men they humble.

All this is to say that active participation in competitive sports may have lost much of its gender-role segregating capacity.

PAPER TIGERS AND PATSIES

Cinematic horror does not have the indicated problems. Gender-role segregation can be accomplished by sitting still in front of a screen. Nobody is left out. Segregation comes at a minimum of skill and a maximum of convenience. And in contrast to the risk of bodily injury in daring activities, the experience is marked by extreme safety. Nobody comes to harm—in a physical sense.

How are men socialized? All they have to do to meet societal precepts concerning their emotional reactions to the terror on the screen is not to blink an eye, not to flinch, and certainly not to scream in distress. Mastery of distress is expected of men who are to radiate the capacity to protect.

How are women socialized? By the opposite behavior. By flinching and screaming in response to the terror on the screen. No mastery of distress is expected of them. On the contrary: They are to express their dismay as best they can; they are to signal a need for support and comfort; they are to show dependence—emotional dependence.

The horror film thus may be viewed as a significant forum for the gender-specific socialization of fear and its mastery in modern times, a last vestige of ancient rites of passage. It is a most popular forum that provides boys with the opportunity to develop, through habituation of the excitatory response associated with fear and distress (Grings & Dawson, 1978), mastery of any disturbance from terrifying events. At the same time, it provides girls the opportunity to practice the expression of distress, whether actually felt or play-acted. If Ovid's earlier discussed convictions have any merit, the horror film will bring young men and women romantically closer. Like obedient dolls, the distressed ladies are to seek comfort from their male dates who became instant heroes by not blinking an eye when heads were rolling. Zillmann and Weaver (chap. 6, this volume) pursue these possibilities further and review the research evidence pertaining to them.

ALTERNATIVE VIEWS

Those who have pondered the appeal of horror as entertainment, the presumed enjoyment of horror movies in particular, have invariably concentrated on emotional benefits for the terrified individual, benefits that are derived entirely from exposure to the terrifying material. Social factors that might influence appeal and enjoyment were simply ignored.

The most popular view is probably that of hostility catharsis. The idea that witnessing violence and mayhem might prompt a purgation of the onlookers' own violent inclinations, usually attributed to Aristotle, has been extended by the presumption that such purgation is pleasurably experienced (Clarens, 1967). Despite a wealth of evidence challenging beliefs in the cathartic process (Geen & Quanty, 1977; Zillmann, 1979), this view has been even more liberally expanded to include purgation from a variety of fears and phobias. It has been suggested, for instance, that people are inflicted with an ancient and hereditary fear of the dark, capable of converting into modern political and social anxieties, from which horror could provide pleasurable relief (Douglas, 1966). Even more particular, it has been suggested that terror directed at promiscuous women is pleasantly experienced by men, because it eases their anxieties about women's increasing sexual assertiveness (Tudor, 1989). Moreover, the recurrent theme of monstrous transformations in horror movies has been said to relieve teenagers' apprehension about their own transformations, especially those concerning sexual maturation (Evans, 1984).

Others have resisted assumptions about hidden anxieties and violent urges as causal conditions for people's fascination with horror. Berlyne (1967, 1971), for instance, suggested that the experience of relief in and of itself is gratifying, but that, in order to attain gratification from relief, noxious experiences are a necessary prerequisite. This reasoning accepts that horror is horrifying—that is, that the reaction to horror is a thoroughly aversive experience. It is the *termination* of this aversive state that is expected to prompt pleasurable relief. In this view, the enjoyment of horror is akin to the pleasures of the sudden end to a bad toothache—which should leave people in hopes for recurrences.

Yet others dug deeper and suggested that horror produces anxieties that motivate added deliberation that eventually results in gratification. Rosenbaum (1979), for example, accused scientific technology of destroying with its logical explanations all beliefs in the mysterious forces of evil, forces deemed essential for the worship of benevolent beings capable of overcoming evil. The popularity of horror movies is viewed as a religious phenomenon, giving the rationally spoiled a glimpse of the inexplicable evil and restoring their longing for a superior entity to restrain the demonic forces. The ultimate yield ought to be feelings of security. According to this elaborate formula, then, people seek terror to gain a sense of spiritual safety and are gratified thereby.

In connection with safety, the concepts of *vicarious experience* and *identification* have been heavily called on to explain the enjoyment of horror. King (1981) asserted that viewers of horror movies identify, in the sense of placing themselves into others and sharing their feelings, with monsters and killers. They are said to attain an aberrant pleasure by this process. The postulated process of identification essentially allows them to experience the joys of sadism, although only vicariously. Numerous writers of psychoanalytic persuasion similarly argued that horror's appeal derives from a fascination with the forbidden. More specifically, it is thought to derive from the vicarious breaking of taboos, especially of uncounted sexual taboos that, with the utmost of imagination, are spotted in more or less all evil and demonic actions (Wood, 1984). If not taboos, any number of anxieties, buried deep in the subconscious, are held accountable (Derry, 1987). These anxieties are presumed to be too severe to surface in realistic discourse and thought to require the nonauthenticity of the horror tale for expression and elaboration. Rockett (1988), director of the celebrated *Nightmare on Elm Street*, endorsed such views when he contended that exposure to artificial horror "exorcises fears and doubts that are going on in a person's subconscious. It brings them out in an entertaining manner and resolves the fears in a way that seems to wrap them all up" (p. 3). The postulated resolution of fear is, of course, nothing other than the catharsis doctrine.

Others have emphasized the absence of risk in "playing with death" (Dickstein, 1984, p. 69), demons, and the supernatural generally (Heller, 1987), but left unclear why, without the benefit of any purgation, such play would be enjoyable.

Those with a more biological orientation invoked a need for stimulation, excitement, and challenge that is seen to derive from coping with danger in prehistoric times. Specifically, the organism is thought to be equipped to continually confront life-threatening dangers and to act on them with some degree of success. The scarcity of such dangers in modern life places few demands on these dormant capabilities, prompting individuals to seek danger and to create challenges in daring ventures (Zuckerman, 1979). Although this proposal focuses on the appeal of activities that are truly dangerous, such as parachute jumping, it applies to horror films in the sense that the observed scary happenings call for the analysis of dangerous situations and the conception of effective coping reactions. One might wonder, however, about the extent to which danger seekers can find fulfillment in witnessing mayhem from a "safe distance" and handling threats in fantasy only.

HORROR IN THE GENDER-SOCIALIZATION SCHEME

The gender-socialization approach that we have pursued makes assumptions that differ sharply from those of models projecting the purgation of violent urges and overt or covert anxieties. They also differ from models projecting a lingering need for fear and danger.

In agreement with Berlyne's (1967, 1971) proposal, we assume, with the likely exception of deviant subpopulations such as sadists, that horror is terrifying in the sense that it liberates empathetic distress with those victimized and evokes apprehensions about victimization (Zillmann, 1991a, 1991b).

However, in contrast to Berlyne's view, we do not assume that the termination of exposure to horror fosters relief sufficient to account for the enjoyment experience. Analogous to suspenseful drama, horror often features some sort of satisfying resolution, a resolution that may be enjoyed for what it is and whose enjoyment may be intensified by residual excitation from preceding terror (see Zillmann, 1991b, for a theoretical model of these processes). More importantly, we propose that enjoyment of horror derives in part from successfully behaving, under emotionally taxing circumstances, in accordance with societal precepts.

The precept for boys and men stipulates that exposure to horror be nondistressing. Their show of mastery of distress in the face of terror should please them and favorably impress others. Gratification is thus self-generated and of a social nature. The precept for girls and women, in contrast, stipulates that exposure to horror be distressing and duly expressed as such. Their show of appropriate sensitivity—dismay, disgust, and contempt—should give them pleasure and favorably impress others. Gratification is again self-generated and social in kind.

The existence and consequences of these precepts are demonstrated elsewhere (Zillmann & Weaver, chap. 6, this volume). Suffice it here to suggest that the projected gender differences do exist in the vast majority of cultures. Whether or not they *should* exist is a matter of values. In light of contentions, such as that gender-role socialization—to which cinematic horror may contribute—has no longer functional utility but is perpetuated in order to maintain male supremacy (Chodorow, 1971), the issue certainly demands reflection.

REFERENCES

Barry, H., Bacon, M. K., & Child, I. L. (1957). A cross-cultural survey of some sex differences in socialization. *Journal of Abnormal and Social Psychology, 55*, 327-332.

Barry, H., Bacon, M. K., & Child, I. L. (1959). Relation of child training to subsistence economy. *American Anthropologist, 61*, 51-63.

Bem, S. L. (1981). Gender schema theory: A cognitive account of sex typing. *Psychological Review, 88*, 354-364.

Benedict, R. (1955). Continuities and discontinuities in cultural condition. In M. Mead & M. Wolfenstein (Eds.), *Childhood in contemporary cultures* (pp. 21-30). Chicago: University of Chicago Press.

Berlyne, D. E. (1967). Arousal and reinforcement. In D. Levine (Ed.), *Nebraska Symposium on Motivation* (Vol. 15, pp. 1-110). Lincoln: University of Nebraska Press.

Berlyne, D. E. (1971). *Aesthetics and psychobiology*. Englewood Cliffs, NJ: Prentice-Hall.

Bernstein, J. S. (1987). The decline of masculine rites of passage in our culture: The impact on masculine individualization. In L. C. Mahdi, S. Foster, & M. Little (Eds.), *Betwixt & between: Patterns of masculine and feminine initiation* (pp. 135-158). LaSalle, IL: Open Court.

Bettelheim, B. (1975). *The uses of enchantment: The meaning and importance of fairy tales*. New York: Vintage Books.

Brockett, O. G. (1982). *History of the theatre* (4th ed.). Boston: Allyn & Bacon.

Brody, L. R. (1985). Gender differences in emotional development: A review of theories and research. *Journal of Personality, 53*(2), 102-149.

Burton, R. V., & Whiting, J. W. M. (1971). The absent father and cross-sex identity. *Merrill-Palmer Quarterly, 7*, 85-95.

Cantor, J. (1991). Fright responses to mass media productions. In J. Bryant & D. Zillmann (Eds.), *Responding to the screen: Reception and reaction processes* (pp. 169-197). Hillsdale, NJ: Lawrence Erlbaum Associates.

Catlin, G. (1848). *Illustrations of the manners, customs, and conditions of the North American Indians* (5th ed.). London: Cattup & Windus.

Chodorow, N. (1971). Being and doing: A cross-cultural examination of the socialization of males and females. In V. Gornick & B. Moran (Eds.), *Woman in sexist society* (pp. 173-197). New York: Basic Books.

Cialdini, R. B. (1985). *Influence: Science and practice*. Glenview, IL: Scott, Foresman.

Clarens, C. (1967). *An illustrated history of the horror film*. New York: Putnam.

Dahlberg, F. (Ed.). (1981). *Woman the gatherer*. New Haven, CT: Yale University Press.

Daly, M., & Wilson, M. (1978). *Sex, evolution and behavior: Adaptations for reproduction*. North Scituate, MA: Duxbury Press.

Derry, C. (1987). More dark dreams: Some notes on the recent horror film. In G. A. Waller (Ed.), *American horrors: Essays on the modern American horror film* (pp. 162-174). Urbana: University of Illinois Press.

Dickstein, M. (1984). The aesthetics of fright. In B. K. Grant (Ed.), *Planks of reason: Essays on the horror film* (pp. 65-75). Metuchen, NJ: Scarecrow Press.

Douglas, D. (1966). *Horror!* New York: Macmillan.

Droogers, A. (1980). *The dangerous journey: Symbolic aspects of boys' initiations among the Wagenia of Kisangani, Zaire*. The Hague: Mouton Publishers.

Erikson, E. H. (1963). *Childhood and society* (2nd ed). New York: Norton.

Evans, W. (1984). Monster movies: A sexual theory. In B. K. Grant (Ed.), *Planks of reason: Essays on the horror film* (pp. 53-64). Metuchen, NJ: Scarecrow Press.

Feather, N. T. (1984). Masculinity, femininity, psychological androgyny, and the structure of values. *Journal of Personality and Social Psychology, 47*, 604-621.

Friedl, E. (1975). *Women and men: An anthropologist's view*. New York: Holt, Rinehart & Winston.

Frisbie, C. J. (1990). Anthropological perspectives on the subordination of women. In S. Ruth (Ed.), *Issues in feminism* (pp. 163-172). Mountain View, CA: Mayfield.

Geen, R. G., & Quanty, M. B. (1977). The catharsis of aggression: An evaluation of a hypothesis. In L. Berkowitz (Ed.), *Advances in experimental social psychology* (Vol. 10, pp. 1-37). New York: Academic Press.

Gennep, A. van. (1960). *The rites of passage* (M. B. Vizedom & G. L. Caffee, Trans.). Chicago, IL: University of Chicago Press.

Grings, W. W., & Dawson, M. E. (1978). *Emotions and bodily responses: A psychophysiological approach.* New York: Academic Press.

Guttmann, A. (1978). *From ritual to record: The nature of modern sport.* New York: Columbia University Press.

Guttmann, A. (1986). *Sports spectators.* New York: Columbia University Press.

Hammond, D., & Jablow, A. (1976). *Women in cultures of the world.* Menlo Park, CA: Cummings.

Harris, H. A. (1972). *Aspects of Greek and Roman life.* Ithaca, NY: Cornell University Press.

Heald, S. (1986). The ritual use of violence: Circumcision among the Gisu of Uganda. In D. Riches (Ed.), *The anthropology of violence* (pp. 70-85). Oxford, UK: Blackwell.

Heller, T. (1987). *The delights of terror: An aesthetics of the tale of terror.* Urbana: University of Illinois Press.

Kernodle, G. R. (1989). *The theatre in history.* Fayetteville: University of Arkansas.

King, S. (1981). *Danse macabre.* New York: Everest.

Lang, A. (1968). *Custom and myth.* New York: AMS Press.

Lewis, H. B. (1976). *Psychic war in men and women.* New York: New York University Press.

Lidz, T., & Lidz, R. W. (1989). *Oedipus in the Stone Age: A psychoanalytic study of masculinization in Papua New Guinea.* Madison, CT: International Universities Press.

Maccoby, E. E., & Jacklin, C. N. (1974). *The psychology of sex differences.* Stanford, CA: Stanford University Press.

Marvin, G. (1986). Honour, integrity and the problem of violence in the Spanish bullfight. In D. Riches (Ed.), *The anthropology of violence* (pp. 118-135). Oxford, UK: Blackwell.

Mead, M. (1949). *Male and female.* New York: William Morrow.

Mercatante, A. S. (1978). *Good and evil: Mythology and folklore.* New York: Harper & Row.

Midwinter, E. (1986). *Fair game: Myth and reality in sport.* London: Allen & Unwin.

Miller, N. (1928). *The child in primitive society.* New York: Bretano.

Mischel, W. (1970). Sex-typing and socialization. In P. H. Mussen (Ed.), *Carmichael's manual of child psychology* (3rd ed., Vol. 2, pp. 3-72). New York: Wiley.

Nevin, J. A. (1973). Conditioned reinforcement. In J. A. Nevin (Ed.), *The study of behavior: Learning, motivation, emotion, and instinct* (pp. 155-198). Glenview, IL: Scott, Foresman.

Puhvel, J. (1987). *Comparative mythology.* Baltimore: Johns Hopkins University Press.

Rockett, W. H. (1988). *Devouring whirlwind: Terror and transcendence in the cinema of cruelty.* New York: Greenwood Press.

Rosenbaum, R. (1979, September). Gooseflesh. *Harpers,* pp. 86-92.

Sansone, D. (1988). *Greek athletics and the genesis of sport.* Berkeley: University of California Press.

Schlegel, A., & Barry, H. (1979). Adolescent initiation ceremonies: A cross-cultural code. *Ethnology, 18,* 199-210.

Schlenker, B. R. (1980). *Impression management: The self-concept, social identity, and interpersonal relations.* Monterey, CA: Brooks/Cole.

Skinner, B. F. (1969). *Contingencies of reinforcement: A theoretical analysis.* New York: Appleton-Century-Crofts.

Smith, H. (1831). *Festivals, games and amusements, ancient and modern.* London: Henry Colburn & Richard Bentley.

Snyder, M. (1981). Impression management: The self in social interaction. In L. S. Wrightsman & K. Deaux (Eds.), *Social psychology in the 80s* (pp. 90-123). New York: Wiley.

Spence, J. T., & Helmreich, R. L. (1978). *Masculinity and femininity: Their psychological dimensions, correlates and antecedents.* Austin: University of Texas Press.

Tudor, A. (1989). *Monsters and mad scientists: A cultural history of the horror movie.* Oxford, UK: Blackwell.

Weitzman, L. J. (1984). Sex-role socialization: A focus on women. In J. Freeman (Ed.), *Women: A feminist perspective* (pp. 157-237). Palo Alto, CA: Mayfield.

Wickham, G. (1985). *A history of the theater.* Cambridge, UK: Cambridge University Press.

Wood, R. (1984). An introduction to the American horror film. In B. K. Grant (Ed.), *Planks of reason: Essays on the horror film* (pp. 164-200). Metuchen, NJ: Scarecrow Press.

Yearsley, P. M. (1968). *The folklore of fairy-tale.* Detroit: Singing Tree Press.

Zillmann, D. (1979). *Hostility and aggression.* Hillsdale, NJ: Lawrence Erlbaum Associates.

Zillmann, D. (1990). Die Beanblossom-Hypothesen. *Semiosis, 15*(1/2), 69-73.

Zillmann, D. (1991a). Empathy: Affect from bearing witness to the emotions of others. In J. Bryant & D. Zillmann (Eds.), *Responding to the screen: Reception and reaction processes* (pp. 135-167). Hillsdale, NJ: Lawrence Erlbaum Associates.

Zillmann, D. (1991b). The logic of suspense and mystery. In J. Bryant & D. Zillmann (Eds.), *Responding to the screen: Reception and reaction processes* (pp. 281-303). Hillsdale, NJ: Lawrence Erlbaum Associates.

Zillmann, D., Weaver, J. B., Mundorf, N., & Aust, C. F. (1986). Effects of an opposite-gender companion's affect to horror on distress, delight, and attraction. *Journal of Personality and Social Psychology, 51,* 586-594.

Zuckerman, M. (1979). *Sensation seeking: Beyond the optimal level of arousal.* New York: Wiley.

Chapter
3

Content Trends in Contemporary Horror Films

Barry S. Sapolsky
Florida State University
Fred Molitor
Bowling Green State University

In this chapter we look at the evolution of the horror film with special attention to conditions that facilitated the emergence of exploitation "teenpics." One teenpic subgenre that emerged in the 1960s following the critical and commercial success of Hitchcock's *Psycho* was gore cinema. Gore films, so named for their attention to the gross-out butchering and even eating of human flesh, pushed the limits of on-screen violence. By the 1970s the outgrowth of gore cinema was the so-called "slasher" movie. Critics have blasted the producers of slasher films, claiming these films disproportionately portray vicious attacks on women and tie images of extreme violence to scenes of sexual titillation and precoital behavior. We examine the results of recent content analyses of slasher movies to test the validity of the assumptions made about violence to women and the linkage of sex and violence.

FROM TRANSYLVANIA TO THE BATES MOTEL

The horror movie genre was established in the 1930s with the release of *Dracula* and *Frankenstein*. Within 10 years, horror films were to become highly derivative, replete with recycled characters and themes, and "strangled by riding a few once-successful types into the ground, exhausting their novelty and coaxing sighs instead of screams" (Kendrick, 1991, p. 221). Intent on not offending their audiences, producers avoided images of bloodshed or dismemberment; the "blunting of horror for the sake of universal appeal" (Kendrick, 1991, p. 222) had, by the late 1940s made the horror movie nearly extinct.

By 1950, in the aftermath of World War II and the detonation of the A-bomb, a subgenre of science fiction horror was born. Zombies, werewolves, and mummies were replaced by mammoth insects and alien beings. Such films vented fears of the atomic menace and, allegorically, communism, and expressed a general mistrust of science and technology (Doherty, 1988; Kendrick, 1991).

Social and industry developments in the late 1940s and 1950s would irrevocably change the nature of the production of and audience for motion pictures. The *Paramount* decision of 1948 ended Hollywood's vertical integration; its exhibition arm was wrested from the control of the studios. Television quickly grew to challenge movies as a source of universal entertainment for the mass audience. Faced with increasing foreign film competition, the move of creative talent to newlyformed independent production companies, and House UnAmerican Activities Committee witchhunts, the old Hollywood studio system was in decline and confronting serious financial difficulties.

American society was undergoing important post-WWII lifestyle changes as well. The growth of suburbia and changing leisure habits contributed to lower theater attendance and a growing fixation on the free entertainment of television. Foremost among the changes that would influence the production of horror movies was the rise of a separate teen culture (Hogan, 1986). America's privileged teenagers were the "one group with the requisite income, leisure and garrulousness to support a theatrical business" (Doherty, 1988, p. 3). Thus, the convergence of Hollywood's structural and financial problems with the growing recognition that teenagers represented the core of Hollywood's audience led to the creation of the "exploitation teenpic" (Doherty, 1988; Hogan, 1986).

A new generation stood at the ready to be frightened by the horror film. In need of capital, Hollywood sold its motion picture libraries to its former archenemy, television. Stations aired vintage horror films to 1950s teenagers. So-called "chiller theater" shows were ratings hits. A new audience's appetite was whetted for Gothic horror.

The 1957 release of *The Curse of Frankenstein* by Britain's Hammer films began a cycle of "horror teenpics" (Doherty, 1988). Stylish and serious, Hammer films shocked their audience by showing the blood and gore of horror in color. Hammer's "most important innovation . . . is that when ghastliness occurs the camera doesn't shy away or fade to black: it zooms in" (Kendrick, 1991, p. 229).

Fittingly, the success of *The Curse of Frankenstein* was soon followed by American International Pictures' (AIP) *I Was a Teenage Werewolf* and *I Was a Teenage Frankenstein*. AIP perfected the teen exploitation film through its canny marketing and obsession with the teen audience. The exploitation film could be boiled down to three key ingredients: "(1) controversial, bizarre or timely subject matter amenable to wild promotion . . .; (2) a substandard budget; and (3) a teenage audience" (Doherty, 1988, p. 8).

Economic and competitive factors in the motion picture industry facilitated the ascendance of horror teenpics. Hollywood answered the challenge of television by channeling its resources into a smaller number of "big" films. The elimination of "B" movies led to a dearth of product for exhibitors. The answer was the relatively inexpensive films turned out by independent producers, many of whom catered to the growing teen market.

Hollywood also attempted to outdo its rival television by tackling previously untouchable mature content. The extremely proscriptive Motion Picture Production Code was relaxed in the 1950s. Both the Supreme Court's 1952 ruling that motion picture content is included within free speech guarantees and the strong impact of provocative foreign films led to more and more films being released without a Code seal (Farber, 1972). Film producers dared to feature previously taboo themes, behaviors, and images.

In the early 1960s movies became increasingly explicit in their portrayals of sex. Horror films were no exception. *Beauty and the Robot* and *The Incredibly Strange Creatures Who Stopped Living and Became Mixed Up Zombies* featured "overripe, underdressed chorus girls" (Hogan, 1986, p. 130). A new level of explicitness extended to violence as well. One film that singlehandedly launched a new subgenre of "gore" horror movies appeared in 1960: Alfred Hitchcock's *Psycho*.

Psycho marked a turning point for two reasons. First, as a highly popular motion picture by a noted director, *Psycho* legitimized blood and gore as a film's *raison d'etre*. Second, Hitchcock's classic invited imitation—horror films in its wake featured psychopathic killers and concentrated on the lurid details of mutilation and murder (Kendrick, 1991).

GORE FILMS

Whereas horror films in the 1930s and 1940s tastefully avoided images of dismemberment and blood, the gore films of the 1960s revolved around grisly slaughter. Ever more inventive special effects pushed the limits of realistic gruesome images. A trendsetter in gore was 1963's *Blood Feast*. It depicted the stalking, attack, and mutilation of beautiful women:

> One girl is attacked as she necks with her boyfriend . . . the top of her head chopped off and her brain left to lie in the sand. Another young lady is . . . hacked to bits, and turned into a stew. Perhaps the best bit involves . . . Astrid Olson, whose tongue is pulled from her head in closeup and without camera cuts. (Hogan, 1986, p. 237).

Even more influential than *Blood Feast* was *Night of the Living Dead* (1968), which featured hideous, decaying zombies eating human entrails and severed limbs (McCarty, 1984). The film's popularity was enhanced through its wide distribution, cult status, and critical success. *Night of the Living Dead* inspired many imitative flesh-eating zombie movies (Newman, 1988).

The level of gore intensified in the 1970s. The extremes of explicit bloodletting were abetted by special effects wizardry. Notable in the progression are *The Texas Chainsaw Massacre* (1974) and *Dawn of the Dead* (1978). In the view of one critic, *The Texas Chainsaw Massacre* is:

> . . . The most affecting gore thriller of all and, in a broader view, among the most effective horror films ever made. . . . The girl watches as her unconscious boyfriend is cut into filets by a chain saw. As the afternoon wears into night, more of the youngsters are stalked and murdered. . . . What is remarkable . . . is that its outrageous horrors seem entirely real. . . . Unlike the villains in most other gore films, Hooper's fiends are not sexually motivated. The driving force of *The Texas Chain Saw Massacre* is something far more horrible than aberrant sexuality: total insanity. (Hogan, 1986, pp. 247-249)

By the end of the 1970s, movies such as *The Texas Chainsaw Massacre* had set the stage for an even more specialized subgenre of horror—the slasher film.

THE SLASHER FILM

The slasher film evolved out of the explicit gore served up in the 1960s and 1970s. Slasher movies have been credited to Herschell Gordon Lewis (1960s producer of *Blood Feast* and *2000 Maniacs*, among others) who recognized that a "combination of pretty girls and crazy violence makes for good box office" (Hogan, 1986, p. 241). Later movies, typified by *Halloween* (1978), *Friday the 13th* (1980) and *Maniac* (1980), were strongly criticized for their frequent portrayal of vicious attacks on females, their linkage of sex to violence, and their savage destruction of innocent characters.

It has been observed that the mayhem in slasher movies is nearly always carried out by a "psychokiller who slashes to death a string of mostly female victims, one by one, until he is subdued and killed, usually by the one girl who has survived" (Clover, 1992, p. 21). The superhuman monster or male typically wields axes, chainsaws, power drills, knives, pitchforks, and the like, weapons guaranteed to exact a maximum of splatter. Another common element in slasher films is said to be postcoital death, especially for instances of "illicit" sex (Clover, 1992). Thus, these movies are at their core eviscerating tales of madness and death.

WOMEN, SEX, AND VIOLENCE

Slasher movies have been the target of heavy criticism from the popular media. Complaints have centered in part on the level of violence that is said to be unique to this subgenre. Unlike classic horror films, slasher films are said to contain acts of *extreme* violence (e.g., beheading and mutilations) portrayed in graphic detail (Bass, 1988; "Child's play," 1987; Continelli, 1989; Maslin, 1981, 1982; Meyer, 1988; Nordheimer, 1987; Shalit, 1980; *Sneak Previews*, 1980; Stein, 1982). Actually, slasher films are the natural progression from gore cinema. Film directors and special effects magicians have lavished these films with "extravagant displays of imitation human bodies getting mauled in ever more outlandish ways" (Kendrick, 1991, p. xix).

Another condemnation of slasher movies is the widely-held view that they single out women for injury and death (Clover, 1992; Continelli, 1989; Maslin, 1982; Nordheimer, 1987). For example, Pat Broeske (1984), film critic for the *Los Angeles Times*, claimed that the "brutal victimization of women [is] a recurring and obviously popular theme in such films" (p. 19). During the ABC news show *Nightline*, correspondent Gail Harris summarized the content of slasher films with the statement, "Almost all of these films are short on plot and long on brutality and violence, much of it sexual, almost all of it directed at women" (cited in Meyer, 1988). Some have labeled this subgenre "violence-to-women" (Worsham, 1982) or "women-in-danger" (*Sneak Previews*, 1980) films. Others have gone so far as to say that, in slasher films, the "victim is always a woman" (Bass, 1988, p. B3).

Slasher films have also been criticized in the popular press for mixing extreme violence with sex (Bass, 1988; Clover, 1992; Continelli, 1989; Meyer, 1988; Nordheimer, 1987). *New York Times* film critic Janet Maslin (1982) characterized the violence in slasher films: "The carnage is usually preceded by some sort of erotic prelude: footage of pretty young bodies in the shower, or teens changing into nighties for the slumber party, or anything that otherwise lulls the audience into a mildly sensual mood" (p. 13).

Social scientists have primarily focused their attention on the negative effects slasher films may have on audiences. These researchers have largely subscribed to film critics' and journalists' claims about the content of slasher movies. For example, Oliver (1994) stated that "extreme violence may be the defining characteristic of films in this genre" (p. 1). Linz and Donnerstein have consistently reported that females are inequitably portrayed as the victims of violence in slasher films. They define the subgenre as films that contain "explicit scenes of violence in which the victims are nearly always female" (Linz, Donnerstein, & Penrod, 1984, p. 137) and state that the violence is "overwhelmingly directed at women" (Donnerstein, Linz, & Penrod, 1987, p. 113).

In regard to the linkage of sex and violence, these same researchers have stated that slasher films "frequently include the mutilation of women in scenes that juxtapose the violence with sexual content" (Linz, Donnerstein, & Adams, 1989, p. 510). Violence in slasher films is said to often occur "during or juxtaposed to mildly erotic scenes" (Linz, Donnerstein, & Penrod, 1988, p. 759) and the "films often juxtapose a violent scene with a sensual or erotic scene (e.g., a woman masturbating in the bath is suddenly and brutally attacked)" (Linz, Donnerstein, & Penrod, 1984, p. 137). Oliver (1994) likewise accepted the view that slasher films contain "erotic scenes often occurring prior to or during victimization" (p. 1).

Taken together, the notions expressed by film critics and social scientists lead to the following assumptions regarding the content of slasher movies: These films (a) portray extreme violence that (b) is primarily directed at women and (c) often occurs during or after sexual or erotic images. In the remaining pages we utilize the findings of three recent content analyses to empirically test these assumptions.

SELECTION OF FILMS FOR STUDY

Before examining the results of three slasher film content analyses in detail, let us first delineate the subgenre. Slasher films can be characterized as commercially released, feature-length films containing suspense-evoking scenes in which an antagonist, who is usually a male acting alone, attacks one or more victims. The accent in these films is on extreme violence. Scenes that dwell on the victim's fear and explicitly portray the attack and its aftermath are the central focus of slasher films. Thus, according to Tudor (1989), the tension in slasher films derives from the question: "Who will the central villain get next and by what method?" (p. 198). This definition also circumscribes what are not slasher films: films in which the antagonist is of nonhuman form, for example, a monster, animal, or zombie.

Content analyses of films conforming to the preceding description offer a means to test the validity of key assumptions that have been made about the subgenre. Cowan and O'Brien (1990) randomly selected 56 films from a list of 100 horror movies available at local video outlets. Weaver (1991) examined the 10 slasher films with the highest box-office earnings through 1987. Molitor and Sapolsky (1993) utilized 30 commercially successful slasher films, 10 each from 1980, 1985, and 1989.

For example, Molitor and Sapolsky's selection of 30 films involved the following procedures. First, all potential slasher films appearing in *Variety's* weekly listing of "Top 50 Grossing Films" (for every week in 1980, 1985, and 1989) and weekly listing of "Top 40 Videocassette Rentals" (for every week in 1985 and 1989; *Variety's* weekly list was not published in 1980) were

TABLE 3.1
Slasher Films Selected for Analysis by Molitor and Sapolsky (1993)

Films	Ranking[a]	Total Acts of Violence	Seconds Females Seen in Fear	Seconds Males Seen in Fear
1980 Releases				
Silent Scream [b]	1	28	410	0
Friday the 13th [b,c]	1	28	907	0
Don't Go in the House	3	35	136	0
Prom Night [b,c]	3	35	625	95
Terror Train	3	21	379	19
Motel Hell	3	60	237	0
Mother's Day	5	98	2822	0
He Knows You're Alone	5	25	785	17
The Boogey Man	5	23	189	0
Don't Answer the Phone	9	52	621	0
1985 Releases				
Friday the 13th V	1	46	415	348
Nightmare on Elm Street 2	2	43	544	413
A Nightmare on Elm Street	6	20	942	36
Night Train to Terror	6	74	305	51
The Mutilator	13	24	236	141
Evils of the Night	13	70	573	14
Basket Case	17	18	136	251
The Hills Have Eyes 2	19	35	362	72
Friday the 13th VI	23	82	625	234
House on the Edge of the Park	27	63	370	0
1989 Releases				
Halloween 5	2	83	1241	67
Shocker	2	131	119	541
A Nightmare on Elm Street 5	3	43	346	152
Friday the 13th VIII	3	119	1016	494
Hellbound: Hellraiser II	6	61	1002	180
Child's Play	15	48	127	218
The Horror Show	15	41	326	69
Halloween 4	24	22	124	0
Out of the Dark	29	113	1035	0
Hell High	30	33	29	0

[a] Highest box-office or video rental ranking.
[b] Coded by Cowan and O'Brien (1990).
[c] Coded by Weaver (1991).

identified. To be selected for this preliminary list a film had to be classified as a "horror" movie in the *Video Source Book* (1990) or be classified as a "women-in-danger" film by Siskel and Ebert in their 1980 special edition *Sneak*

Previews program devoted entirely to criticism of such movies. Slasher films as identified by Linz, Donnerstein, and Penrod (1984, 1988) were also included in this preliminary list, as were films with titles that suggested they contain scenes of violence and death. A total of 148 films were contained in the preliminary list, 48 in 1980, 35 in 1985, and 62 in 1989. The films within each year were then rank-ordered according to box office and rental revenue.

Second, using national newspaper movie reviews (*NewsBank*, 1990), each film was evaluated (beginning with the top-ranked film) using the definition of slasher films outlined earlier. Accordingly, the 10 most successful slasher films appearing in 1980, 1985, and 1989 were identified (see Table 3.1).

WOMEN AS VICTIMS

The three content analyses provide body counts—the number of males and females injured or killed in slasher films. Table 3.2 presents the mean number of victims by sex found in the samples of slasher movies. No significant differences were found between the number of male and female victims. These findings, based on a total of 83 *different* films coded across the three studies, leads to the conclusion that, contrary to popular belief, females are not singled out for attack in slasher films.

TABLE 3.2
Victims of Violence by Sex

Sex	Cowan & O'Brien (1990)	Weaver[a] (1991)	Molitor & Sapolsky (1993)
Males	4.3	3.0	7.3
Females	4.1	3.8	5.9

Note. Means do not differ significantly (vertical comparisons).
[a]Only includes characters who were killed.

LINKING VIOLENCE AND SEX

In addition to coding the number of females killed, each of the three studies noted whether acts of violence occurred during or after sexual or erotic images. Thus, data from the three content analyses allow us to explore the extent to which violence is connected to sex in slasher films. As can be seen in the upper portion of Table 3.3, between one sixth and one third of the murdered females were presented in a sexual or erotic situation before or at the time of the attack. Although these figures might be interpreted as "high," they are dependent on the total number of females killed per film. To determine the *frequency* with which sex and violence are linked in slasher films, we believe that the important question must be: How many times, on average, is a female seen killed either during or after sex? The figures presented in the lower portion of Table 3.3 provide an answer to this question. The three content analyses found that juxtapositions of sex and violence only occur about one time per film. Of course, murder is only one, albeit the ultimate, form of violence; the Molitor and Sapolsky study found only two instances of major injury during or after a sexual display in the 30 films coded (Weaver and Cowan and O'Brien do not provide comparable data).

TABLE 3.3
Juxtaposition of Sex and Violence

	Cowan & O'Brien (1990)	Weaver (1991)	Molitor & Sapolsky (1993)
Percentage females killed for whom death was connected to sex	34.0%	16.7%	33.3%
Average number of female deaths per film connected to sex	1.1	0.6	1.3

The content analyses also found that direct acts of sexual aggression are not commonly portrayed in slasher films. Cowan and O'Brien found 15 instances ($M = 0.27$) of "forced sex" in the 56 films they examined. Weaver reports two scenes ($M = 0.20$) of sadomasochism as the only depictions of sexual violence in 10 slasher films. In the 30 films coded by Molitor and Sapolsky, five ($M = 0.17$) occurrences of rape were observed, along with 19 ($M = 0.63$) instances involving a female forced to kiss and/or endure fondling against her will. Given these findings, and the rare instances wherein a female is killed during or after a sexual situation, it can be concluded that the oft-repeated claim that sex and violence are frequently linked in slasher films is unfounded.

To summarize, three recent content analyses show that females are victims of slashers as often as males, and sex and violence are not commonly linked in slasher films. Neither Cowan and O'Brien nor Weaver addressed the third assumption that has been made regarding the content of slasher films—that they contain acts of extreme violence. The Molitor and Sapolsky content analysis attempted to do so by noting the frequency with which different types of violent acts were committed in popular slasher movies.

THE BRUTALITY OF SLASHERS

To ascertain the level of brutality in slasher films, Molitor and Sapolsky categorized violent behavior as follows: verbal abuse, beating, kicking, strangling, burning, beheading, bludgeoning, hanging, dismembering, stabbing, or shooting. A total of 1,573 violent acts were coded across the 30 slasher films, for an average of 52.4 acts per film. Table 3.4 offers a profile of the mayhem. The most frequently appearing categories of violent behavior include beating (32.3% of all violent acts), stabbing resulting in major injury or death (21.6%), and shooting (18.0%). Assaults perpetrated without some type of weapon (beating, choking/strangling, kicking, threats, and verbal abuse) represent more than 4 in 10 (43.1%) violent acts. Those acts clearly more "extreme" (stabbing resulting in major injury or death, burning, dismemberment, beheadings, and bludgeonings) are found, on average, 14 times per film, and represent 26.7% of all violent behaviors coded. Thus, the third assumption made in the popular press and academic literature concerning the content of slasher films appears to be valid—one fourth of the violent acts coded by Molitor and Sapolsky could be defined as extreme brutality or sadistic victimization.

TABLE 3.4
Violent Acts Coded in 30 Slasher Films

Violent Act	Percentage ($n = 1573$)
Beating	32.3
Stabbing (Major injury or death)	21.6
Shooting	18.0
Choking/Stangling	4.6
Kicking	2.9
Restraining	2.6
Threat	2.3
Burning	1.8
Stabbing (Minor injury or other)	1.8
Dismemberment	1.4
Verbal Abuse	1.0
Beheading	1.0
Electrocution	0.9
Bludgeoning	0.9
Poisoning	0.8
Hanging	0.7
Other/Unknown	4.7

Note. From Molitor and Sapolsky (1993). Percentages do not sum to 100% due to rounding.

TRENDS IN SLASHER VIOLENCE

An examination of additional variables coded by Molitor and Sapolsky offers a better indication as to what types of content are featured in slasher films. Moreover, by comparing the data collected across 3 years (1980, 1985, and 1989), we can see whether levels of victimization and the linkage of sex and violence have changed over time, possibly in response to the previously discussed criticisms found in the popular press.

The first such comparison looks at the number of violent acts committed against males and females. For each act of violence, Molitor and Sapolsky made a judgment as to whether the perpetrator and the recipient were portrayed as "good" or "bad" characters. This distinction allows those violent behaviors committed against innocent victims to be differentiated from those directed at deserving targets (e.g., a cruel bully or the central villain). However, if the central villain was shown in a "flashback" from childhood being beaten, for example, he would be judged as an "innocent" victim in this context. The outcome of each attack was also noted: escape, minor injury, major injury (requiring medical treatment), or death.

TABLE 3.5
Violent Acts Committed Against Innocent Victims Compared by Sex and Year

Outcome	1980	1985	1989	Combined
Males				
Minor Injury	5.1	7.2	7.8	6.7^b
Major Injury	1.1	1.8	6.1	3.0^a
Death	5.1	6.7	7.7	6.5^b
Combined	11.3^b	15.7^b	21.6^c	16.2^B
Females				
Minor Injury	9.5	3.4	2.1	5.0^b
Major Injury	0.5	2.0	0.5	1.0^a
Death	4.6	4.2	2.5	3.8^b
Combined	14.6^b	9.6^b	5.1^a	9.8^A
Total	25.9	25.3	26.7	26.0

Note. Means with different superscripts differ significantly by $p < .05$. Uppercase superscripts compare the combined means by sex. Lowercase superscripts compare the means for the interaction of sex by year.

The 30 slasher films were found to portray a total of 938 acts of violence directed at innocent victims. Minor and major injury and death were the result of an overwhelming number (83%) of these violent acts. Escape, although an outcome for 7% of all violent acts, was disproportionately depicted across the sample—three films contained all the instances where a victim escaped from the intended attack. The remaining outcomes were unknown or coded as "other." Before examining the data across the 3 years, it is interesting to note that innocent males were found to suffer more from attacks that ended in injury or death than did innocent females (refer to Table 3.5). This finding provides further evidence that contradicts the contention that females are more often the victims in slasher films.

Table 3.5 reveals that the average number of violent acts committed against innocent victims, when examined by outcome, tends to increase over the 3 years for males, but tends to decrease (except for major injury) for females. For films released in 1989, males suffered significantly more injuries and deaths than did females.

As previously discussed, there was no significant difference in the number of males and females injured or killed in the sample of slasher films coded by Molitor and Sapolsky. However, when looking at the number of victims by sex across the 3 years (see Table 3.6), it can be seen that, in 1989, there were significantly fewer female victims of violence.

TABLE 3.6
Victims of Violence Compared by Sex and Year

Sex	1980	1985	1989	Combined
Males	4.7^a	7.9^a	9.4^b	7.3
Females	5.3^a	7.4^a	4.9^a	5.9
Combined	10.0	15.3	14.3	13.2

Note. Means with different superscripts differ significantly by $p < .05$. Comparisons should be made vertically.

A similar trend is evident for the amount of time during which images of dead bodies or body parts were depicted (refer to Table 3.7). There were no significant differences for sex or year of release for the amount of time (in seconds) in which the camera lingered on victims after they had been killed. However, in 1989 the camera dwelled on dead males ($M = 34.1$ seconds) significantly longer than dead females ($M = 13.5$ seconds).

The results of year-to-year comparisons suggest that highly vocal complaints raised over the content and impact of slasher films may have been responsible for producers altering their portrayals of violence, and, in particular, the depiction of women as victims. Whereas the amount of victimization has remained stable throughout the 1980s, males have had to endure a greater share of the brutality as producers appear to have toned down their attacks on females.

TABLE 3.7
Duration of Display of Dead Bodies Compared by Sex and Year

Sex	1980	1985	1989	Combined
Males	35.5[a]	24.6[a]	34.1[b]	31.4
Females	44.9[a]	29.4[a]	13.5[a]	29.3
Combined	80.4	54.0	47.6	60.7

Note. Means with different superscripts differ significantly by $p < .05$. Comparisons should be made vertically.

Molitor and Sapolsky also recorded the amount of time during which victims were shown in fear of violence (see Table 3.1). Duration of threat or fear was recorded whether the victim was aware or unaware of the presence of the attacker. The sample of 30 slasher films contains an average of 679.8 seconds of perceived threat per film (see Table 3.8). Females were shown in fear significantly longer than were males. Moreover, it was found that the average number of seconds of threats directed at males was significantly shorter than the threats directed at females for films released in both 1980 and 1985. Thus, the portrayal of fear is one form of victimization wherein females have clearly received more attention.

TABLE 3.8
Duration of Victims Seen in Fear Compared by Sex and Year

Sex	1980	1985	1989	Combined
Males	13.1[a]	156.0[a]	172.1[a]	113.7[a]
Females	711.1[b]	450.8[b]	536.5[a]	566.1[b]
Combined	724.2	606.8	708.6	679.8

Note. Means with different superscripts differ significantly by $p < .05$. Comparisons should be made vertically.

CONCLUSIONS

The results from three separate empirical studies refute two of the assumptions that have been made by film critics, journalists, and social scientists regarding the content of slasher films. Females have not been found to be the primary victims in slasher films. In fact, when examining the number of violent acts committed against innocent victims, Molitor and Sapolsky (1993, 1994) reported that males were more often singled out for injury and death. The Cowan and O'Brien (1990), Weaver (1991), and Molitor and Sapolsky (1993) content analyses also indicate that sex and violence are not frequently connected in slasher films.

Content analyses of slasher movies have consistently shown that the basic assumptions regarding slasher films are unfounded. Why, then, are these assumptions carried forward (see Oliver, 1994)? Perhaps those scenes that dwell on the woman's terror, prolonging her suffering and the uncertainty as to the outcome of her plight, are more offensive to many viewers than are more direct acts of physical violence. Cowan and O'Brien (1990) offered one possible explanation: "Women murdered in a sexualized context may be simply more noticeable (salient and memorable) than men getting killed and noneroticized killings" (p. 187).

The issue of whether or not slasher films "often" pair images of sex and violence is an important one from a theoretical standpoint. Findings that males register more favorable reactions to slasher films after prolonged exposure have been accounted for through the processes of classical conditioning and extinction (cf. Donnerstein, Linz, & Penrod, 1987). Slasher films are said to "contain scenes of explicit violence . . . often occurring during or juxtaposed to strongly erotic scenes" (Donnerstein, Linz, & Penrod, 1987, p. 123). The arousal from sexual images, it is argued, is classically conditioned to subsequent violent scenes, thus leading males to offer more favorable judgments of scenes of extreme violence and degradation directed at women.

In general, the relatively infrequent pairing of sex and violence and the rare appearance of sexual violence in slasher films calls into question the proposal that classical conditioning may explain the reported desensitizing effects of slasher films (Linz, Donnerstein, & Penrod, 1984, 1988). A more plausible explanation may derive from the extinction process (cf. McCutcheon & Adams, 1975). Accordingly, depictions of violence directed at women as well as the substantial amount of time devoted to images of women in terror (which may or may not conclude with injury and death) may reduce the viewer's anxiety, which in turn may lead to a dampened response to subsequently viewed violence, especially violence directed at females. Sensual or erotic displays need not be a part of the stimulus for extinction to occur.

Molitor and Sapolsky found that slasher films do contain a substantial amount of extreme violence. An important question now becomes: To what extent does the extreme violence appearing in popular slasher films differ from that contained in other R-rated violent film genres? For example, there may in fact be a set of slasher films that possess content quite different from those coded by Molitor and Sapolsky (cf. Molitor & Sapolsky, 1994). This may be the case for the slasher films that have been used as stimuli in experimental studies of males' reactions to film violence (e.g., *Friday the 13th: Part 2, I Spit on Your Grave, Maniac, Nightmare, Texas Chainsaw Massacre, Toolbox Murders,* and *Vice Squad* from Linz, Donnerstein, & Penrod, 1984, 1988). These films may in fact dwell on women as victims, and often do so in the context of sexual activity. Other violent horror movies that might be compared to the more popular slasher films are those that have duplicated the plot (i.e., dead zombies eating victims) of *Night of the Living Dead* (e.g., *Return of the Living Dead, Dawn of the Dead,* and *Day of the Dead*), and the *Faces of Death* series, which includes actual footage of gruesome accidental deaths, autopsies, and executions. Although these types of films have not been as popular in theatrical release, they may have received wider exposure through videotape rentals.

It is obvious that different conclusions about the level of extreme violence and the level of violence directed at women may be drawn, depending on which films are included in what we have referred to as the slasher subgenre. One characteristic that would appear to be important, for example, is the number of female characters present in a film and thus available to serve as targets of extreme violence (Molitor & Sapolsky, 1994). We anticipate that further analyses of film content will reveal subtle distinctions in what have to date been broadly defined as slasher movies.

REFERENCES

Bass, A. (1988, December 19). Do slasher films breed real-life violence? *Boston Globe* [from service *Newsbank*, FTV, 1989, fiche No. 5, grid B2-B4].

Broeske, P. H. (1984, September 2). Killing is alive and well in Hollywood. *Los Angeles Times*, pp. 19-22.

Child's play. (1987, June 1). *Time*, p. 31.

Clover, C. J. (1992). *Men, women and chain saws: Gender in the modern horror film.* Princeton, NJ: Princeton University Press.

Continelli, L. (1989, May 7). Are "slasher" movies numbing us to violence? *Bufflo News* [from service *Newsbank*, FTV, 1989, fiche No. 63, grid A7-A9].

Cowan, G., & O'Brien, M. (1990). Gender and survival vs. death in slasher films: A content analysis. *Sex Roles, 23,* 187-196.

Doherty, T. (1988). *Teenagers and teenpics: The juvenilization of American movies in the 1950's.* Boston: Unwin Hyman.

Donnerstein, E., Linz, D., & Penrod, S. (1987). *The question of pornography.* New York: The Free Press.

Farber, S. (1972). *The movie rating game.* Washington, DC: Public Affairs Press.

Hogan, D. J. (1986). *Dark romance: Sexuality in the horror film.* Jefferson, NC: McFarland & Company.

Kendrick, W. (1991). *The thrill of fear: 250 years of scary entertainment.* New York: Grove Press.

Linz, D., Donnerstein, E., & Adams, S. M. (1989). Physiological desensitization and judgments about female victims of violence. *Human Communication Research, 15,* 509-522.

Linz, D., Donnerstein, E., & Penrod, S. (1984). The effects of multiple exposures to filmed violence against women. *Journal of Communication, 34*, 130-147.

Linz, D., Donnerstein, E., & Penrod, S. (1988). Effects of long-term exposure to violent and sexually degrading depictions of women. *Journal of Personality and Social Psychology, 55*, 758-768.

Maslin, J. (1981, November 1). Tired blood claims the horror film as a fresh victim. *New York Times*, Section 2, pp. 15, 23.

Maslin, J. (1982, November 21). Bloodbaths debase movies and audiences. *New York Times*, Section 2, pp. 1, 13.

McCarty, J. (1984). *Splatter films: Breaking the last taboo of the screen.* New York: St. Martin's.

McCutcheon, B. A., & Adams, H. E. (1975). The physiological basis of implosive therapy. *Behavior Research Therapy, 13* (2-3), 93-100.

Meyer, M. (1988, March). Keeping a lid on gore and sex. *Video Magazine*, pp. 75-76.

Molitor, F., & Sapolsky, B. S. (1993). Sex, violence, and victimization in slasher films. *Journal of Broadcasting & Electronic Media, 37*, 233-242.

Molitor, F., & Sapolsky, B. S. (1994). Violence towards women in slasher films: A reply to Linz and Donnerstein. *Journal of Broadcasting and Electronic Media, 38*, 247-250.

Newman, K. (1988). *Nightmare movies.* London: Bloombury.

NewsBank [Database]. (1990). New Canaan, CT: Author.

Nordheimer, J. (1987, May 18). Rising concern with VCR's: Violent tapes and the young. *New York Times*, pp. A1, B9.

Oliver, M. B. (1994). Contributions of sexual portrayals to viewers' responses to graphic horror. *Journal of Broadcasting & Electronic Media, 38*, 1-17.

Shalit, G. (1980, October). Movie violence: The offense to your children; what you can do. *Ladies Home Journal*, pp. 12, 16.

Sneak Previews [Television]. (1980, October 24). Alexandria, VA: Public Broadcasting System.

Stein, E. (1982, June 20). Have horror films gone too far? *New York Times*, Section 2, pp. 1, 21.

Tudor, A. (1989). *Monsters and mad scientists.* New York: Basil Blackwell.

Video source book (11th ed.). (1990). Detroit, MI: Gale Research.

Weaver, J. B., III. (1991). Are "slasher" horror films sexually violent? A content analysis. *Journal of Broadcasting & Electronic Media, 35*, 385-392.

Worsham, D. G. (1982, May 20). Films show disturbing trend toward violence against women. *Oakland Tribune* [from service *Newsbank*, FTV, 1981-82, fiche No. 148, grid E1-E2].

Chapter
4

The Economics of the Horror Film

Douglas Gomery
University of Maryland

The horror film has its origins in the rise of popularity of the novel and theatre as mass entertainment. Throughout the 19th century, English Gothic novels (and their stage adaptions) made early mass culture entrepreneurs rich. Thus it was not surprising that at the turn into the 20th century, with the rise of the cinema, this wealth of accumulated horror plots would be fashioned into moving pictures. The horror genre had long proven it could raise an intended fear and dread in audiences (as well as profits), most frequently from an abnormal threatening monster disturbing the "natural" order (Carroll, 1990).

The horror film ranks certainly as one of the most popular and profitable of film genres. Hollywood has long exploited interest in monsters and mayhem to make money. Indeed through the production, distribution, and exhibition of motion pictures in the United States, motion picture entrepreneurs have regularly utilized the profit-maximizing possibilities of horror movies. This chapter seeks to understand how the U.S. film industry has come to produce, distribute, and exhibit horror films. Specifically my goal will be to seek to understand how the horror film has fit into the economic history of motion pictures, leaving to Carroll and others (see the other fine chapters that follow in this anthology) to fathom the anthropological, psychological, and social implications of cinematic horror.

MOVIE INDUSTRY ECONOMICS

Before directly answering my research question, I lay out a method by which to analyze the economics of Hollywood film genres. How can one best understand the American movies as a business, where economic decisions by corporate leaders lead to the production, distribution, and exhibition of certain types of Hollywood films?

During the decade of the 1910s Hollywood arose as an industry to define the cinema of the United States as well as proper motion pictures throughout the world. Stars like Charlie Chaplin and Mary Pickford became as well known as kings, queens, and presidents. Inexorably the American cinema came to dominate and indeed define Southern California studios as the world center of film production.

Movie Industry Phases

But Hollywood was (and still is) simply more than a set of moviemaking companies all nestled together in the Los Angeles environs. Any movie industry—Hollywood or other—includes three phases: production, distribution, and exhibition.

Production. Films are planned, shot, edited, and copied. Since the early 1910s this has been done in studios in and around Los Angeles—an area generically known as Hollywood, although it encompasses more than that city section: Universal City for Universal Studios, Burbank for Warner Bros., and an actual Hollywood address for RKO. Through its popular film genres, Hollywood defines popular cinema around the world.

Distribution. Then Hollywood companies peddle copies of these films around the world. Indeed, worldwide distribution has long been the core basis of Hollywood's longstanding economic power, based on a principle of economies of scale. During the 1920s Hollywood companies came to dominate cinema markets from England to Ethiopia, from South America to South Africa, from Afghanistan to Asia. No other film industry has been so far reaching.

Exhibition. Finally, films are shown to audiences. Prior to the television age, films were shown principally in theaters. The exhibition section moved from nickelodeons to movie palaces to multiplexes. Today the vast majority of movie audiences watch motion pictures on television. Whatever the exhibition conditions, these sites are where the public envelops its favorites, from comedies and westerns to science fiction and horror films.

Economic History of the Movie Industry

To analyze changing conditions of production, distribution, and exhibition I shall divide up the economic history of Hollywood into four stages. Once we understand the key differences among these four stages we can properly seek to understand what economic conditions led to the production, distribution, and exhibition of specific types of films.

Stage 1. From the turn of the century to the Great Depression Hollywood as an industry sought to establish itself. The Great Depression brought to a halt this expansion and growth, a 30-year rise that crested with the coming of sound. By 1930 eight studio corporations had survived and begun to dominate in what we know as the studio system. As Hollywood was growing into an oligopolistic system of powerful studios, executives borrowed works of fiction from popular genres formulated in other media, principally the theater and novel. The so-called silent era is thus one of experimentation, not because films were silent, but because the Hollywood industry was growing, groping, and finally consolidating.

Stage 2. From 1930 through 1950 the U.S. film industry functioned as a tight-knit oligopoly in which eight corporations dominated the film industry and formed the studio system. The coming of sound had solidified Hollywood's control over the world market. Thereafter the "Big Five" of Paramount, Loew's (parent company for the more famous MGM), Fox Film (later Twentieth Century-Fox), Warner Bros., and RKO ruled by not only making the most expensive feature films, but also distributing them around the world and owning and operating the key movie houses in the United States and parts of Europe.

From their theatres the Big Five took in three quarters to seven eighths of all dollars. Only after they granted their own theatres first runs and soaked up as much of the box-office grosses as possible did they permit smaller, independently owned theaters to scramble for the remaining bookings, sometimes months, or even years, after a film's premiere.

The remaining three major Hollywood moviemaking firms—Universal Pictures, Columbia Pictures, and United Artists—did not own theatres and thus had to cozy up to the Big Five to secure bookings in the best theaters. There were more companies in Hollywood than these eight, but they—as exemplified by Republic Pictures and Monogram Pictures—were left only the rural markets where little money was made.

The Hollywood production executives, with guaranteed screen time, embraced film genres. Once a hit had set off a new round of popularity of a kind of motion picture, the studio boss would order sequels. The studio system can best be seen as a 20-year history of the testing, exploiting, and abandoning of a plethora of film genres.

Stage 3. After World War II, the U.S. film industry began to change. Loyal film fans began to look for other things to do: starting families, finding nicer homes in the suburbs, buying cars and refrigerators. Movie attendance in the United States crested in 1946 and then began to steadily fall, so by 1963 it settled at 1 billion theatrical tickets sold per year. The causes of this postwar transformation have been much debated. Most commentators generally blame television, but in most parts of the United States television did not become a viable entertainment alternative until long after the decline in moviegoing was well underway. Americans tempered their love affair with the movies because of a fundamental sociological shift.

First, they secured homes in the suburbs, free from city congestion and noises. In the late 1940s and 1950s Americans moved in record waves to new suburban subdivisions. By 1963, just as theatrical American moviegoing was hitting a nadir not experienced since the days of the nickelodeon, more Americans owned homes than rented for the first time in the nation's history.

They filled these new homes with children in record numbers. Women married at younger ages, and the birth rate increased as never before or since. Better educated couples had larger families. As a consequence, the typical moviegoer of the past (better educated, richer, middle class) was precisely that individual who most embraced the suburban ideal—with its sizable mortgage and the family of three children (Gomery, 1991).

These two factors—suburbanization and the baby boom—directly led to a decline in theatrical moviegoing and would have done so even without the coming of television. The U.S. film industry responded and provided auto-oriented theaters close to the new suburbs. The drive-in offered an open space where parked cars filled with movie fans could watch double and triple features on a massive screen. By 1963, the very height of suburbanization and the baby boom, the number of drive-ins in the United States crested at nearly 5,000 and for the first time more fans went to the movies during the summer than colder times of the year.

A longer term solution offered by movie exhibitors came in the late 1960s with the shopping center theater. By the mid-1970s, with thousands of new shopping malls in place, the locus of theatrical movie attendance permanently shifted. With acres of free parking and computer plotted "ideal" access by highway, the shopping mall—America's new downtown—accommodated thousands of indoor screens and became the center of America's moviegoing habit.

The baby boom of the 1950s drained the traditional movie theater of a generation of young adults who before (and after) formed the core moviegoing population. Well-educated, middle-class Americans looked to entertainment at home—in the suburbs—involving their growing families. In the late 1940s and even into the first few years of the 1950s, they turned on the radio, but during the 1950s middle-class suburbanites, who had already abandoned the movies, substituted television watching for radio listening. The Late Show fed their appetite for movie watching.

At the same time the U.S. government was separating Hollywood moviemaking from theatrical exhibition. Simply put, the government split the major Hollywood companies in two: One division handled production and distribution, another movie theaters. Surviving Hollywood film companies retained a measure of control of their markets through continued oligopoly in distribution. They still made the most expensive motion pictures and could dictate booking terms.   The Hollywood oligopoly was not broken by the *Paramount* decision, just wounded.

But the change in U.S. society and the government dictated division of corporate organization did open up the movie market to independent filmmakers. Many new circuits were started, especially those centered around the only new type of profitable theater, the drive-in, and these exhibitors needed "product." New entrepreneurs stepped in and produced the popular genre films that would draw suburbanites out of the house. From 1950 through 1975 a new age of opportunity existed in the U.S. movie market, a sharp contrast to the closed years of the studio system.

Stage 4. This stage of transformation came to an end during the summer of 1975 when the era of the blockbuster—in which we are still live—commenced. That summer *Jaws* (which some have called a horror film) demonstrated that one film could make hundreds of millions of dollars for a studio and formulate a positive balance sheet for a complete fiscal year. The key economic decision became finding a formula for this year's mass appeal blockbuster. Few doubted that a new stage of Hollywood's economic history had begun when George Lucas' *Star Wars* (1977) topped even the success of Steven Spielberg's *Jaws*.

Something as radical was happening in film exhibition as well. During the late 1970s satellite distribution and videotape recorders initiated a wave of at-home film viewing unprecedented in film history. With the rise of new technologies—distribution by satellite, and exhibition at home on a VCR and through cable television—film viewers entered a new world.

Americans have never been more fascinated with the movies, but not at a theater. In 1986, on average, nearly 20 million fans journeyed each week to nearby multiplex cinemas to relish Hollywood studio-sponsored theatrical blockbusters such as Paramount's *Star Trek* in its multiple versions; but this number paled when compared to the millions more who turned on a television set and watched films at home.

In the mid-1970s, Time, Inc. initiated a change in how and where we view films. Home Box Office, which, for a monthly fee of about $10, offered cable television subscribers recent Hollywood motion pictures—uncut, uninterrupted by commercials, and not sanitized to please network censors. For the first time, a profit-making method had been found to make viewers directly pay for what they watched in their living rooms. As "pay television," Home Box Office drew back the older movie fan who did not want to go out to a theatre but loved watching second-run films on television at home.

Cable television offered the film fan even more than Home Box Office. Ted Turner took a typical independent station, complete with its around-the-clock-reruns of old movies, and beamed it to all America via the satellite to fashion his famous "superstation." Turner went so far as to purchase MGM, not for its current productions, but for access to its library of old films. With the addition of competing superstations, Americans in the 1980s had for the first time a rich, repertory cinema in the home. Old Hollywood films, the best and worst, ran all day long. A quick survey of *TV Guide* reveals that about a quarter of the average television broadcast day is devoted to rerunning Hollywood feature films.

However, the greatest movie watching impact was still to come. In 1975 the Sony Corporation introduced its Betamax ½-inch home video cassette recorder. Originally priced at more than $1,000 (double that in today's dollars adjusted for inflation), the cost of the Beta machines and their newer rivals from VHS dropped to just over $300 per machine by the mid-1980s. An enthusiastic U.S. public (plus millions in other nations) snapped up so many machines that by the 1990s fully three quarters of American households were equipped to run prerecorded tapes of movies. Watching classic horror films (as well as new releases) became as simple as finding a parking space at the local video store.

These four stages codify the changing economics of Hollywood production, distribution, and exhibition; but in this chapter we need to be more specific. Certain types of films (e.g., horror films) form a logical extension of a profit-seeking motion picture industry needing predictable fare, presold to a mass audience. The familiar expectations of genre films accomplish this task. But money-making moviemakers also need a continual string of "new" products. This is where the ever-changing themes and variations of a film genre seek to make the seemingly "natural" movie conventions new and exciting (Gomery, 1989).

HORROR FILM ECONOMICS

By examining the ebb and flow of the production, distribution, and presentation of horror films within the four stages of economic development already outlined. we can understand how economics plays a role in the creation of horror films.

Economic History of Horror Films

Stage 1. As Hollywood rose to power as the world motion picture capital, its competing firms searched popular story genres to locate a regular basis for making movie profits. From the early days the horror genre was attractive because it drew from literary sources that were known and generally royalty free. *Dr. Jekyll and Mr. Hyde,* for example, had been filmed, released, and sent to theatres in six different versions by 1920. This half dozen "Dr. Jekylls and Mr. Hydes" came from pioneering film companies such as Selig and Thanhauser in the United States and Nordisk in Europe. It was altogether appropriate that in 1920 the most powerful motion picture company of the day, Paramount, launched its version, starring noted stage actor John Barrymore (Huss & Ross, 1972).

The early Hollywood tapped all possible literary horror sources, from werewolf tales to a score of versions of *Frankenstein*, from the tales from Edgar Allan Poe to the supernatural speculations of Jules Verne. Yet unlike the western with *The Covered Wagon* and *The Iron Horse*, no Hollywood company could establish the horror film as a consistently popular film genre. That would only begin with the Universal Pictures' innovations in the early 1930s. In the silent Hollywood, a set of business enterprises was still exploring for a profitable mix of filmed genres (Wood, 1988).

Stage 2. The Golden Age of the Hollywood studio system, from 1930 to 1950, set up the initial Golden Age of the horror film. In particular, Universal Pictures during the early 1930s established the horror film as a key motion picture genre and then a decade later a producer at RKO, Val Lewton, refined it into a complex formula second to none. Both these studios, Universal and RKO, took up and relied on their genre innovations because of profit-maximizing economic considerations.

During the difficult days of the Great Depression Universal Pictures could never hope to match the economic muscle of an MGM or Paramount. Simply put, Universal did not own a chain of theaters and so had to rely on the favors of Paramount, Loew's, Twentieth Century-Fox, Warner Bros., or RKO for optimal bookings. Although Universal Pictures could trace its roots to founder Carl Laemmle's successful fight against the Motion Picture Patents Company, this company would play only a marginal role during the lucrative Studio Era. Indeed Universal only prospered with weekly serials such as *Flash Gordon* and *Jungle Jim*, a discount newsreel service, Woody the Woodpecker cartoons, feature film comedies, and horror films.

The Great Depression battered an already ailing Universal. In 1929 the elder Laemmle had mistakenly appointed his son, Carl Laemmle, Jr., as head of production at the studio. The inexperienced 21-year-old "Junior" Laemmle turned Universal from a marginally profitable operation into a gigantic corporate loser, willing to try anything. Thus, on Valentine's Day 1931 a struggling Universal Pictures released the filmed version of *Dracula*. An American stage production of the Bram Stoker novel, starring Bela Lugosi, had been mounted on Broadway 5 years earlier, and despite unfavorable reviews ran for a year in New York and 2 years on tour.

Still, Universal executives were surprised when the filmed *Dracula* turned into a money maker; but they knew what to do with this unexpected hit: Turn out more. As a result, the invasion of the normal world by the supernatural was followed by a version of the Mary Shelley tale, *Frankenstein*, starring Boris Karloff as the monster. This version of the oft-filmed *Frankenstein* also proved popular and helped establish the movie icons of the mad scientist, the out-of-control monster, and the dangerous, dark, murky foreign setting.

Universal was off and running. The next year brought *The Mummy* (1932, starring Karloff), and *The Old Dark House* (1932, also with Karloff, and created by James Whale, director of *Frankenstein*). Money was now available for original scripts; it was not until *The Mummy* that an important U.S. horror film was made from other than a literary source. In time even critics praised Universal's continuing efforts. *The Black Cat* (1934, directed by Edgar G. Ulmer and starring both Karloff and Lugosi), and *The Bride of Frankenstein* (1935, directed by James Whale and starring Boris Karloff) rank as two of the best ever created in the horror film genre (Schaefer, 1991).

After these money-minting successes for weak Universal, the Big Five even began to make and distribute horror films. In 1932 Paramount released *Island of Lost Souls* (with Charles Laughton and Bela Lugosi) and yet another version of *Dr. Jekyll and Mr. Hyde* (this time starring Fredric March). Warner Bros. issued *Dr. X* (with Lionell Atwill). However, this burst of activity by members of the Big Five proved only temporary; profits proved too small. It was left to Universal to mine the horror film genre.

Universal mined the genre. In time it developed new antagonists in *The Wolfman* (1941, with Lon Chaney, Jr.) and *Frankenstein Meets the Wolfman* (1943, also starring Chaney). Later, Universal melded its top stars in *Abbott and Costello Meet Frankenstein* (1948), *Abbott and Costello Meet the Invisible Man* (1950), *Abbott and Costello Meet the Mummy* (1955), and *Abbott and Costello Meet the Killer, Boris Karloff* (1949). Universal made money on all of these.

Universal was attracted to the horror film because of the low costs of production. Screenplays were cheap to develop because the literary sources were no longer under copyright protection. Horror film stars may have become well known in time, but even at their height Karloff and Lugosi never commanded the salaries of the luminaries of comedy or the western. For example, at the height of his fame, Boris Karloff was paid about a tenth as much as musical star Betty Grable. In addition, the horror genre could make efficient use (with judicious placement of light and shadow) of existing studio sets and thus save thousands of dollars in basic production costs (Gomery, 1986).

After this burst of activity in the early 1930s the major Hollywood studios generally shied away from the horror film. Again it took needs of economy and special circumstances to foster a notable exception—Val Lewton's fascinating cycle of horror films made at RKO during the years of World War II. Radio-Keith-Orpheum had been formed in 1928 so that electronic giant RCA could market its sound equipment, Joseph P. Kennedy could sell his studio, and the Keith-Albee-Orpheum vaudeville theaters could be converted into movie houses. RKO's corporate business history proved dismal. During its first 2 years of existence, RKO battled on an equal footing with Paramount and MGM, but thereafter RKO struggled.

RKO produced the best and worst feature films because its owners and managers were always under the gun to find ways to turn a quick profit or be fired. Rarely was a management team in place for more than a few years when myopic owners replaced them with studio bosses with different ideas. So when George Schafer came on as head of production at RKO in 1938, he sought to bring "class" by attracting noted figures from Broadway to produce prestige films. Schafer wanted to make RKO the next MGM.

He failed. Surely *Abe Lincoln in Illinois* (1940), and *Citizen Kane* (1941) brought lines of critical praise, but unfortunately they were money losers. George Schafer was fired in 1942 and replaced by Charles Koerner, who turned the studio on its head, demanding cheaply done, predictably profitable films. Koerner's first big hit came with *Hitler's Children* (1943), an anti-Nazi melodrama that cost $200,000 to make but grossed more than $3 million in an entertainment starved World War II United States. However, not all these cheap features were created by second-rate talents; Jean Renoir's *This Land Is Mine* (1943) and Robert Siodmak's *The Spiral Staircase* (1946) were both made during Koerner's tenure.

The best of the Koerner inexpensive fare came with the horror tales produced by Val Lewton, beginning with *Cat People* in 1942. Here were cinematic gems made on a shoestring budget. Lewton, a former script editor for David O. Selznick, took a mere $80,000 to film *The Cat People*, which then grossed in excess of $1 million. Lewton then went on to produce *I Walked with a Zombie* (1943), *The Leopard Man* (1943), *The Seventh Victim* (1943), *The Ghost Ship* (1943), *The Curse of the Cat People* (1944), *The Body Snatcher* (1945), and *Isle of the Dead* (1945). All were highly profitable.

For these "B" films, Lewton kept costs low. He was expected to use already existing sets, employ contract actresses and actors, and find and develop inexpensive scripts. To take advantage of a multitude of standing sets at RKO, Lewton situated his horror films within the modern world. Fear of the unknown and terror in a changing modern world replaced threatening vampires and werewolfs. In *Cat People* a woman cannot deal with her obsession with cats; in *The Seventh Victim* the heroes are menaced by diabolic cults. Lewton did not have the resources to overwhelm the audience with the shocks of spectacular sequences of terror, so he encouraged his screenwriters to create and maintain tension throughout the film and no unit ever did it better (Gomery, 1986).

Stage 3. After World War II, Hollywood could not protect a Val Lewton. Corporate executives faced a new and difficult age of adjustment. They worked to produce, distribute, and exhibit films that would attract growing families who spent all their money on a move to the suburbs, their expanding family, and their acquisition of material goods including a new television set. However, the U.S. government had opened up the marketplace to entrepreneurs not connected to the Big Five. Marginal movie producers aped Universal and RKO and tendered cheaply made fare for the thousands of drive-ins springing up from Bangor, Maine to San Diego, California. Typical of their efforts were *I Was a Teenage Frankenstein* and *I Was a Teenage Werewolf*, both released in 1957.

The 1950s was also an era of rapidly changing motion picture technology. Filmgoers saw everything from 3-D to CinemaScope, from VistaVision to Panavision. In this period of technical change, the horror film proved an appropriate vehicle. Warner Bros. made and released *House of Wax* as one of the first entries in the short-lived 3-D wars of 1953 and 1954. Universal followed with *Creature From the Black Lagoon*, also in 3-D. But these were experiments in audience and technical change. A longer term solution was needed. Bold entrepreneurs embraced fresh approaches.

One way that movie production costs could be cut was to "run away" and shoot films in Europe. As the Americans invaded Europe, Europeans in turn sought ways to break into the lucrative U.S. market. In the 1950s and 1960s age of experimentation came a cycle of horror films from Hammer Films from Great Britain.

The first Hammer horror film came in 1957 with *The Curse of Frankenstein*. Again, here was a minor operation attracted by the public domain status of Mary Shelley's story as Universal had been 25-years earlier. Both the Hammer and Universal versions of *Frankenstein* have nearly the same plot; the British version, which played in U.S. drive-ins, was an "update" in color. Peter Cushing starred as Baron Victor Frankenstein; Christopher Lee played his monster. Both Cushing and Lee became the stars of the Hammer horror cycle. *The Curse of Frankenstein* became the top-grossing British film of 1957.

Hammer executives turned to *Dracula* (1958), made with virtually the same cast with equal economic success. Again in color, differentiating it from the Universal classic, Hammer had another box office winner. The economic formulae that followed seemed predictable: *The Revenge of Frankenstein* (1958), *The Mummy* (1959), *The Man Who Could Cheat Death* (1959), *The Stranglers* (1960), *The Curse of the Werewolf* (1960), *The Brides of Dracula* (1960), *The Two Faces of Dr. Jekyll* (1960), *The Terror of the Tongs* (1961), *Kiss of the Vampire* (1964), *The Evil of Frankenstein* (1964), *The Curse of the Mummy's Tomb* (1964), *Dracula-Prince of Darkness* (1966), *Dracula Has Risen From the Grave* (1968), and *Frankenstein Must Be Destroyed* (1969). The cycle ended in 1974 with Peter Cushing starring in *Frankenstein ... and the Monster from Hell*.

The Hammer company was able to penetrate the U.S. market during the transitional television era by cheaply producing the films in Europe and then distributing them in the United States through a deal made first with Warner Bros., then Columbia Pictures, and then finally with Universal. In time Hammer was even able to obtain advance production monies from these Hollywood studio patrons. The Hammer horror cycle lasted until Hollywood's new blockbusters began to demand screen time in new U.S. multiplex theatres (Eyles, 1984).

One U.S. producer was able to successfully match Hammer's efforts. Roger Corman, entrepreneur on a shoestring budget, crafted a series of horror films, from *A Bucket of Blood* (1959) to *Masque of the Red Death* (1964), for production budgets rarely extending beyond $100,000. Mainline Hollywood of the 1950s and 1960s seemed to be more interested in science fiction films or Alfred Hitchcock's special brand of suspense, leaving the pure Hollywood-made horror niche to Corman (Wood, 1988).

In 1954, Corman, after some training at the major studios, set off, producing and directing low-budget genre films—from westerns such as *Five Guns West* (1955) to science fiction efforts such as *It Conquered the World* (1956). His horror films represented but one of the genres he utilized. However, Corman was most skillful in his adaptation of the macabre tales of Edgar Allan Poe.

Corman's first Poe horror film was *The Fall of the House of Usher* (1960). Thereafter in *The Pit and the Pendulum* (1961), *The Premature Burial* (1962), *Tales of Terror* (1962), *The Haunted Palace* (1963), and *The Raven* (1963), Corman adapted Poe using out-of-favor actors (from Ray Milland to Peter Lorre) and 3-week shooting schedules. Sometimes he went overboard and so his *The Fall of the House of Usher* came in at a record $300,000; triple the average for Corman's American International Pictures. For a reported $27,000 he was able to fashion the ultimate horror film spoof, *The Little Shop of Horrors* (1960; Butler, 1967; McGee, 1988).

It took a great deal to "out do" Hammer or Roger Corman, but in the movie business of the 1950s and 1960s some tried. Take for example George Romero's independent *Night of the Living Dead* (1968) shot and distributed from, of all places, Pittsburgh, Pennsylvania. Romero had made 8mm shorts, TV commercials, and industrial films in western Pennsylvania before he crafted, on a minimalist budget, what is now considered a horror classic. Shot in black and white with money from family and friends, *Night of the Living Dead* was made in 30 days, during free time on weekends. *Night of the Living Dead* earned an estimated $30 million in a then-thriving campus film society scene. Few were able to match this achievement from Pittsburgh, but Tobe Hooper with his *The Texas Chainsaw Massacre* of 1974 and Romero's own

Dawn of the Dead (1978), a *Night of the Living Dead* sequel, almost did (Gagne, 1987).

Stage 4. In 1975 with *Jaws,* Hollywood entered a new phase, the era of the blockbuster. Television was left for the routine TV movie; the theatrical movie industry turned to trying to create special blockbuster events. When an attempt succeeded, such as with *Jaws* or *E.T.*, millions, almost billions, could be made. This new Hollywood of the late 1970s and 1980s led to the now familiar cycle of the sequel. As of 1991, there had been three *Halloweens* (1978, 1981, and 1983) and nine *Friday the 13ths* (beginning in 1980).

The horror film was revived early on with *The Exorcist* (1973). William Peter Blatty's novel on film was released during the Christmas season of 1973 and went on to make millions for the then-new Warner Communication empire. There was a sequel, *Exorcist II*, released in 1977 that did not do well at the box office, but Warner proved that the correct vehicle could be turned into a multimillion-dollar popular culture event (Sackett, 1990).

However, we cannot set the genesis of the blockbuster era with *The Excorist* because it was not released in the summer; *Jaws* (1975) takes that honor. *Jaws,* with its "monster" shark, set off Hollywood studio executives looking for architects of terror. There were werewolves in Joe Dante's *The Howling* (1981) and John Landis' *American Werewolf in London* (1981); vampires in John Badham's *Dracula* (1979) and Tony Scott's *The Hunger* (1983); zombies in George Romero's *Dawn of the Dead* (1979) and John Carpenter's *The Fog* (1980; Schaefer, 1991).

The monster conventions of the horror film were crossbred with other genres, particularly the science fiction film as in *Alien* (1979) and *Aliens* (1986). This variation then led to the alien who is friendly, giving rise to the most popular movie of the 1980s and one of the most popular of all time—Steven Spielberg's *E.T.* (1982). This transplanted horror film plot appealed to the core teenaged audience because it implanted its horror within a parable about coming of age.

Less successful have been other attempts to utilize the horror formula. In 1974 Mel Brooks made millions with his parodies *Blazing Saddles* (the western) and *Young Frankenstein* (the horror film), the second and third highest box office films of that year. The idea of remaking *Frankenstein* in a send-up was not new. Andy Warhol had done it in 3-D, but Brooks made money using regulars Gene Wilder and Madeline Kahn and carefully duplicated the look and feel of the black-and-white Universal "original." He went so far as to borrow sets from Universal.

However, the send-up of all send-ups for the horror film came with *The Rocky Horror Picture Show* (1975). This musical spoof made its millions the hard way, from single screenings each week, held at midnight on Saturday nights. The same people, by 1977 in costumes matching the movie's characters, returned every Saturday night and by 1980 had made *The Rocky Horror Picture Show* into a major hit.

The other variant of the blockbuster version of the horror genre must be credited to the fertile imagination of Steven Spielberg. This one-man studio has already been properly been credited with *Jaws* and *E.T.* here, but he made a pure film of terror by monster with his production of *Gremlins*. However, even the magician Spielberg could not make *Gremlins II* (1989) into a second blockbuster. Yet we can be sure that Spielberg—or another aspiring "movie brat"—will seek to craft a horror blockbuster for the 20,000 available movie screens and millions of television sets of the 1990s.

CONCLUSIONS

As the analyst looks for the end of Stage 4, the economics of the horror film remain firmly in place. We do not know when and where the next stage in its economic development will occur, but in times of need the horror film has certainly been a genre to which filmmakers and film studios have looked to increase profits. So when Hollywood hits the doldrums—as it invariably does—we can be sure that the horror film will invade our theatrical and television screens.

What about possible changes? One place we can look to see change is in the forums for presentation to watch films. New forums create new film forms. For example, today Hollywood creates twice the number of TV movies as theatrical features. Some critics dismiss these low-budget TV movies and productions as the disease or scandal of the week. But from an economic point of view today's made-for-TV dramas are successors to Hollywood's "B" movies of yore. They surely boost ratings, which is why they arrive with *Frankenstein: The True Story* (1973), and *Dracula* (1973), two early movies made for television, and 1990's *Stephen King's IT*, in two parts, the third and 11th highest rated TV movies of the 1990-1991 television season.

Because the turnaround time from production to presentation is so short, made-for-TV films can deal with topical issues and even, like the immensely popular *The Day After* (1983), provoke discussion of important ideas. However, TV movies also rely on formulae. So for Halloween 1991 the Fox network broadcast *Frankenstein: The College Years*, and producers will surely continue to tap the horror genre to make TV movie hits of the future.

The other fundamental new Hollywood transformation will come from new owners, with fresh corporate strategies. In the late 1980s Japan's Sony Corporation purchased Columbia Pictures and Matsushita acquired Universal Pictures. No doubt these new corporate chieftans will refocus on their subsidiaries' bottom lines and seek a new genre of blockbusters. It will not be the first time the Japanese have borrowed from the horror genre; during the

1950s Japanese filmmakers crafted *Godzilla*. Surely they will borrow again and the horror film will continue as a staple strategy of motion picture economics (Hardy, 1991).

REFERENCES

Butler, I. (1967). *The horror film*. London: A. Zwemmer.

Carroll, N. (1990). *The philosophy of horror*. New York: Routledge.

Eyles, A. (1984). *The house of horror*. London: Lorrimer.

Gagne, P. R. (1987). *The zombies that ate Pittsburgh*. New York: Dodd, Mead.

Gomery, D. (1986). *The Hollywood studio system*. New York: St. Martin's.

Gomery, D. (1989). Media economics: Terms of analysis. *Critical Studies in Mass Communication, 6*, 43-60.

Gomery, D. (1991). Who killed Hollywood? *Wilson Quarterly, 15*(3), 106-112.

Hardy, Q. (1991, October 25). Godzilla is back in his 18th film, to take on city hall. *Wall Street Journal*, pp. A1, A7.

Huss, R., & Ross, T. J. (1972). *Focus on the horror film*. Englewood Cliffs, NJ: Prentice-Hall.

McGee, M. T. (1988). *Roger Corman*. Jefferson, NC: McFarland.

Sackett, S. (1990). *The Hollywood reporter book of box office hits*. New York: Billboard Books.

Schaefer, A. (1991, November). Ten Best. *Premiere*, p. 121.

Wood, G. C. (1988). Horror film. In W. D. Gehring (Ed.), *Handbook of American film genres* (pp. 211-228). Westport, CT: Greenwood Press.

Chapter 5

Developmental Differences in Responses to Horror

Joanne Cantor
University of Wisconsin, Madison
Mary Beth Oliver
Virginia Polytechnic Institute and State University

> When I was about eight years old I watched a film . . . about a little doll that comes alive and terrorizes the owner. Many of the actions of the doll seemed real to me. This was particularly scary because my parents had just returned from Mexico and had brought me a doll that I thought looked just like the crazy doll in the film. For months after watching the film I could hardly sleep and I would definitely remove the doll from my bedroom when I wanted to sleep. . . . Eventually my parents took it away so I could feel safer and more relaxed in my room. (College Student)[1]

Almost everyone seems to be able to remember an occasion in their childhood when an especially terrifying mass media portrayal took hold of their consciousness and left them frightened, shaken, and troubled for a considerable period of time. Many researchers have reported that such enduring fright reactions, which often involve sleep disturbances and nightmares, are not at all uncommon (Blumer, 1933; Cantor & Reilly, 1982; Eisenberg, 1936; Hess & Goldman, 1962; Himmelweit, Oppenheim, & Vince, 1958; Johnson, 1980; Palmer, Hockett, & Dean, 1983; Preston, 1941).

Although, for ethical reasons, children's responses to the horror genre per se have rarely been investigated directly, a considerable amount of research and theoretical speculation has been conducted on fright reactions to media presentations in general and on children's fright reactions to media fiction specifically. Much of this research is applicable to the question of how children

---

[1]The quotes from students are from essays in which students reported on one mass media offering that had frightened them. The contributions of these students are gratefully appreciated. The film titles in parentheses indicate the film referred to, if known.

respond to horror films. As seen from the following discussion, "classic" horror films share basic elements with other genres such as psychological thrillers, slasher films, and other fright-inducing fare, and it is reasonable to assume that to a great extent, similar processes are involved in producing the fright reactions to these genres. In this chapter, therefore, the phrase *horror film* will be used broadly to encompass a variety of genres whose main or prominent theme is the induction of terror.

In this chapter we review theories and research on media and fright to address the question of how children and adolescents respond to horror films. To do so, we first consider the question of why horror films should be frightening at all, and then explore why developmental differences in responses to horror might be expected. Finally, we address some possible implications of exposure to horror. In addition to reporting on the findings of systematic research, we illustrate various points by quoting from college students' retrospective reports of their own intense emotional reactions to horror.

WHY FILMS INDUCE FRIGHT

I remember feeling physically nauseous, crying, sweating and sitting up very tense (*The Accused*).

At the moment Michael picked her face out of the water, my stomach dropped and I thought I was going to faint (*Halloween*).

The movie was so intense and suspenseful that immediately after the show, I broke into tears (*Cape Fear*).

To anyone who has felt the intense feelings that horror films can generate, it might seem ridiculous to pose the question of why such feelings occur. However, if we look at the film viewing situation in a detached fashion, the fright response seems a bit absurd, particularly as far as adults are concerned. Typically, people watch horror films by choice, for purposes of entertainment. Under these circumstances, they understand full well that what is being depicted is not actually happening—no threatening agent will leap off the screen and attack them. Moreover, in many cases, they know that what they are seeing is the product of someone's imagination and never actually happened; often, they know that it never could happen. Objectively speaking, then, the viewer is not in any danger. Why then, does the fright reaction occur so intensely and so reliably?

In a recent chapter (Cantor, 1994), we proposed that such fright reactions can be at least partially explained on the basis of classical and operant conditioning and on principles of stimulus generalization (see Pavlov, 1927; Razran, 1949). The basis of the argument is that certain stimuli elicit fear when they are encountered in the real world. These stimuli may be unconditioned fear stimuli, such as an attacking animal, or stimuli that have come to evoke fear through conditioning. According to the notion of stimulus generalization, if a stimulus evokes either an unconditioned or a conditioned emotional response, other stimuli that are similar to the eliciting stimulus will evoke similar, but less intense emotional responses. This principle leads to the conclusion that, because the stimulus on film is perceptually similar to the real stimulus it represents, any stimulus that would evoke a fright response if experienced firsthand will evoke a similar, albeit less intense response when encountered via the mass media. In other words, stimuli and events that cause fear in the real world will produce a fear response when they appear in movies. It may be argued that horror movies, for the most part, present images that tend to be perceptually realistic, and that this visual realism should enhance the tendency to generalize from the real to the mediated stimulus.

In our conditioning explanation, we proposed categories of stimuli and events that tend to induce fear in real-life situations and that are frequently depicted in frightening media productions. These categories were based on a review of research on the sources of real-world fears and on the effects of frightening media. The categories are *dangers and injuries, distortions of natural forms,* and *the experience of endangerment and fear by others.* As detailed in the following, these elements comprise what may be considered the *essence* of the horror film genre.

Prevalence of Dangers and Injuries

Stimuli that are perceived as dangerous should, by definition, evoke fear. If any such threats were witnessed firsthand, the onlooker would be in danger, and fear would be the expected response. Through stimulus generalization, it is logical to expect mediated depictions of danger or injury to produce fright reactions as well.

The depiction of events that either cause or threaten to cause great harm is so essential to the horror film that it is inconceivable that a horror film could exist without them. This genre, perhaps more than any other, provides abundant opportunity for viewers to experience fear in response to injury and danger, as one of the defining characteristics is the portrayal of victimization and death (Schoell, 1985). In a recent content analysis of 56 slasher films, Cowan and O'Brien (1990) counted 474 characters who were portrayed as threatened or frightened by a killer. This amounts to more than eight threatened characters per movie. Moreover, this analysis revealed that 86% of threatened characters portrayed did not survive their victimization.

In addition to portrayals of dangerous (often fatal) situations, horror films also graphically illustrate the injuries that cause the demise of most victimized characters. Rather than presenting violence in a sanitized form, horror films dwell on gruesome and bloody depictions. As vivid examples a character in

Friday the 13th suffers a blow to the face with an ax, a character in *Halloween, Part III* has his head ripped from his body, a character in *Texas Chainsaw Massacre* is hoisted upon a meat hook and left to die; and several characters in *Slumber Party Massacre, Part II* are murdered with an oversized drill attached to the end of a guitar.   As Schoell (1985) described: "Stalk-and-slash" and "splatter" movies have gone as far as they can go.   Every type of death imaginable has been lovingly recreated on the screen.   Nothing is left to our imagination any more: disembowelments, beheadings, amputations, entrail eating. Nothing is out of bounds" (p. 149).

Distortions of Natural Forms

Distortions and deformities naturally produce fear, anxiety, and negative affect in general.   Hebb (1946) observed that even baby chimpanzees exhibit fear responses to deformities, and argued that such responses are spontaneous, in that they do not require conditioning.   Organisms that have been mutilated as a result of injury could be considered to fall into this category as well as the previous category.   More importantly, distortions that are not the result of injury are often encountered in horror films, in the form of realistic characters like dwarves, hunchbacks, and mutants, or in the form of monsters.   Monsters are unreal creatures that are similar to natural beings in many ways, but deviant from them in other ways, such as through distortions in size, shape, skin color, or facial configuration.   It may be argued that such distortions are especially typical in classic horror films.   However, a variety of frightening genres involve characters with grotesque and distorted features.

   In slasher films, although some villains are depicted as appearing ominously normal or commonplace, most killers evidence some physical abnormality or distortion that sets them apart from the characters they victimize.   For example, the killer in *The Burning* is characterized by a face that is scorched and scarred beyond recognition, as is Freddy Krueger from the *Nightmare on Elm Street* series.   Other villains' facial features are distorted by masks or costumes (Dika, 1990).   As prominent examples: Michael Myers, the killer in the *Halloween* series, is disguised by an expressionless white mask; Jason Vorhees from the *Friday the 13th* series is characterized by a hockey mask; and Leatherface from *The Texas Chainsaw Massacre* sports a rotting and grotesque mask made from the skin of his former victims.

Focus on the Fear and Endangerment of Major Characters

Although in some horror movies, viewers seem to respond directly to depictions of fear-evoking stimuli, in most such films, these stimuli are shown to have profound effects on the emotional responses and outcomes of depicted characters. In many cases, the viewer can be said to respond *indirectly* to the stimuli through the experiences of the characters. One mechanism underlying such responses is *empathy*. Although there is controversy over the origins of empathic processes (see Berger, 1962; Hoffman, 1978), it is clear that under some circumstances, people experience fear as a direct response to the fear expressed by others. Many horror films seem to stress characters' expressions of fear in response to dangers at least as much as the perceptual cues associated with the threat itself.

Even though, as mentioned previously, many characters in this genre are eventually killed by the villains, a considerable amount of time is often devoted to the victims' frantic attempts to ward off their tormentors or to escape from the perilous situations. For example, in a content analysis of 10 slasher films, Weaver (1991) reported that the average length of the scenes involving the death of male characters was 108 seconds and the average length of the scenes involving the death of female characters was 218 seconds. Certainly, with this much screen time devoted to portrayals of death, a considerable amount of attention is given to the victims' expressions of fear and agony.

In addition to scenes involving death, a common characteristic of the horror film genre is the portrayal of the prolonged terrorization of a lone character (usually a heroine) who remains alive after his or her friends have been murdered (Dika, 1987). Typically, this terrorization involves the heroine hysterically attempting to escape or hide from the villain, with the focus of suspense concentrated on the victim's fear and panic rather than on actual scenes of death or injury. Instances of this type of prolonged terrorization and "stalking" are abundant in the slasher film genre. For example, a particularly noteworthy scene in *Halloween* involves Jamie Lee Curtis' character anxiously attempting to suppress her screams as she hides in a closet from the killer who is but a few feet away. Although it is clear that danger is imminent, the focus of the scene is on Curtis' fearful reactions rather than on the graphic display of injury or on the killer himself.

Arousal-Enhancing Stylistic Techniques

An additional reason to expect fright reactions to horror films is that this genre usually involves a variety of visual and auditory techniques, in addition to basic plot elements, to increase and maintain the viewer's arousal response. This increased arousal is then available to energize and intensify, via excitation transfer (e.g., Zillmann, 1978), the viewer's feelings of fear that are produced by the various plot elements. Some of these techniques seem to be built on stimuli that humans are predisposed to fear spontaneously (see Bowlby, 1973; Yerkes & Yerkes, 1936). For example, sudden loud noises and music that mimics the alarm signals of animals are typical in horror films. Perhaps the best example of a fear-provoking soundtrack is Bernard Herrmann's often imitated musical score for the film *Psycho*. In particular, the infamous shower scene portraying the brutal death of Janet Leigh's character was made considerably more terrifying by the screeching violins that accompanied her screams.

Darkness, obscured vision, and ominous shadows are visual elements that we are predisposed to fear and that are also prevalent in horror films. An examination of horror film titles supports the idea that this genre often features scenes taking place in darkness or at night. Such titles include *The Dark, Dark Places, Dead of the Night, Fear in the Night, Hell Night, Near Dark, Night of Bloody Horror, Night of the Living Dead, Night Screams, One Dark Night*, and *Out of the Dark*, among many others (Martin & Porter, 1990).

> It wasn't so much Freddy (the evil main character who arose from the dead) as it was the ways in which he jumped out of nowhere and hid behind corners ready to attack his victims. The music which began to play before something scary or unforeseen happened also made me feel anxious and scared (*Nightmare on Elm Street*).

In sum, fright-inducing elements abound in horror films. These films focus on dangers and graphic displays of injuries, grotesque distortions, and expressions of terror. Moreover, typically used stylistic techniques are well designed to enhance viewers' emotional reactions.

The stimulus generalization approach to understanding media-induced fear falls short of fully explaining adults' reactions to horror films, however, because it leads to the expectation that through stimulus discrimination, adults should become less and less responsive to horror films over time, as they learn that the reinforcement contingencies associated with real dangers are vastly different from those associated with fright-inducing stimuli depicted on screen.

One way to explain the fact that adults continue to respond with fear to horror is to take motivations for media exposure into account. As Zillmann (1982) has argued, mature viewers often seek out media programming for entertainment and arousal. In order to enhance the emotional impact of a drama they may, for example, adopt the "willing suspension of disbelief" by cognitively minimizing the effect of knowledge that the events are mediated. In addition, mature viewers may enhance their emotional responses by generating their own emotion-evoking visual images or by cognitively elaborating on the implications of the portrayed events. On the other hand, mature viewers who seek to avoid intense arousal may employ other appraisal processes (see Zillmann, 1978), to diminish fright reactions to media stimuli by using the "adult discount," for example (see Dysinger & Ruckmick, 1933), and concentrating on the fact that the stimuli are only mediated. Research by Lazarus and his co-workers has shown that adults can modify their emotional responses to stressful films by adopting different "cognitive sets" (e.g., Koriat, Melkman, Averill, & Lazarus, 1972).

Another factor that should influence whether adults respond with fear to horror films involves whether or not a depicted threat is realistic, in that the events could conceivably happen in real life. Knowledge that the terrible situation being witnessed is being performed by actors should not necessarily prevent the viewer's emotional response if the depiction reminds the viewer of his or her own vulnerability to similar threats. Often in horror films, there are elements of reality even within highly unrealistic plots. For example, even though viewers know that homicidal maniacs cannot return from the dead as they do repeatedly in the *Halloween* series, they know that psychopathic murderers do exist and pose potential threats to innocent, unsuspecting victims.

As we argued in our stimulus generalization rationale (Cantor, 1994), the more similar a depicted stimulus is to those stimuli that provoke fear in a particular individual, the greater the fear response should be. This principle predicts that horror films that focus on fears already resident in the viewer will produce more intense reactions than those that focus on other fear-evoking events. It may well be that an enhanced feeling of personal vulnerability is one of the most potent sources of fright among adults who view horror films.

I believe *The Accused* frightened me so much because it portrayed a woman's nightmare. The worst rape scenario I'd ever imagined. Also, one of my girlfriends from High School had recently been raped by two men while she was running.

EXPECTATIONS OF DEVELOPMENTAL DIFFERENCES

Given the previous explanations for adults' responses to horror films, there are a variety of reasons to expect differences in responses to such presentations as a function of age. These differences are based both on principles of stimulus generalization and on theories of cognitive development. The next portion of this chapter presents a series of proposed developmental differences and cites theoretical arguments and research results to support them. Again, anecdotal accounts are presented for illustration.

1. *Viewers of different ages will be frightened by different components of horror films, just as they are frightened by different real-world stimuli.* Research shows that there are consistent developmental trends in the stimuli and issues that evoke fear (e.g., Angelino, Dollins, & Mech, 1956; Maurer, 1965). According to a variety of studies using diverse methodologies, children from approximately 3 to 8 years of age are frightened primarily by animals; the dark; supernatural beings, such as ghosts, monsters, and witches; and by anything that looks strange or moves suddenly. The fears of 9- to 12-year-olds are more often related to personal injury and physical destruction and the injury

and death of relatives. Adolescents continue to fear personal injury and physical destruction, but school fears and social fears arise at this age, as do fears regarding political, economic, and global issues (see Cantor, Wilson, & Hoffner, 1986, for a review).

These age differences in the sources of fears suggest that horror films abound in elements that should be particularly frightening to young children and adolescents. Children up to age 8 should be especially terrified by the fantastic and grotesque monsters that populate such films—even if they do not understand critical elements of the plot.

> Of all the effects on myself from television that I am aware of . . . the most profound effect had to do with the influences from the movie *The Wizard of Oz*. . . . That old witch scared me so much that I had recurring nightmares about her for about three or four weeks after each showing. . . . The dream would always climax with my perspective being that of Dorothy's and the Witch saying in an extremely grotesque way, "come my prittee." At this point, I would awake screaming and crying.

Also according to developmental research on fears, elementary school children and adolescents should be especially frightened by the physical injury and death that are so common in horror films.

> The horror film, *Friday the Thirteenth, Part II* produced a great deal of fear and anxiety in me when I saw it at the age of 12. . . . The most frightening parts were the murders that occurred at night, with haunting music and dark sets. . . . My thoughts were on what I would do if I was in the same situation as the victims.

Finally, older children and adults should be especially sensitive to films depicting devastating global consequences.

> While I was in high school, the made-for-TV movie *The Day After* aired, and it left an impact on me that is still present. To be honest, I did not watch the whole show. I stopped watching it a few segments after a nuclear bomb decimated an entire countryside. When the bomb landed, the television screen turned white and then everything was gone. I never really imagined the full effects a nuclear explosion could have. I could not picture that in a few seconds everything in existence could be obliterated.

    2. *Younger children will be more responsive than older children and adults to the visually grotesque aspects of horror film stimuli.* This proposition is based on our finding that the relative importance of the immediately perceptible components of a fear-inducing media stimulus decreases as a child's age increases. Research on cognitive development indicates that, in general, very young children react to stimuli predominantly in terms of their perceptible

characteristics and that with increasing maturity, they respond more and more to the conceptual aspects of stimuli. Piaget referred to young children's tendency to react to things as they appear in immediate, egocentric perception as *concreteness* of thought (see Flavell, 1963). Bruner (1966) characterized the thought of preschool children as *perceptually dominated*. A variety of studies have shown that young children tend to sort, match, and remember items in terms of their perceptible attributes, and that around age 7 this tendency is increasingly replaced by the tendency to use functional or conceptual groupings (e.g., Melkman, Tversky, & Baratz, 1981).

The notion of a developmental shift from perceptual to conceptual processing has been tested in terms of the impact of visual features of a stimulus. Our research findings support the generalization that preschool children (approximately 3 to 5 years old) are more likely to be frightened by something that *looks* scary but is actually harmless than by something that looks attractive, but is actually harmful; for older elementary school children (approximately 9 to 11 years), appearance becomes less influential, relative to the behavior or destructive potential of a character, animal, or object.

One set of data that supports this generalization comes from a survey (Cantor & Sparks, 1984) asking parents to name the programs and films that had frightened their children the most. In this survey, parents of preschool children most often mentioned offerings with grotesque-looking, unreal characters, such as the television series *The Incredible Hulk* and the feature film *The Wizard of Oz*; parents of older elementary school children more often mentioned movies (like *The Amityville Horror*) that involved threats without a strong visual component, and that required a good deal of imagination to comprehend.

A second investigation that supports this generalization was a laboratory study involving an episode of the *Incredible Hulk* series (Sparks & Cantor, 1986). In this study, we concluded that preschool children's unexpectedly intense reactions to this program were partially due to their overresponse to the visual image of the Hulk character. When we tracked subjects' levels of fear during different parts of the program, we found that preschool children experienced the most fear after the attractive, mild-mannered hero was transformed into the monstrous-looking Hulk. Older elementary school children, in contrast, reported the least fear at this time, because they understood that the Hulk was really the benevolent hero in another physical form, and that he was using his superhuman powers on the side of "law and order" and against threats to the well-being of liked characters.

In another study (Hoffner & Cantor, 1985), we tested the effect of appearance more directly, by creating a story in four versions, so that a major character was either attractive and grandmotherly looking or ugly and grotesque. The character's appearance was factorially varied with her behavior—she was depicted as behaving either kindly or cruelly. In judging how nice or mean the character was and in predicting what she would do in the subsequent scene, preschool children were more influenced than older children (6-7 and 9-10 years) by the character's looks and less influenced than older children by her kind or cruel behavior. As the age of the child increased, the character's looks became less important and her behavior carried increasing weight. A follow-up study revealed that all age groups engaged in physical appearance stereotyping in the absence of information about the character's behavior.

Taken together, these findings suggest that younger children should be particularly sensitive to the grotesque and distorted nature of horror characters.

3. *Younger children will be more responsive than older children and adults to blatantly fantastic happenings. Older children and adults will be more sensitive to the objectively threatening aspects of plots.* Our research has led to the conclusion that as children mature, they become more responsive to realistic threats, and less responsive to fantastic dangers depicted in the media. The data on trends in children's fears suggest that very young children are more likely than older children and adolescents to fear things that are not real, in the sense that their occurrence in the real world is impossible (e.g., monsters). The development of more "mature" fears seems to presuppose the acquisition of knowledge regarding the objective dangers posed by different situations.

One important component of this knowledge includes an understanding of the distinction between reality and fantasy. Much research has been conducted on the child's gradual acquisition of the various components of the fantasy-reality distinction (see Flavell, 1963; Kelly, 1981; Morison & Gardner, 1978). Before a child understands the distinction, he or she will be unable to comprehend that something that is not real cannot pose a threat, and thus, the reality or fantasy status of a media depiction should have little effect on the fear it evokes. As the child comes increasingly to understand this distinction and increasingly appreciates the implications of real-world threats, depictions of real dangers should gain in fear-evoking potential relative to depictions of fantasy dangers.

This generalization is supported by our survey of parents, mentioned earlier (Cantor & Sparks, 1984). In general, the tendency to mention fantasy offerings, depicting events that could not possibly occur in the real world, as sources of fear, decreased as the child's age increased, and the tendency to mention fictional offerings, depicting events that might possibly occur, increased with age. Further support for this generalization comes from an experiment (Cantor & Wilson, 1984) in which a reminder that the happenings in *The Wizard of Oz* were not real reduced the fear of older elementary school children but did not affect preschool children's responses.

This reasoning leads to the expectation that aspects of horror films that are patently fantastic should diminish in their ability to frighten as children mature. However, real dangers that pose physical threats to the well-being of characters, especially those threats that are less visually apparent (e.g., the mad scientist planning to blow up the world or the soon-to-be-violent stalker) should upset older children more than younger ones. Also, because as children mature they become more and more aware of threats to their own lives, realistic threats that have the capacity to harm them, (e.g., murderers, kidnappers, and rapists) should come to have more fright-inducing power than other depicted dangers.

Examples of blatantly fantastic happenings abound in recollections of fright from the early years:

> We were watching a horror story on television. The lead woman character turned into a werewolf. She did this whenever she became mad or angry at someone. Before she became a werewolf, however, she became a series of other faces besides, for example, a man, frog, skeleton, and then progressed to the werewolf face. The woman werewolf was attacking young girls.

Realistic threats are more typical of fright in the teen years:

> I was 14 when I saw *Wait Until Dark*. To make a long movie short, it is about a defenseless blind woman that two men are trying to murder. At the climax of the movie the murderer's hand grabs ahold of the woman's ankle in the darkness of her room. I have always had a fear of a hand doing the identical thing to me when I'm alone in the dark.

4. *The terrorized reactions of threatened protagonists should frighten older children and adults more than younger children.* Our research indicates that there are developmental differences in the tendency to empathize with a film protagonist's fear. In an experiment (Wilson & Cantor, 1985), preschool and older elementary school children were exposed to a videotape of either a frightening stimulus alone (a large, menacing killer bee), or to a character's fear response to the frightening stimulus. In line with predictions based on a cognitive-developmental approach to the process of empathy, younger children were less emotionally aroused by the character's fear than by the fear-provoking stimulus. In contrast, older children responded similarly to the two versions of the videotape. The difference was not due to younger children's failure to identify the emotion the protagonist was feeling. Both age groups were aware that the character was frightened.

> Last year's thriller *Silence of the Lambs* had me on the edge of my seat nonstop. . . . Tension was increased through identification with the character Clarice. Her curiosity, determinedness and desire for success in addition to

inexperience, left her in a vulnerable position relying on the trust of a brilliant yet psychotic cannibalistic madman.

5. *Abstract elements of threats will be more frightening for older children and adults than for the youngest children.* Another generalization from our research is that as children mature, they become frightened by media depictions involving increasingly abstract concepts. This generalization is clearly consistent with the general sources of children's fears, cited earlier. It is also consistent with theories of cognitive development (e.g., Flavell, 1963), which indicate that the ability to think abstractly emerges relatively late in cognitive development.

Data supporting this generalization come from a survey we conducted on children's responses to the television movie *The Day After* (Cantor et al., 1986). Many people were concerned about young children's reactions to this movie, which depicted the devastation of a Kansas community by a nuclear attack, but our research led us to predict that the youngest children would be the least affected by it. We conducted a telephone survey (using random sampling) the night after the broadcast of this movie. As we predicted, children under 12 were much less disturbed by the film than were teenagers, and parents were the most disturbed. The very youngest children were not upset or frightened at all. Most of the parents of the younger children who had seen the film could think of other shows that had frightened their child more during the preceding year. Most of the parents of the teenagers could not. We concluded that the findings were due to the fact that the emotional impact of the film comes from the contemplation of the potential annihilation of the earth as we know it—a concept that is beyond the grasp of the young child. The visual depictions of injury in this movie were quite mild compared to what most children have become used to seeing on television.

Thus, the depiction of invisible, but potent threats such as radiation, chemical warfare, or deadly diseases is expected to frighten older children more readily than younger ones.

6. *Older children and adults' fright responses are more likely than those of young children to be mediated by their motivations for media exposure.* Research has shown that young children are less able than older children and adults to modify their thought processes when viewing frightening media. Thus, their responses are not as likely to be affected by their motivations for exposure. In a study of children's ability to modify their fright reactions (Cantor & Wilson, 1984), older elementary school children who were told to remember that the movie they were seeing was not real showed less fear than their classmates who received no instructions. Children who were told to try to put themselves mentally in the threatened protagonist's position showed more

fear than those in the control condition. The same instructions had no effect on the fear of preschoolers, however.

POTENTIAL LONG-TERM EFFECTS OF EXPOSURE TO HORROR

It is not unusual to hear the argument that "a good scare" never hurt anyone, and that it is silly to be concerned about children's exposure to frightening movies. Therefore, it is reasonable to inquire whether fright responses to mass media horrors exert any long-term emotional effects, and whether such intense fright experiences produce any important negative behavioral consequences.

Both questions are difficult to answer.   For ethical reasons, it is inappropriate to assess whether fright induced in the laboratory lasts a long time. We simply cannot expose children to intensely frightening fare and then send them home without taking steps to alleviate their fright, for the purpose of determining how severe their nightmares were. The best we can do is to ask children about their longer term reactions to shows and media events that they exposed themselves to on their own. The evidence on this question is mixed, because controlled studies conducted shortly after traumatic media events have typically found only mild reactions among the children in their samples. A review of research on reactions to the movie *The Day After*, and news coverage of the space shuttle *Challenger* disaster and the Three Mile Island nuclear accident (Cantor, 1992) reported that minor and short-lived reactions were typical (see also Schofield & Pavelchak, 1985).

The mild nature of these observed reactions may be due to several factors. First, all three offerings dealt with technology gone awry, and thus the implications of the events were abstract and difficult to comprehend. Second, all children who were exposed to these media events were in the presence of adults or discussed the events with an adult shortly after exposure. Finally, there was an exceptionally high level of parental concern over the impact of these events on children, and this concern may have led parents to help their children deal with their fears. Research on coping with media-induced fears indicates that the presence of a caring adult and discussion with a parent are potent fear reducers for children (Cantor & Wilson, 1988).

The mild and short-lived nature of these reactions contrasts with the intensity typical of responses measured retrospectively. When Johnson (1980) asked a random sample of adults whether they had ever seen a motion picture that had disturbed them "a great deal," 40% answered in the affirmative, and the median length of the disturbance was 3 days. Based on the type, intensity, and duration of the symptoms, Johnson concluded that almost half of these respondents (or 19% of the random sample) had experienced a "significant stress reaction" lasting for at least 2 days as the result of viewing a movie.

The retrospective descriptions that many college students give of their reactions also suggest that intense and long-lasting emotional responses are not unusual.

> I remember seeing that horrible face in my dreams for several nights afterward, always waking just as the creature was about to grab me (*The Twilight Zone*).

What is especially interesting about the descriptions is how many of them refer to effects that have lasted to the present time:

> To this day I remember that movie like it was yesterday, and I still am uneasy when I am by myself at night (*When a Stranger Calls*).
> To this day I still wonder if the bees couldn't be heading this way (*Killer Bees*).

There is anecdotal evidence of severe disturbances requiring medical treatment. The most extreme reactions reported in the literature come from psychiatric case studies in which acute and disabling anxiety states enduring several days to several weeks or more are said to have been precipitated by the viewing of horror movies such as *The Exorcist* and *Invasion of the Body Snatchers* (Buzzuto, 1975; Mathai, 1983). A recent case reported in the *British Medical Journal* (Simons & Silveira, 1994) involved a 10-year-old's reaction to a program with the title *Ghostwatch*. The child was diagnosed as suffering from television-induced post-traumatic stress disorder, and required 8 weeks of hospitalization. Most of the patients in the psychiatric cases that have been reported had not had previously diagnosed psychiatric problems, but the viewing of the film was seen as occurring in conjunction with other stressors in the patients' lives.

An example of a major behavioral effect of exposure to horror was recounted on a popular television talk show by Myra Lewis Williams (ex-wife of rockstar Jerry Lee Lewis). In response to an audience question, Ms. Williams confided that she had married at the age of 13 because she had seen the global holocaust movie *On the Beach*, and had concluded that because the world was going to end soon, she had better get on with her life (*Phil Donahue Show*, 1986).

A recent experiment provides some support for the potential of scary movies to influence children's everyday behavior in negative ways. In that study (Cantor & Omdahl, 1991), children were exposed to fictional depictions of realistic life-threatening events (either a fatal house fire from *Little House on the Prairie*, or a drowning from *Jaws II*) or to benign scenes involving fire or water. Afterward, children exposed to a particular threat subsequently rated similar events as more likely to occur in their own lives, considered the potential consequences to be more severe, and reported more worry about such happenings than subjects exposed to neutral depictions. Moreover, liking for activities closely related to the observed threats was reduced. Subjects who had seen a drowning indicated less desire to go canoeing than those who had not. Subjects who had seen a fatal house fire reported less desire to build a fire in a fireplace than those who had not. Although only short-term effects were assessed and responses were given in the form of self-reports only, the notion that fright reactions to horror could have long-lasting behavioral effects is consistent with many of the self-reports of college students.

> Even though I knew there was no Great White Shark in Maynard Lake on that summer afternoon, I still made my friends go back to my house and get our canoe to paddle out to that island and pick me up (*Jaws*).
>
> The frightening effect it had on me was that I would always check the toilet and swimming pools for alligators. I was also hesitant to go too close to any sewers (*Alligator*).
>
> The movie has installed a permanent fear in me . . . I like to hunt [but] I am perpetually afraid to grab any duck or goose that isn't absolutely dead. I keep picturing the birds in the movie *The Birds* biting people.
>
> Ever since that night, whenever I enter an apartment which reminds me of the one Stewart lived in, I first of all close all of the shades and then I look in the closets (*Rear Window*).
>
> I still can't sleep without something covering me, even on a hot night, because of the fear that movie produced (title unknown).
>
> My phobia of taking a shower without anyone in the house began in October of 1973. . . . No matter how silly and childish it may seem, 5 years older and wiser, I still find myself peering around the shower curtain in fear of seeing the beholder of my death (*Psycho*).

The studies and anecdotes reported here are not meant to imply that all children should be prevented from seeing horror films. For one thing, some very intense fright reactions have been shown to result from what have appeared to be fairly innocuous presentations, so it would be difficult to know where to draw the line. For another, many children like horror films, and most do not want their viewing to be restricted (Cantor, 1994). The findings are suggestive, however, of the fact that emotional responses can endure well beyond the time of viewing, and that these reactions can involve intense negative affect and, at times, the avoidance of activities that would otherwise be deemed nonthreatening.

The findings suggest that parental involvement is appropriate in the selection of films for children, to improve the chances that the child will experience a pleasurable and short-lived emotional reaction, rather than long-term feelings of threat and anxiety. The findings of research on the elements of horror films that are most likely to frighten children at different ages should be helpful. It should be recognized, however, that children are exposed to many programs and films without their parents' knowledge. The pervasiveness of multiple television sets in the home as well as the saturation of cable television, increases the opportunities for children to be exposed to a wide variety of horrific images. In addition, there is much anecdotal evidence of the prevalence of peer pressure as the force behind children's exposure to films they would otherwise avoid.

Because even the most cautious parents are likely to find themselves confronted with a child whose fright was caused by horror films, parental involvement will also be necessary to help children cope with whatever fright reactions do occur. Studies have shown that a variety of strategies can be effective in reducing media-induced fright, and that different strategies are appropriate for children of different ages (Cantor & Wilson, 1988).

REFERENCES

Angelino, H., Dollins, J., & Mech, E. V. (1956). Trends in the "fears and worries" of school children as related to socio-economic status and age. *Journal of Genetic Psychology, 89*, 263-276.

Berger, S. M. (1962). Conditioning through vicarious instigation. *Psychological Review, 69*, 450-466.

Blumer, H. (1933). *Movies and conduct.* New York: Macmillan.

Bowlby, J. (1973). *Separation: Anxiety and anger.* New York: Basic Books.

Bruner, J. S. (1966). On cognitive growth I & II. In J. S. Bruner, R. R. Oliver, & P. M. Greenfield (Eds.), *Studies in cognitive growth* (pp. 1-67). New York: Wiley.

Buzzuto, J. C. (1975). Cinematic neurosis following "The Exorcist." *Journal of Nervous and Mental Disease, 161*, 43-48.

Cantor, J. (1994). Fright reactions to mass media. In J. Bryant & D. Zillmann (Eds.), *Media effects: Advances in theory and research* (pp. 213-245). Hillsdale, NJ: Lawrence Erlbaum Associates.

Cantor, J. (1992). Children's emotional responses to technological disasters conveyed by the mass media. In J. M. Wober (Ed.), *Television and nuclear power: Making the public mind* (pp. 31-53). Norwood, NJ: Ablex.

Cantor, J., & Omdahl, B. L. (1991). Effects of televised depictions of realistic threats on children's emotional responses, expectations, worries, and liking for related activities. *Communication Monographs, 58*, 384-401.

Cantor, J., & Reilly, S. (1982). Adolescents' fright reactions to television and films. *Journal of Communication, 32*(1), 87-99.

Cantor, J., & Sparks, G. G. (1984). Children's fear responses to mass media: Testing some Piagetian predictions. *Journal of Communication, 34*(2), 90-103.

Cantor, J., & Wilson, B. J. (1984). Modifying fear responses to mass media in preschool and elementary school children. *Journal of Broadcasting, 28*, 431-443.

Cantor, J., & Wilson, B. J. (1988). Helping children cope with frightening media presentations. *Current Psychology: Research & Reviews, 7*, 58-75.

Cantor, J., Wilson, B. J., & Hoffner, C. (1986). Emotional responses to a televised nuclear holocaust film. *Communication Research, 13*, 257-277.

Cowan, G., & O'Brien, M. (1990). Gender and survival vs. death in slasher films: A content analysis. *Sex Roles, 23*, 187-196.

Dika, V. (1987). The stalker film, 1978-81. In G. A. Waller (Ed.), *American horrors: Essays on the modern American horror film* (pp. 86-101). Chicago: University of Illinois Press.

Dika, V. (1990). *Games of terror: "Halloween," "Friday the 13th," and the films of the stalker cycle.* Cranbury, NJ: Associated University Presses.

Dysinger, W. S., & Ruckmick, C. A. (1933). *The emotional responses of children to the motion picture situation.* New York: Macmillan.

Eisenberg, A. L. (1936). *Children and radio programs.* New York: Columbia University Press.

Flavell, J. (1963). *The developmental psychology of Jean Piaget.* New York: Van Nostrand.

Hebb, D. O. (1946). On the nature of fear. *Psychological Review, 53,* 259-276.

Hess, R. D., & Goldman, H. (1962). Parents' views of the effects of television on their children. *Child Development, 33,* 411-426.

Himmelweit, H. T., Oppenheim, A. N., & Vince, P. (1958). *Television and the child.* London: Oxford University Press.

Hoffman, M. L. (1978). Toward a theory of empathic arousal and development. In M. Lewis & L. A. Rosenblum (Eds.), *The development of affect* (pp. 227-256). New York: Plenum.

Hoffner, C., & Cantor, J. (1985). Developmental differences in responses to a television character's appearance and behavior. *Developmental Psychology, 21,* 1065-1074.

Johnson, B. R. (1980). General occurrence of stressful reactions to commercial motion pictures and elements in films subjectively identified as stressors. *Psychological Reports, 47,* 775-786.

Kelly, H. (1981). Reasoning about realities: Children's evaluations of television and books. In H. Kelly & H. Gardner (Eds.), *Viewing children through television* (pp. 59-71). San Francisco: Jossey-Bass.

Koriat, A., Melkman, R., Averill, J. R., & Lazarus, R. S. (1972). The self-control of emotional reactions to a stressful film. *Journal of Personality, 40,* 601-619.

Martin, M., & Porter, M. (1990). *Video movie guide: 1991.* New York: Ballantine Books.

Mathai, J. (1983). An acute anxiety state in an adolescent precipitated by viewing a horror movie. *Journal of Adolescence, 6,* 197-200.

Maurer, A. (1965). What children fear. *Journal of Genetic Psychology, 106,* 265-277.

Melkman, R., Tversky, B., & Baratz, D. (1981). Developmental trends in the use of perceptual and conceptual attributes in grouping, clustering and retrieval. *Journal of Experimental Child Psychology, 31,* 470-486.

Morison, P., & Gardner, H. (1978). Dragons and dinosaurs: The child's capacity to differentiate fantasy from reality. *Child Development, 49,* 642-648.

Palmer, E. L., Hockett, A. B., & Dean, W. W. (1983). The television family and children's fright reactions. *Journal of Family Issues, 4,* 279-292.

Pavlov, I. P. (1927). *Conditioned reflexes* (G. V. Anrep, Trans.). London: Oxford University Press.

Phil Donahue Show. (1986). Transcript #05196. New York: Multimedia Entertainment.

Preston, M. I. (1941). Children's reactions to movie horrors and radio crime. *Journal of Pediatrics, 19,* 147-168.

Razran, G. (1949). Stimulus generalization of conditioned responses. *Psychological Bulletin, 46,* 337-365.

Schoell, W. (1985). *Stay out of the shower: 25 Years of shocker films beginning with "Psycho."* New York: Dembner Books.

Schofield, J., & Pavelchak, M. (1985). "The Day After": The impact of a media event. *American Psychologist, 40,* 542-548.

Simons, D., & Silveira, W. R. (1994). Post-traumatic stress disorder in children after television programmes. *British Medical Journal, 308*(6925), 389-390.

Sparks, G. G., & Cantor, J. (1986). Developmental differences in fright responses to a television program depicting a character transformation. *Journal of Broadcasting and Electronic Media, 30,* 309-323.

Weaver, J. B., III. (1991). Are "slasher" horror films sexually violent? A content analysis. *Journal of Broadcasting and Electronic Media, 35,* 385-393.

Wilson, B. J., & Cantor, J. (1985). Developmental differences in empathy with a television protagonist's fear. *Journal of Experimental Child Psychology, 39,* 284-299.

Yerkes, R. M., & Yerkes, A. W. (1936). Nature and conditions of avoidance (fear) response in chimpanzee. *Journal of Comparative Psychology, 21,* 53-66.

Zillmann, D. (1978). Attribution and misattribution of excitatory reactions. In J. H. Harvey, W. Ickes, & R. F. Kidd (Eds.), *New directions in attribution research* (Vol. 2, pp. 335-368). Hillsdale, NJ: Lawrence Erlbaum Associates.

Zillmann, D. (1982). Television viewing and arousal. In D. Pearl, L. Bouthilet, & J. Lazar (Eds.), *Television and behavior: Ten years of scientific progress and implications for the eighties* (Vol. 2, pp. 53-67). DHHS Publication No. ADM 82-1196. Washington, DC: U.S. Government Printing Office.

Chapter 6

Gender-Socialization Theory of Reactions to Horror

Dolf Zillmann
University of Alabama
James B. Weaver, III
Auburn University

This chapter extends the proposal that adolescent enthrallment with horror, with cinematic horror in particular, derives from the rites of passage in ancient societies characterized by strong gender segregation along protector-protectee lines (Zillmann & Gibson, chap. 2, this volume). More specifically, it is suggested that the practice of gender segregation in hunter-gatherer cultures may have undergone changes, but that it has never been abolished and that modern society has continued to place men into agonistic and women into sedentary roles. Although the utility of such segregation has been compromised, the archaic dichotomization has persisted. Societal precepts still force men into provider and protector roles, and they still encourage women to seek men's protection and to show dependence in these terms. As in earlier times, adolescent men and women are expected to prepare for these societally prescribed gender roles. However, unlike earlier times, formal rituals testing their accomplishments in this regard—rites of passage into adulthood—no longer exist. Adolescents of modern society have to demonstrate their compliance with societal precepts in alternative social contexts, and we suggest that going to the movies provides such a context. Societally prescribed emotional maturation may be exhibited to peers and others, for instance, by laughing, crying, and cussing at appropriate times during exposure to events featured in cinematic fiction. More important here, fearlessness and the ability to protect may be signaled by not blinking an eye when confronted with cinematic horror. Analogously, fearfulness and a need for protection may be signaled by showing acute distress. Could it be, then, that the horror movie, by providing a forum for the exhibition of societally appropriate emotional maturation, serves as a rite of passage for modern times? Could it be that this genre provides male adolescents the forum for learning to master distress and for expressing their mastery? Analogously, might this genre provide the forum for female adolescents to hone their skills at play-acting dismay and signaling a need for protection?

The chapter addresses these issues. We first present a theory of the gender socialization of affective behaviors and displays through the consumption of horror films. Special attention is given to emotional displays that are pertinent to the protector-protectee dichotomy. We then explore implications of the social consumption of cinematic horror for interpersonal attraction and interaction. Focus is on compliance with, and violation of, societally prescribed display rules for affect and emotion. Finally, pertinent research evidence is presented in support of the proposed gender-socialization function of cinematic horror.

PRELIMINARY CONSIDERATIONS

The analysis by Zillmann and Gibson (chap. 2, this volume) should leave no doubt about the fact that gender segregation along protector-protectee lines has been practiced in the vast majority of ancient cultures. Suffice it here to refer to general demonstrations of the practice in question.

The comparative assessment of socialization in more than 100 cultures (Barry, Bacon, & Child, 1957) shows compellingly that, starting at the age of 4 and extending beyond puberty, children have been treated in a highly gender-specific manner. Boys have been trained to be assertive and self-reliant, girls to be supportive and nurturing. In cultures where agonistic skills were essential, such as for hunting and warfare, this gender segregation has been particularly strong, and considerable pressures were brought to bear on compliance with designated gender roles. In particular, the expression of fear by boys was disallowed and duly punished. Girls, in contrast, were free to express their anxieties, even encouraged to do so.

Little seems to have changed. In contemporary societies, boys are still expected to inhibit any display of fear, and girls are still expected to exhibit distress and apprehensions (Brody, 1985; Maccoby & Jacklin, 1974; Saarni, 1988, 1989; Shennum & Bugental, 1982). However, the enforcement of societal precepts concerning the display of fear have changed drastically. Following the abandonment of formal rites of passage in which boys could be ridiculed and whipped for crying and their parents, brothers, and sisters could be shamed into seclusion, alternative conventions and institutions emerged for the display of fear and fearlessness. The horror tale, told by the fearless to the fearful, initiated a transition to informal control of compliance with expected displays of emotion. The horrifying fairy tale is analogously associated with informal control. Boys expressing distress and fear in response to horrifying tales are no longer whipped by elders or similarly punished by parents, although these former agents of control may intentionally or inadvertently make their displeasure and stern disapproval known. Nonetheless, cinematic horror is to be considered the latest manifestation of tale telling, where the telling occurs under conditions that give minimal, if any, control to chaperons. Does this mean that the gender-specific reinforcement contingencies that promote fearlessness in boys and squeamishness in girls have been removed? Not at all. It seems that merely a changing of the guard has taken place: The contingencies that used to be enforced by elders and parents are now enforced by peers, without apparent loss of effect. Boys must prove to their peers, and ultimately to themselves, that they are unperturbed, calm, and collected in the face of terror. Girls must similarly demonstrate their sensitivity by being appropriately disturbed, dismayed, and disgusted. Such demonstration seems important enough to adolescents to make them seek out horror and to subject themselves to cinematic torment. In fact, if the societally prescribed display rules for fear and fearlessness could readily be mastered by all, cinematic horror would fail to constitute a challenge or test that some master and others flunk. The 18-year-old founder of a German horror video club appreciated these circumstances. He focused on men's bragging about their mastery of fear and disgust, stating that a horror film is most enjoyed when it gives a boy a chance to claim: "Everybody threw up. But not me!" ("Alle haben gckotzt," 1984, authors' translation).

In summing up, then, it appears that cinematic horror does provide a forum, akin to rites of passage, for male and female adolescents to practice and demonstrate mastery of societally defined gender-specific expressive displays. In contrast to formal rites, however, this forum is used voluntarily. Moreover, the social agents enforcing contingencies of reinforcement are adolescent peers, not elders.

GENDER SOCIALIZATION OF AFFECT AND ITS EXPRESSION

It may be considered well established that different cultures and subcultures regulate the public display of affect and emotion differently, and that gender-specific display rules are part and parcel of culture-specific regulation (Harris, 1989; Izard, 1991; Morawski, 1987; Zammuner, 1987). Some cultures, for instance, severely curtail the expression of anger, whereas others allow or invite such expression (Averill, 1982). Similarly, in some cultures and subcultures women are expected to inhibit their enjoyment of sexual humor, whereas in others they are free to laugh with the boys (van Alphen, 1988). The same variance is found in the cultural control of the expression of fear and presumably the precipitating experience of fear (Izard, 1991).

Expressive expectations are implicit in the public behavior of the emotionally mature.   They are defined in adult interactions rather than in clearly articulated prescriptions (Saarni, 1979).   Behavior in specific situations defines the coward, the weakling, the hero, and the macho guy.   It also defines the accommodating, supportive, nurturing woman versus the assertive, uppity, if not bitchy female.   Surely, these schemata are neither universal nor invariable over time.   They are continually adjusted in the societal struggle toward appropriateness, and they shift in accordance with whatever perceptions seem consensually held.   But modifiable as they may be, these schemata of the emotionally mature adult world set the maturation goals for adolescents and children.   If good men do not cry when injured, and if they do not show fear in situations of grave danger, then that is what a boy has to shoot for.   Likewise, if admired women come apart in hostile encounters and tragic happenings, then that's the sensitivity that a girl has to acquire and exhibit.

All this is to make the point that children and young adolescents, who strive toward man- or womanhood, seek to adopt the expressive behavior exhibited by those who (a) have apparently managed the transition to adult already and (b) share their social identity (Abrams & Hogg, 1990; Turner, 1985).   The first stipulation allows for the emulation of expressive behavior by young adults who are admired and therefore come to serve as models.   The latter stipulation ensures that boys take cues from men and girls from women; but it also applies to matching ethnic and other subculture identities.

Given that adolescents strive to acquire the expressive repertoire of esteemed young and not-so-young adults, it must be expected that failure to conform with emotional display rules is unpleasantly experienced, especially when witnessed by peers.   Analogously, it must be expected that success in conforming with such rules is pleasantly experienced, again especially when witnessed by peers.   The presence of peers striving to accomplish the same goals, then, may be assumed to enhance greatly the self-administered operant reinforcement (Nevin, 1973; Zillmann, 1988).

It should also be recognized that schemata concerning the perception of appropriate emotional displays by adults are formed on the basis of media presentations, fiction included, as much as on actual interactions and observations.   This is so, simply because actual experience with emotion-evoking circumstances, especially with life-threatening, fear-inducing conditions, is severely limited.   The media, in contrast, are virtually unrestricted in their ability to confront respondents with emotion-stirring happenings and in showing how others are dealing with the circumstances at hand.   Media presentations thus demonstrate appropriate emotional reactions and displays in uncounted situations that are alien to the respondents' realm of experience and thereby prepare them to display affect appropriately in similar, but to them novel, situations.

CINEMATIC HORROR AND GENDER SOCIALIZATION

These considerations of the gender socialization of affect and its expression lead to the following assumptions and propositions concerning use and effects of cinematic horror.

Assumption 1. The informative function of social-learning theory (Bandura, 1969, 1971) projects that children and adolescents extract information about prevailing contingencies of reinforcement from the behavior of models, adult models in particular. Accordingly, displays of fear and dependence or fearlessness and dominance are deemed *appropriate* when consistently witnessed to yield reward, and they are deemed *inappropriate* when consistently witnessed to yield punishment. Motivation to conform with displays identified as appropriate, and to avoid displays identified as inappropriate, also follows from recognition of prevailing contingencies of reinforcement.

Assumption 2. Children and adolescents identify prevailing contingencies of reinforcement as gender specific and apply to themselves those matching their gender identity. Thus, boys emulate behaviors and adopt emotional displays that they have identified as appropriate and rewarding for men, and girls emulate behaviors and adopt emotional displays that they have identified as appropriate and rewarding for women.

Assumption 3. To the extent that gender-segregated emotional displays of fearlessness and dominance by men and fearfulness and dependence by women continue to be prevalent in the child's or adolescent's social and media environments, boys seek to display men's fearlessness and dominance and girls women's fearfulness and dependence.

Proposition 1. Cinematic horror, by featuring death and bodily mutilation in countless variations and with great frequency, constitutes modern society's most convenient testing ground for the display of appropriate emotional reactions to situations posing grave danger.

Proposition 2. Cinematic horror thus provides a forum for boys to practice and achieve the display of fearlessness and protective competence. It provides a forum for girls to practice and achieve the display of fearfulness and protective need.

Proposition 3. The successful performance of appropriate emotional displays in the face of terror on the screen is pleasantly experienced. Performance failure is unpleasantly experienced. These reactions are enhanced by the presence of witnesses, especially peer witnesses.

Proposition 4. Gratification from the successful performance of appropriate emotional displays is likely to be misconstrued as enjoyment of cinematic horror. Performance failure is likely to foster disinterest in, if not condemnation of, cinematic horror.

Proposition 5. The presence of others, especially peers, is likely to influence the enjoyment of cinematic horror. Male adolescents who have acquired the skill of displaying fearlessness and protective competence in the face of terror on the screen enjoy cinematic horror more, the greater the number of male and/or female companions who display distress. In contrast, female adolescents who have acquired the skill of displaying fearfulness and protective need in the face of terror on the screen enjoy cinematic horror less, the greater the number of male and/or female companions who display distress.

It should be pointed out that excitatory habituation (Grings & Dawson, 1978, Zillmann, 1979), that is, the successive diminution of the intensity of the initial distress reaction that comes with repeated exposure to horror, assists the achievement of mastery of displays of fearlessness. With repeated consumption of horror films, then, even squeamish boys should soon be able not to express any residual distress. Eventually, they should not experience distress and be at ease signaling protective competence. Girls should analogously experience a lessening of distress reactions. Their task of exhibiting dismay and helplessness may prove difficult after habituation, and demands on play-acting may ultimately be greater on them than on boys. Interestingly, and presumably the result of much display practicing by female adolescents, research with college students shows that women are significantly more confident than men about their ability to express fear and fear-related emotions. In contrast to women, men appear to have great difficulty expressing feelings of vulnerability (Blier & Blier-Wilson, 1989).

SOCIAL CONSEQUENCES OF APPROPRIATE AND INAPPROPRIATE DISPLAYS

Proposition 3 is not only preparatory for the predictions of immediate gratification from exposure to horror that are expressed in Propositions 4 and 5; it also leads to the prediction of more lasting benefits from appropriate emotional display by self and secondarily from inappropriate emotional display by others, as well as to that of drawbacks from inappropriate emotional display by self and secondarily from appropriate emotional display by others. A most direct implication of the successful or unsuccessful performance of appropriate, gender-specific displays concerns confidence and self-esteem. Cognizance of progress toward achieving, or ultimately of achieving, societally prescribed display skills may be expected to manifest itself in increased self-esteem.

Proposition 6. Successful performances of appropriate emotional displays in the face of terror on the screen heighten self-esteem. Performance failures lower it. These reactions are enhanced by the presence of witnesses, especially peer witnesses.

Further implications concern social perception, disposition formation, and interaction. Specifically, those who are able to exhibit great skill in displaying appropriate emotions should impress others, their peers in particular, in specific ways. Obviously, a boy who is unperturbed in the face of terror projects traits that are markedly different from those of a boy who cannot (or will not) cover up his distress. Likewise, a girl who is or pretends to be disturbed by such terror projects traits that are different from those of a girl who is unperturbed (or pretends to be so). It also seems to matter greatly whether traits are judged by members of the same or the opposite gender. Finally, one should expect that the perception of traits influences a person's appeal and, along with it, dispositions for forthcoming interactions with that person.

Proposition 7. Boys and male adolescents who are witnessed displaying fearlessness and protective competence in the face of terror on the screen are more favorably evaluated by male and female peers and nonpeers than their counterparts who are witnessed displaying distress.

Proposition 8. Girls and female adolescents who are witnessed displaying fearfulness and protective need in the face of terror on the screen are more favorably evaluated by male and female peers and nonpeers than their counterparts who are witnessed displaying no distress.

Proposition 9. Boys and male adolescents who show fearfulness in the face of horror, and girls and female adolescents who show fearlessness, are perceived as rule violators and accordingly condemned as being effeminate or uppity, respectively.

Proposition 10. The intergender appeal of boys and male adolescents is greater for those able to express fearlessness and protective competence than for those less able or unable to manage such expression. Analogously, the intergender appeal of girls and female adolescents is greater for those able to express fearfulness and protective need than for those less able or unable to manage such expression.

Proposition 11. Boys and male adolescents who have been witnessed exhibiting fearlessness in the face of cinematic horror are more intimidating and hence achieve more compliance with behavioral expectations than their squeamish counterparts. Girls and female adolescents who have been witnessed exhibiting fearfulness are less intimidating and hence achieve less compliance than their fearless counterparts.

Because the heterosexual adolescent couple defines a typical consumer unit for cinematic horror, it would seem justified to posit consequences of consumption for romantic attraction specifically.

Proposition 12. Male adolescents are most attracted to females who express fearfulness and protective need in the confrontation with horror. Other things equal, they are least attracted to females who express fearlessness. In contrast, female adolescents are most attracted to males who express fearlessness and protective competence in the confrontation with horror. Other things equal, they are least attracted to males who express fearfulness.

APPARENT REASONS FOR HORROR'S APPEAL

Those who pondered the appeal of horror tales and cinematic horror have often resorted to global, untestable explanations that, on closer inspection, actually restate the phenomenon to be explained. Clarens (1967), for instance, sought to explain the fascination with horror as "a constant, everpresent yearning for the fantastic, for the darkly mysterious, for the choked terror of the dark" (p. xi). There are allusions to archetypal images of fright (Conrad, 1974) deep in human subconsciousness (Clarens, 1967), and there is the presumed hereditary fear of the dark (Douglas, 1966), the unknown (Brosnan, 1976), and the future (Douglas, 1966). Brosnan (1976) simply asserted a uniquely human capacity for converting fear to pleasure: "The ability to *enjoy* being frightened is surely one of the things, along with a sense of humor, that makes man a race apart" (p. 253; see also Ratzke, 1984, on the concept of Angstlust). Alewyn's explanatory attempt projects a depth of thought that is not atypical in this realm: The appeal of horror is said to be a "neurosis of abstinence of an aging enlightenment" (cited in Conrad, 1974, p. 49). Most writers, however, resort to the catharsis doctrine for explanation (Brosnan, 1976; Clarens, 1967; Douglas, 1966; Farber, 1979; Greenberg, 1975, 1983). This doctrine has failed to attract empirical support of any kind (Geen & Quanty, 1977), but is used nonetheless to suggest that the consumption of horror is beneficial by relieving deep-rooted anxieties, and that the experience of relief makes for the genre's attractiveness.

Compared to such uncurtailed speculations, the empirical exploration of why children, adolescents, and other people watch horror films and videos is rather mundane. An obvious approach is, of course, to bypass the hermeneutical analyses and solicit explanations directly from those who should know best: consumers of horror, especially avid consumers (see Lawrence & Palmgreen, chap. 10, this volume, for the systematic assessment of consumer interpretations).

Regarding reasons given for the consumption of horror, the most detailed, seemingly exhaustive analysis of viewer interpretations was conducted by Brosius and Hartmann (1988) and Brosius and Schmitt (1990). These investigators worked with male and female adolescents aged 11 to 17, more than 90% of whom were 15 years of age. They solicited these students' reactions to a long list of potential motives for watching horror films and videos. Among them were plain curiosity, that such films are spine tingling, that one can talk about them with peers, suspense, that one can impress friends, because other films are not stimulating, to learn about one's own reactions, to show others that one is not a coward, because friends go see such movies, because the forbidden is tempting, to experience the limits of one's own reactivity, and because they are funny. The predictive value of all these possible motives was determined by regression analysis. Specifically, it was determined to what extent the consumption of cinematic horror can be projected on the basis of the students' implication of particular motives. Only three motives emerged as reliably associated with horror consumption: suspense, superior stimulation, and proof of courage (or noncowardness).

Both males and females thought the suspense in horror to contribute significantly to their attraction to this genre (β = 0.29 and β = 0.22, respectively). Surely, there is much suspense in horror movies, and it stands to reason that empathic distress is extremely high and often enough converts to great euphoria when protagonists escape impending disaster, if only temporarily (Sparks, 1991; Zillmann, 1991). That suspense contributes to the enjoyment of horror thus is to be expected. It should be recognized, however, that suspense does not sufficiently define horror. It is not specific to horror, and the revelation that suspense may critically contribute to horror's appeal can be construed as complicating the issue. This revelation places even greater demands on explaining why, specifically, the portrayal of postsuspense activities in which dreaded things are actually happening—blood is squirting, limbs are flying, and the bodies of perfectly nice people are dropping—are not deterring youngsters from returning to similar mayhem—in fact, why they come back time and time again.

Females, but not males, thought horror appealing because it is more stimulating than "normal" movies (β = 0.21). This finding is puzzling in that female children and adolescents are known to react more negatively to fear-inducing media fare than their male counterparts. For instance, second-grade girls were found to express more fear in response to frightening programming than their male peers (Palmer, Hockett, & Dean, 1983; see also Cantor, 1991). Weiss (1990), working with 14- and 15-year-olds, reported gender differences that leave no doubt that females respond unfavorably to horror. Specifically, Weiss reported that, concerning positive reactions to horror, males consistently outdo females. Concerning negative reactions, however, the reverse applies. Girls, compared to boys, were found to feel markedly less well, more afraid, more disgusted, and they eventually had more nightmares. Thus, if female adolescents deem horror appealing because of its stimulating quality, it seems unlikely that they had blood and gore as such in mind, and it remains to be found out exactly what it was that may have favorably colored the concept of stimulation.

The finding that females grant positive stimulus quality to horror also clashes with reports that girls are mostly drag-alongs of boys eager to be accompanied to horror movies (Brosius & Schmitt, 1990; Luca-Krueger, 1988; Weiss, 1990), an observation, it should be noted, that is most consistent with our gender-socialization proposal.

The third motive implicated by the students was the proof of courage. This motive emerged for males only, and it proved to project appeal negatively (β = -0.22). Proof of courage thus appears to be thought a motive for beginners only (i.e., boys without much horror experience). The negative relationship between test-of-courage interpretations and horror consumption is possibly explained by beginners' admissions and veterans' indifference or denial. After all, denial is self-serving in that, should horror function as a test of courage and bravery under emotionally taxing conditions, it prevents recognition of the shallowness of the proof.

This latter point is of considerable interest. If boys do use cinematic horror as a test of courage, as has been suggested on occasion (Armbruster & Kuebler, 1984; Orwaldi, 1984), those who mastered the challenge should indeed show little interest in retrospectively belittling their "bravery" by associating it with enduring a horror movie. If queried about horror as test of courage, the proven courageous thus should deny the test function. This does not mean, however, that horror failed them, or that it failed others, in this capacity. In fact, numerous behavioral observations show that horror veterans place themselves above squeamish and cowardly novices, thereby indicating that they think of themselves as members of a fearless elite that have successfully passed the initiation rite. Brosius and Schmitt (1990), for instance, reported that interviewed students were eager to volunteer stories of classmates who were grossed out and acutely distressed by particularly vivid horror scenes—clearly implying their own superior maturity. Boys, as a rule, do not relate difficulties that they themselves may have experienced. Such admissions are for girls and women, and they are often enough exploited by boys to build up their masculine image. The aforementioned 18-year-old founder of a horror video club, for example, enlisted female help in determining the quality of his rental holdings. The more a female screamed in utter dismay, the more certain he was to have a hit on his hands ("Alle haben gekotzt," 1984).

In contrast to abundant anecdotal evidence of male denial and female articulation of distress from horror, little has been said or written about men's signaling of protective competence and women's signaling of protective dependence. A rare exception is a report by Lavery (1982), who observed that theater attendants, in reacting to a particularly frightening scene of *Don't Look Now*, sought reassurance and comfort from companions, even from strangers: "Perfect strangers were reaching out to each other in the packed theatre for comfort, actually grabbing onto the nearest possible person in the hope that their terror might be so relieved" (p. 54). Unfortunately, this observation of a mass reaction is not specific about the gender of the comfort seekers. It can only be speculated that female attendants were in greater need, and less reluctant to express it, than their male counterparts; furthermore, that they turned to friends and companions before seeking comfort from strangers.

Nonetheless, the observation points to the significance of companionship in the confrontation with cinematic horror. This companionship seems exploitable, giving the advantage to those who can signal fearlessness and protective competence. Among male cohorts, for instance, the squeamish might find comfort in the presence of unperturbed peers and come to admire their maturity. More likely, however, the accomplished, callous youths will display their superior handling of terror and let the others feel the intimidating sting of immaturity. Such bragging displays by callous male youths are also to be expected in mixed-gender groups. Emerging heroes (and leaders) are likely to be those who manage to laugh about terror on the screen, not those who display empathic sensitivity or deem horror in poor taste and disgusting. In this connection it should be pointed out that the exhibition of amusement over utter mayhem is a most compelling and also a convenient demonstration of accomplished callousness. It should not be surprising, therefore, to find that amusement and laughter are popular male reactions to the grossest of cinematic horror. In fact, horror aficionados often explain their devotion to the genre by claiming horror to be extremely amusing. Notwithstanding such interpretations, laughter in response to terror is an obtrusive, effective display of fearlessness and thus a signal of protective competence.

Viewers' assumptions about their motives may often obscure actual motives for the consumption and enjoyment of particular genres of entertainment (Zillmann, 1985). Claiming that horror is grand comedy or insisting that its appeal is mostly or totally due to "special effects," which is a typical male contention (Farber, 1987), may miss the mark. On occasion, however, adolescent horror buffs seem to be on target. In interviews with youngsters waiting to see *A Nightmare on Elm Street 3: Dream Warriors*, conducted by Maryanne Russell, 14-year-old Nicole Memoli explained her attraction to the genre as follows: "They're fun to watch. You go with your friends and try to get scared and everything. And you can just be rowdy. You can get all rowdy with boys and jump into their lap, and they can comfort you. They say, 'Don't worry, I can protect you'" (Farber, 1987, p. 109). Such analysis leaves no doubt that she understood the expressive and behavioral roles that boys and girls are supposed to play in horror movies. Moreover, 18-year-old Rosemarie Ferranto showed tacit knowledge of our Proposition 12. She explained her love for watching horror with a companion in these terms: "I like everyone yelling and screaming. I like going with my boyfriend and pulling him close in the scary parts" (p. 109). Male interviewees were surprisingly uninsightful, hiding behind special effects and the like. However, the boys must also have some understanding of a scared girl's inclination to snuggle up on a fearless guy. Why else would they be so eager to drag girls to horror movies?

RESEARCH DEMONSTRATIONS

Many of the propositions of the outlined gender-socialization model of horror have not as yet been subjected to rigorous empirical examination. Although consistent with much anecdotal observation, their predictive value remains to be determined. However, the propositions concerning intergender effects, Propositions 7 through 12 and Proposition 5 in part, have been put to the test in an elaborate experiment conducted by Zillmann, Weaver, Mundorf, and Aust (1986). These investigators had male and female adolescents watch a horror movie with an opposite-gender peer, ostensibly another research participant but actually an experimental confederate, who either displayed gender-appropriate, gender-inappropriate, or no emotions, and they then ascertained enjoyment of the movie, liking of the cohort, romantic attraction to that cohort, and being intimidated by the cohort.

The horror movie was *Friday the 13th, Part III*. The movie features Jason, a raging killer whose face is always covered by an ice-hockey goalie mask, in pursuit of victims—adolescent couples in a vacation cottage in this case. The segment of interest shows a young woman searching for her companion in the midst of night. She is startled by the body of one of her friends dropping from a tree. The woman, in terror, runs into a farm house where she witnesses the body of her boyfriend flying through a window and slumping onto the floor. Attempting to flee the house, the young woman is attacked by Jason, the masked killer. Cornered in a closet, she pulls a bloody knife from the body of yet another dead friend, charges at the killer, and wounds him in the hand and knee. Despite this, the killer continues to pursue her through the house and its vicinity. Eventually, the young woman hides in the loft of a barn, but the killer quickly locates and attacks her. In the ensuing struggle, she is able to render the killer unconscious by hitting him on the head with a shovel. She then ties a rope around his neck and pushes him out of the barn loft, apparently killing him by hanging. But the killer survives, frees himself, picks up a machete, and continues his attack on the young woman. After bludgeoning to death a man who comes to help the woman, he continues his assault on her. She finds an ax and plants it into the killer's skull. The segment ends showing the killer lying on the barn floor, covered with blood, with the ax protruding from his head. He is apparently dead, and the young woman is apparently out of danger.

The experiment created three display conditions: fearlessness or *mastery of fear*, deemed appropriate for males but inappropriate for females; fearfulness or *distress*, deemed appropriate for females but inappropriate for males; and *indifference* (i.e., no particular affect was displayed). The mastery and distress conditions entailed the display of both verbal and nonverbal reactions to the experimental stimulus on the part of the confederate. Mastery or distress reactions were placed after critical scenes, their distribution being parallel (i.e., associated with the same scenes) in both conditions. In the condition of *indifference*, these reactions were simply omitted, and the confederate gave no indication of responding emotionally. More specifically, the confederate remained silent throughout the presentation. He or she assumed an erect but relaxed posture, exhibiting neither boredom nor excitement. Arm and leg movements were limited to those naturally occurring during an extended period of sitting.

In contrast, in the *distress* condition the confederate verbally indicated dismay during six specific scenes. For example, when the main protagonist removed the bloody knife from her dead friend's body, the confederate, in a shocked and disbelieving manner, exclaimed: "Oh my God!" During another gory scene, the exclamation was: "Yech . . . Oh, how gross!" Nonverbal expressions of distress underscored the verbal ones. With sudden displays of mayhem, such as a bloody corpse crashing through a window, the confederate jerked back in the chair. He or she was sitting in a rigid, erect posture most of the time and showed much restlessness (e.g., fidgeting with the hands, moving hands through face and hair).

In the *mastery* condition, the confederate's verbal and nonverbal responses were designed to show, first of all, that the stimulus failed to induce distress of any kind. Moreover, they were to exhibit true mastery of anxieties, such as those experienced by the endangered parties in the film, by suggestion of preparedness for effective coping with the threats at hand. For example, when the main protagonist removed the knife from her dead friend's body and attacked the masked killer, the confederate encouragingly uttered: "That's the idea . . . use the knife!" Similarly, when the young woman apparently succeeded in incapacitating the killer by striking him in the head with an ax, the confederate, in a congratulating manner, exclaimed: "Alright . . . you got him good this time!" The associated nonverbal expressions of mastery included the adoption of a casual posture (i.e., sitting reclined in the chair with legs extended forward) and occasional slow, methodical movements of arms and legs throughout exposure to the segment.

Enjoyment of the horror film proved to be greatly affected by the emotional displays of an opposite-gender companion. Male respondents enjoyed the same horror virtually twice as much in the presence of an acutely distressed female peer than in the presence of a fearless female peer who, in fact, signaled protective competence. This finding, shown in Fig. 6.1, supports Proposition 5. Also evident from Fig. 6.1 is that female respondents enjoyed horror the least in the presence of a fearful, distressed male. In this condition, it dropped to one third of that observed in the presence of a male companion who showed the societally expected male mastery of fear. This finding also supports Proposition 5. For both male and female respondents, then, enjoyment was the strongest when, as predicted, the companion's emotional display conformed with prevail-

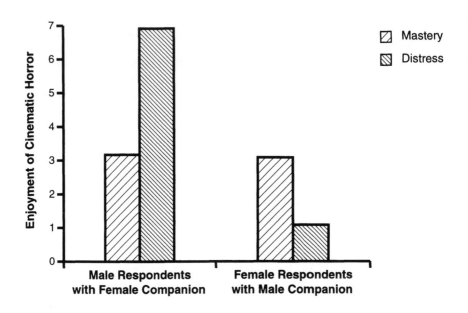

FIG. 6.1. Enjoyment of cinematic horror by male and female respondents as a function of emotional displays to the horror by an opposite-gender companion (data are from Zillmann, Weaver, Mundorf, & Aust, 1986).

ing gender-specific display rules. Watching horror in the company of a terrified woman apparently confirms men's protector role, and any positive affect from recognition of the implicit granting of superior status seems to be misattributed to the film. For women, in contrast, watching horror in the company of a distressed man can only add to their distress from horror. Their enjoyment seems to benefit from the security provided by the presence of an unperturbed guy who must know what to do in situations of danger. Such fear- and disgust-curtailing comfort is apparently appreciated, and this appreciation is misconstrued as enjoyment of the film.

It should be pointed out that enjoyment in the condition without particular emotional displays was very similar to that in the condition of fear mastery. This finding is not surprising. After all, being calm and unemotional in the face of terror is one way of signaling fearlessness and protective competence.

In assessing the appeal of fearless versus fearful cohorts, a peculiar observation was recorded: The appeal of particularly handsome young men and exceptionally cute young ladies seemed unaffected by their emotional displays. Gorgeous men were judged to be gorgeous, even when they were distressed by horror. Similarly, gorgeous women were gorgeous women, even when being uppity by showing mastery of fear. Beautiful people, it seems, can do no wrong!

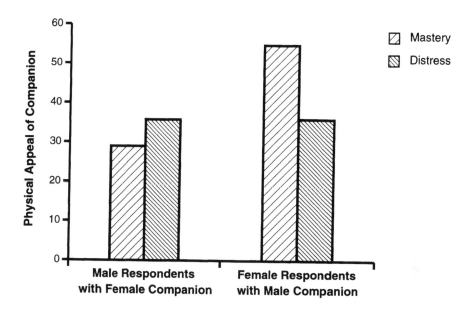

FIG. 6.2. Physical appeal of an opposite-gender companion as a function of the companion's emotional displays to cinematic horror (data are from Zillmann, Weaver, Mundorf, & Aust, 1986).

In contrast, the appeal of persons less blessed with great physique was greatly affected by their show of emotion to horror. As Fig. 6.2 shows, the female respondents were markedly more attracted to a male companion when he exhibited mastery of fear than to the same companion when expressing distress. This finding lends strong support to Proposition 7 and also supports Propositions 9, 10, and 12. Male respondents, in contrast, tended to be more attracted to a female companion when she showed acute distress than to the same companion when unperturbed by terror on the screen. This finding accords with predictions from Propositions 8 through 10 and 12. Gender-specific emotional displays to horror are indeed most conducive to favorable evaluations of physical appeal.

The experiment also assessed the perception of positive behavioral traits. Effects on the appraisal of such traits followed the same pattern as those on physical appeal, further supporting the indicated propositions.

The companion's appeal and traits were ascertained under the guise of a forthcoming cooperation task. Respondents had been told that, because others' appeal might influence performance on such tasks, appeal and perceived traits needed to be measured. Respondents also performed the announced task.

Prior to performing it, the respondents rated the desirability of having the companion for a partner in this task. Effects of emotional displays during the horror movie were still evident. However, the effects no longer followed the appeal and trait pattern. For solving problems together, gender considerations became secondary, and the ability to cope with horror became the primary choice criterion. The capacity to cope with terror on the screen is apparently generalized to problem-solving competence. Distress responses to horror are analogously generalized to overall ineptness. As a result, both fearless men and fearless women were deemed more desirable collaborators than either squeamish men or squeamish women.

If, then, fearless means able and tough and squeamish means inept and weak regardless of gender, one should expect those who were unperturbed by horror to intimidate others more than those who were distressed—regardless of gender. This, however, was not at all the case.

The experimental procedure stipulated that respondent and confederate take turns in estimating the age of persons shown on slides. An estimate was to be suggested by one party; if necessary, it was then to be corrected and given greater accuracy by the other. The procedure was rigged, such that the confederate was to make the first estimates. The estimates were quite obviously grossly in error. The respondents' failure to correct them defined the measures of intimidation and acquiescence with unreasonable requests (i.e., with requests to accept glaringly erroneous assertions as correct).

The findings, shown in Fig. 6.3, leave no doubt about the fact that female respondents were more intimidated by fearless men than by fearful ones. This strongly supports Proposition 11. On the other hand, male respondents tended to be least intimidated by fearless women. They felt compelled, apparently, to resist yielding to a defiant, uppity woman who showed poor judgment. This finding is inconsistent with and challenges the second part of Proposition 11.

The latter finding points to men's difficulty with women in superior roles. Women, whose only fault it was to behave malelike in their confrontation with horror, were treated as if they had violated sacred ground. From such women, men can take no orders!

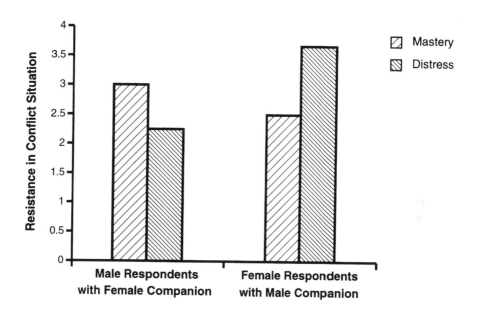

FIG. 6.3. Resistance to acquiescing to suggestions by an opposite-gender collaborator as a function of this collaborator's emotional displays to cinematic horror. Note that intimidation is suggested inversely—that is, the more resistance, the less intimidation (data are from Zillmann, Weaver, Mundorf, & Aust, 1986).

The finding may well require an amendment to Proposition 11. This proposition makes predictions that are indifferent to the gender of intimidated parties. For female respondents it should be the case, as stated, that fearless women are more intimidating than fearful ones, but this prediction should be reversed for male respondents with strong male-dominance acculturation.

Notwithstanding the need for such minor adjustments, the experimental demonstration of the consequences of watching horror with a companion shows that, depending on the companion's emotional reactions, this experience is capable of influencing the enjoyment of horror, the physical appeal of the companion, the perception of the companion's personality traits, and the accommodation of requests, unreasonable ones included, by that companion. Emotional displays to horror thus have social consequences for the displayer, consequences that extend far beyond reactions to events on the screen as such. Most importantly, these consequences are predictable. As the discussed experimental evidence is supportive of the gender-socialization model of horror, this model may be considered to predict many of these consequences accurately.

ADDITIONAL CONSIDERATIONS

This chapter has addressed social motives for the consumption of cinematic horror along with social consequences of such consumption. A theoretical model was presented that is based on a joint dichotomization of gender and display rules pertaining to fear. More specifically, it has been proposed that essentially *all* boys and male adolescents strive to perfect displays of fearlessness and protective competence, whereas essentially *all* girls and female adolescents strive to perfect displays of fearfulness and protective need.

The all-inclusiveness of this proposal is certainly open to challenge. There are, after all, meek and mild-mannered boys and tough tomboys who might never have deemed it desirable to acquire gender-appropriate emotional displays. Exceptions to the gender scheme must be recognized. However, as long as these exceptions constitute only small minorities, and they apparently do, the gender-display dichotomization can be considered statistically justified.

Efforts have been made to identify the *psychological gender* (Bem, 1976, 1985) of persons responding to horror and to determine the implications of discrepancies between psychological and biological gender (Mundorf, Weaver, & Zillmann, 1989). Such assessments invariably show some lack of correspondence between psychological and biological gender, and at times they suggest that psychological gender can exert a stronger influence on gender-typed behavior than biological gender does. To the extent that these suggestions have merit, it could be argued that our proposals should be applied to psychological rather than biological gender. Indeed, if the behavioral implications of biological gender differentiation should ever erode and become irrelevant, and if precepts for affect expression and related behaviors should be determined by whatever determines psychological gender, a substitution of psychological for biological gender would be in order. It should be noted that our model can easily accommodate such substitution. However, as long as the mismatch between psychological and biological gender is limited to comparatively small minorities, and more importantly, as long as prevailing contingencies of reinforcement encourage or dictate adherence to behavioral expectations that are specified for biologically defined groupings, the focus on biological gender is warranted.

Nonetheless, it is worthy to note that our socialization model could be applied to any two groupings, say Group A and Group B, whose precepts regarding the public expression of fear and behaviors in the protector-protectee dichotomy differ sharply. If, for instance, Group A embraces bravery and dominance and Group B sensitivity and tolerance, if not submission, all this regardless of gender considerations, the socialization model would reasonably well predict these groups' behavior in response to horror—if A and B were substituted for boys and girls or men and women.

Returning to gender socialization, it also should be clear that personality assessments other than psychological gender are potentially useful in refining the model. Traits of interest (e.g., extroversion-introversion, psychoticism, neuroticism, empathy, sensation-seeking) vary greatly within gender and have been shown to mediate emotional reactions to cinematic horror (Edwards, 1991; Tamborini, 1991; Weaver, 1991; Zuckerman & Litle, 1986). Variance in pertinent traits presumably does not only influence interest in, and enjoyment of, cinematic horror, but probably modifies social effects as well.

Finally, it must be reiterated that the analysis of the contribution of social factors to the enjoyment of cinematic horror does not lay claim to offering a complete account of the enjoyment of horror. Numerous alternative factors are likely to contribute their part. A prime candidate is the distress-delight conversion predicted by suspense theory (Zillmann, 1980, 1991). The more distress is experienced, the greater the euphoric reaction on its resolution (Sparks, 1991). Cinematic horror offers the needed conditions for such transformation with considerable frequency, but numerous other contributing factors may exist, awaiting discovery.

REFERENCES

Abrams, D., & Hogg, M. A. (Eds.). (1990). *Social identity theory: Constructive and critical advances.* New York: Springer-Verlag.

Alle haben gekotzt, nur ich nicht [All threw up, but not me]. (1984, March 12). *Der Spiegel,* p. 42.

Armbruster, B., & Kuebler, H.-D. (1984). Die Klasse von 1984: Videobewaeltigung in der Schule?—Eine Tagung mit Lehrern. *Medien Praktisch, 2,* 4-9.

Averill, J. R. (1982). *Anger and aggression: An essay on emotion.* New York: Springer-Verlag.

Bandura, A. (1969). *Principles of behavior modification.* New York: Holt, Rinehart & Winston.

Bandura, A. (1971). Analysis of modeling. In A. Bandura (Ed.), *Psychological modeling: Conflicting theories* (pp. 1-62). Chicago: Aldine-Atherton.

Barry, H., Bacon, M. K., & Child, I. L. (1957). A cross-cultural survey of some sex differences in socialization. *Journal of Abnormal and Social Psychology, 55,* 327-332.

Bem, S. L. (1976). Probing the promise of androgyny. In A. G. Kaplan & J. P. Bean (Eds.), *Beyond sex-role stereotypes: Readings toward a psychology of androgyny* (pp. 48-62). Boston: Little, Brown.

Bem, S. L. (1985). Androgyny and gender schema theory: A conceptual and empirical investigation. In T. B. Sonderegger (Ed.), *Nebraska Symposium on Motivation: Psychology and gender* (pp. 176-226). Lincoln: University of Nebraska Press.

Blier, M. J., & Blier-Wilson, L. A. (1989). Gender differences in self-rated emotional expressiveness. *Sex Roles, 21*(3-4), 287-295.

Brody, L. R. (1985). Gender differences in emotional development: A review of theories and research. *Journal of Personality, 53*(2), 102-149.

Brosius, H.-B., & Hartmann, T. (1988). Erfahrungen mit Horror-Videos bei Schülern unterschiedlicher Schultypen. Eine Umfrage unter 12 bis 15jährigen Schülern [Experience with horror videos of students from different types of schools: A survey of students aged 12-15]. *Communications, 14*(3),

91-112.

Brosius, H.-B., & Schmitt, I. (1990). Nervenkitzel oder Gruppendruck?: Determinanten für die Beliebtheit von Horrorvideos bei Jugendlichen [Nerve titillation or social pressure?: Determinants of the appeal of horror videos among adolescents]. In H. Lukesch (Ed.), *Wenn Gewalt zur Unterhaltung wird . . . : Beiträge zur Nutzung und Wirkung von Gewaltdarstellungen in audiovisuellen Medien* (pp. 9-46). Regensburg, Germany: S. Roderer.

Brosnan, J. (1976). *The horror people.* New York: New American Library.

Cantor, J. (1991). Fright responses to mass media productions. In J. Bryant & D. Zillmann (Eds.), *Responding to the screen: Reception and reaction processes* (pp. 169-197). Hillsdale, NJ: Lawrence Erlbaum Associates.

Clarens, C. (1967). *An illustrated history of the horror film.* New York: Putnam.

Conrad, H. (1974). *Die literarische Angst* [Literary anxiety]. Düsseldorf, Germany: Bertelsmann.

Douglas, D. (1966). *Horror!* New York: Macmillan.

Edwards, E. D. (1991). The ecstasy of horrible expectations: Morbid curiosity, sensation seeking, and interest in horror movies. In B. A. Austin (Ed.), *Current research in film: Audiences, economics, and the law* (Vol. 5, pp. 19-38). Norwood, NJ: Ablex.

Farber, J. (1987, July). Blood, sweat, & fears: Why are horror movies such a slashing success? *Seventeen,* pp. 108-109, 140-141, 149.

Farber, S. (1979). The bloody movies: Why violence sells. In A. Wells (Ed.), *Mass media & society* (pp. 332-340). Palo Alto, CA: Mayfield.

Geen, R. G., & Quanty, M. B. (1977). The catharsis of aggression: An evaluation of a hypothesis. In L. Berkowitz (Ed.), *Advances in experimental social psychology* (Vol. 10, pp. 1-37). New York: Academic Press.

Greenberg, H. (1975). *The movies on your mind.* New York: Saturday Review Press/E. P. Dutton.

Greenberg, H. (1983). The fractures of desire: Psychoanalytic notes on *Alien* and the contemporary "cruel" horror film. *The Psychoanalytic Review, 70,* 241-267.

Grings, W. W., & Dawson, M. E. (1978). *Emotions and bodily responses: A psychophysiological approach.* New York: Academic Press.

Harris, P. L. (1989). *Children and emotion: The development of psychological understanding.* Oxford: Basil Blackwell.

Izard, C. E. (1991). *The psychology of emotions.* New York: Plenum.

Lavery, D. (1982). The horror film and the horror of film. *Film Criticism, 7*(1), 47-55.

Luca-Krueger, R. (1988). "Das Gute soll gewinnen". Gewaltvideos im Erleben weiblicher und männlicher Jugendlicher ["The good should win:" Responses of female and male adolescents to violent videos]. *Publizistik, 33,* 481-492.

Maccoby, E. E., & Jacklin, C. N. (1974). *The psychology of sex differences.* Stanford, CA: Stanford University Press.

Morawski, J. G. (1987). The troubled quest for masculinity, femininity, and androgyny. In P. Shaver & C. Hendrick (Eds.), *Sex and gender* (pp. 44-69). Newbury Park, CA: Sage.

Mundorf, N., Weaver, J., & Zillmann, D. (1989). Effects of gender roles and self perceptions on affective reactions to horror films. *Sex Roles, 20,* 655-673.

Nevin, J. A. (1973). Conditioned reinforcement. In J. A. Nevin (Ed.), *The study of behavior: Learning, motivation, emotion, and instinct* (pp. 155-198). Glenview, IL: Scott, Foresman.

Orwaldi, D. (1984). "Ich sehe sie mir gern an, obwohl mir dabei schlecht wird". Zum Gebrauch von Videofilmen durch Kinder und Jugendliche ["I like to see them, although they make me nauseous:" On the consumption of videos by children and adolescents]. *Medium: Zeitschrift für Hörfunk, Fernsehen, Film und Presse, 14,* 31-34.

Palmer, E., Hockett, A. B., & Dean, W. W. (1983). The television family and children's fright reactions. *Journal of Family Issues, 4,* 279-292.

Ratzke, B. (1984). Bedürfnis nach Gewalt. Psychologische Erklärungsversuche zum Konsum von Horrorfilmen [Need for violence. Psychological attempts at explaining the consumption of horror movies]. *Medien Praktisch, 2,* 14-18.

Saarni, C. (1979). Children's understanding of display rules for expressive behavior. *Developmental Psychology, 15,* 424-429.

Saarni, C. (1988). Children's understanding of the interpersonal consequences of dissemblance of nonverbal emotional-expressive behavior. *Journal of Nonverbal Behavior, 12,* 275-294.

Saarni, C. (1989). Children's understanding of strategic control of emotional expression in social transactions. In C. Saarni & P. L. Harris (Eds.), *Children's understanding of emotion* (pp. 181-208). New York: Cambridge University Press.

Shennum, W. A., & Bugental, D. B. (1982). The development of control over affective expression in nonverbal behavior. In R. Feldman (Ed.), *Development of nonverbal behavior in children* (pp. 101-121). New York: Springer-Verlag.

Sparks, G. G. (1991). The relationship between distress and delight in males' and females' reactions to frightening films. *Human Communication Research, 17,* 625-637.

Tamborini, R. (1991). Responding to horror: Determinants of exposure and appeal. In J. Bryant & D. Zillmann (Eds.), *Responding to the screen: Reception and reaction processes* (pp. 305-328). Hillsdale, NJ: Lawrence Erlbaum Associates.

Turner, J. C. (1985). Social categorization and the self-concept: A social-cognitive theory of group behavior. In E. J. Lawler (Ed.), *Advances in group processes: A research annual* (Vol. 2, pp. 77-121). Greenwich, CT: JAI.

van Alphen, I. C. (1988). Wie die Jungen das Lachen lernten—und wie es den Mädchen verging . . . [How the boys learned to laugh—and the girls learned not to . . .]. In H. Kotthoff (Ed.), *Das Gelächter der Geschlechter: Humor und Macht in Gesprächen von Frauen und Männern* (pp. 197-209). Frankfurt: Fischer Taschenbuch.

Weaver, J. B. (1991). Exploring the links between personality and media preferences. *Personality and Individual Differences, 12,* 1293-1299.

Weiss, R. H. (1990). Horror-Gewalt-Video-Konsum bei Jugendlichen: Gefühlsreaktionen-Persönlichkeit-Identifikation Täter/Opfer [Adolescents' horror-violence-consumption: Emotion-personality-identification relations to perpetrator and victim]. In H. Lukesch (Ed.), *Wenn Gewalt zur Unterhaltung wird . . . : Beiträge zur Nutzung und Wirkung von Gewaltdarstellungen in audiovisuellen Medien* (pp. 47-91). Regensburg, Germany: S. Roderer.

Zammuner, V. L. (1987). Children's sex-role stereotypes: A cross-cultural analysis. In P. Shaver & C. Hendrick (Eds.), *Sex and gender* (pp. 272-293). Newbury Park, CA: Sage.

Zillmann, D. (1979). *Hostility and aggression.* Hillsdale, NJ: Lawrence Erlbaum Associates.

Zillmann, D. (1980). Anatomy of suspense. In P. H. Tannenbaum (Ed.), *The entertainment functions of television* (pp. 133-163). Hillsdale, NJ: Lawrence Erlbaum Associates.

Zillmann, D. (1985). The experimental exploration of gratifications from media entertainment. In K. E. Rosengren, L. A. Wenner, & P. Palmgreen (Eds.), *Media gratifications research: Current perspectives* (pp. 225-239). Beverly Hills, CA: Sage.

Zillmann, D. (1988). Mood management: Using entertainment to full advantage. In L. Donohew, H. E. Sypher, & E. T. Higgins (Eds.), *Communication, social cognition, and affect* (pp. 147-171). Hillsdale, NJ: Lawrence Erlbaum Associates.

Zillmann, D. (1991). The logic of suspense and mystery. In J. Bryant & D. Zillmann (Eds.), *Responding to the screen: Reception and reaction processes* (pp. 281-303). Hillsdale, NJ: Lawrence Erlbaum Associates.

Zillmann, D., Weaver, J. B., Mundorf, N., & Aust, C. F. (1986). Effects of an opposite-gender companion's affect to horror on distress, delight, and attraction. *Journal of Personality and Social Psychology, 51,* 586-594.

Zuckerman, M., & Litle, P. (1986). Personality and curiosity about morbid and sexual events. *Personality and Individual Differences, 7,* 49-56.

Chapter 7

A Model of Empathy and Emotional Reactions to Horror

Ron Tamborini
Michigan State Univeristy

The capacity of film to generate strong reactions in audience members has been a mystery to philosophers and psychologists engaged in the study of emotional behavior (cf. Walters, 1989). The difficulty in explaining emotions evoked by imagined events stems from the fact that viewers react while knowing full well that they are safe from any consequence that might befall the characters on screen. In the absence of any consequence, one wonders not only why viewers should respond with great intensity, but why they should respond at all. Nevertheless, the intense reaction produced by film exposure is of particular interest to those concerned with emotional response. Of particular interest here are the characteristics of a film genre that elicit the greatest emotional response. In this regard, perhaps no other film genre inspires reactions as intense as those produced by graphic horror. This chapter develops a model of empathy and emotional reactions to horror in an attempt to explicate processes by which these aesthetic emotions are elicited by imaginative involvement with environments created by film. The model applies cognitive-motivational-relational theory to the aesthetic emotion phenomenon by employing empathy and situational cues provided by film as the antecedent conditions of personality and environment found in the theory by Lazarus (1991).

AESTHETIC EMOTIONAL EXPERIENCE

The perplexing nature of audience reactions to film and to other forms of media entertainment has led some to claim that aesthetic emotional reactions are not real emotions at all, but simply memories of previous experiences that have been activated by observed events (Binkley, 1977; Gombrich, 1962). Other scholars accept these reactions as real emotions, but claim that they are irrational (Rorty, 1978), incoherent (Radford, 1975), or in some way distinct from emotions elicited by events appraised as real (Bell, 1914; Danto, 1964; 1981; Fry, 1920).

The belief that aesthetic emotions are distinct in their character was presented by Frijda (1989). Frijda claimed that film is perceived by audience members as though actual events were occurring in an imaginary world. When exposed to film or to other aesthetic forms, viewers do not perceive unreality, but discount extant unreality cues and engage in the suspension of disbelief—something made possible by the degree to which the film's substance is convincing or "real" enough so that viewers do not need to think about its fictional nature. In this case, the mystery is not how fantasy evokes true emotions, but rather why it does not do so all of the time. According to Frijda, the answer is that film "does not *elicit* emotions by products known to be imaginary, but allows *inhibition* of emotions because the products are known to be imaginary" (p. 1546).

Frijda (1989) suggested that emotions resulting from imagined reality have a particular structure that is distinct from emotions in response to real events—a structure that is determined by one's observational position. The spectator position one takes when viewing a film creates an awareness that appraised events are not relevant to one's own welfare and that actions to intervene are precluded. What Frijda called *complementing emotions* results from one's ability to identify with others and to sense the character's fate (positive or negative), knowing that there is no real need to be concerned about the consequences to oneself. At the same time, an even deeper *responding emotion* can result from the film's ability to create the realization that some meaningful form, idea, or experience exists in the real world, and knowledge of this actuality creates a powerfully felt emotion—one based simply on the knowledge of the object's existence or of the possible consequences it may hold for the viewer. In either case, the capacity for emotions to be influenced by imaginative involvement with such events has great practical and theoretical significance for understanding human behavior. To this extent, it is surprising that so little attention has been paid to the process through which film can influence these emotional experiences.

Lazarus (1991) claimed that the process governing film's impact on the generation of aesthetic emotions can be explained by the same mechanisms controlling the process through which any specific emotion is generated. In his cognitive-motivational-relational theory, Lazarus suggested that antecedent conditions (environmental and personality factors) impact the manner in which one's evaluation of a situation results in an appraisal outcome. This appraisal outcome is a mediating factor that strongly impacts all that follows—including coping behaviors and the specific emotional state (see Fig. 7.1). In the same manner, an aesthetic emotional response to film exposure can be seen as a process determined by the personality traits associated with viewing and the situational cues contained in film content. Appraisal and coping processes determine the relevance of the event for the individual's well-being. These results regulate both the type and the strength of the specific emotion that is experienced. A more detailed understanding of cognitive-motivational-relational theory will improve our comprehension of the processes that govern aesthetic emotional reactions to film.

COGNITIVE-MOTIVATIONAL-RELATIONAL THEORY

According to Lazarus (1991), emotional reactions are associated with a person's relationship to their environment (the person-environment relationship). People attempt to realize personal goals and to manage environmental demands through episodes called adaptational encounters. Ongoing appraisals during these encounters produce a pattern of outcomes that differentiate the emotion experienced. The appraisals made during this process contain three primary components concerned with adaptation motivation; goal relevance, goal (in)congruency, and type of ego involvement. In addition, there are three secondary components concerned with options for coping and expected results: blame/credit, coping potential, and future expectations. The emotion an individual experiences is distinguished by the specific pattern of components resulting from the appraisal process. For example, anger occurs when appraisal determines that an important goal is at stake, environmental conditions are incongruent with attaining this goal, the incongruity creates a threat to one's ego in terms of self-esteem, and blame for this situation can be attributed to someone. If appraisal of coping potential indicates that the offense can be rectified by attack, anger is intensified. If appraisal of future consequences suggests that the benefits of attack are likely to exceed costs, anger will be further facilitated.

Appraisal and coping processes are stimulated by the combined product of personality and environmental factors. The first task, appraisal, is a process of integrating personality and environmental components into a "relational meaning" based on the relevance of events for a person's well-being. This meaning is expressed in a "core relational theme" for each individual emotion, which summarizes the harms and benefits in the person-environment relationship. Returning to the previous example, the core relational theme for anger is perceiving an episode as a demeaning offense against oneself or some entity that one holds dear. In this way, anger is seen as a response to a threat of harm to self-esteem. For certain personality types sensitive to such threats, a variety of environmental events makes experience of the relational theme for anger more common.

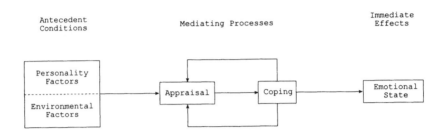

FIG. 7.1. A theoretical schematization of mechanisms involved in the determining of emotional states (*Source*: Adapted from R. S. Lazarus & S. Folkman, *Stress, appraisal, and coping*. New York: Springer, 1984. Used by permission.)

The second task, coping, is a process designed to bring about change that maximizes well-being in response to the appraised relational theme. It essentially enhances beneficial experiences and inhibits harmful ones. Often innate "action tendencies" attached to specific emotions create an immediate action tendency impulse to facilitate this process. In the anger example, if an event is perceived as a demeaning offense, the immediate action tendency is to halt the offense by attacking the blameworthy offender. However, the action will depend on secondary appraisal of the attack's potential utility. If success is appraised as unlikely, the attack will not unfold. In this example, concern for the social and personal reprisal could serve to delay an immediate, direct attack or to prevent it altogether. Under such conditions more deliberate coping takes place that involves a strategic activity to maximize long-term benefits. If cognitive coping strategies in our anger example can either prevent thinking about the offense or change its appraised meaning, they can benefit well-being by inhibiting the experience of anger completely or by limiting it from elevating to dangerous levels of rage.

Coping's impact on the person-environment relationship has an impact on subsequent emotional state. The changed meanings resulting from the employment of coping strategies designed to benefit a person's well-being will modify the outcome of future appraisals resulting from the interaction of personality and environment. The key is the change in relational meaning and the relevance of events for well-being. This influence plays an important part in the experience of core relational themes.

RELATIONAL THEMES IN GRAPHIC HORROR

The experience of specific core relational themes can be expected from exposure to horror. Although appraisal outcomes should vary due to differences in personality and learned associations with environmental cues, generalizable responses might be anticipated to the extent that certain traits and common experiences are shared among individuals. The particular themes expected from horror might include the experience of anxiety and fright. Whereas horror in real life might combine fright and loathing or disgust, horror in film is more likely to be associated with certain aspects of anxiety. Because there are important differences between fright and anxiety, it may be useful to identify them separately and to explain why we might expect these different relations to occur for real life and for film horror.

According to Lazarus (1991), "uncertainty or ambiguity is always a feature of fright because the harm is always in the future. However, since the danger is concrete and sudden and there is little time to reflect, uncertainty is not as prominent in fright as it is in anxiety, where the threat is symbolic, existential, and ephemeral" (p. 235). Thus, both fright and anxiety are concerned with future harm. However, the core theme of fright is threat of imminent physical harm, whereas the theme of anxiety is uncertain, existential threat. In fright we are scared about the immediate prospect of death or injury, whereas anxiety entails symbolic threats of existential danger—a dread of death that Becker (1973) described as a threat to one's ego identity.

The appraisal and coping processes associated with fright and anxiety can be looked at in the same manner as anger. The process for fright begins when appraisal determines that a relevant goal (bodily integrity) is incongruent with environmental conditions (concrete threat of imminent harm). With fright, no further appraisal or coping processes are relevant to its origination, although avoidance or escape would result quickly in its termination. The process for anxiety begins in a similar manner with appraisal determining that a relevant goal (existential meaning) is incongruent with environmental conditions (uncertain, existential threat). In this case, however, the appraisal of ego involvement is crucial to anxiety's origination. Whereas threat to self-esteem and attribution of blame led to the experience of anger, anxiety results from a threat to one's existential well-being (individual identity) with no target for the attribution of blame. What does it mean that such a terrible thing could be caused by forces beyond anybody's control? Is there any escape from such a terrible fate? Blame is impossible because threat is ambiguous, and this uncertainty puts limits on coping. We are made vulnerable by the fact that we only dimly appreciate the nature of our existential relationship to life and to the world. When this is threatened, there is nothing concrete against which to take action—nothing specific from which to escape.

This distinction between fright and anxiety is particularly useful in helping us understand the perplexing issues that surround the aesthetic emotional experiences associated with horror. If anxiety is distinguished by conditions of existential threat, and fright by more concrete danger, viewers are not likely to respond with fright when they know that they are unaffected by the immediate consequences to characters observed in the film. On the other hand, even though viewers are confronted with no immediate concrete threat, the existential threat present in the film is as real as in any other human activity. In fact, because film viewing encourages imaginative contemplation of events that are both real and fantastic, it may be more likely to stimulate thoughts of an existential nature that can lead to the experience of anxiety—the distress associated with contemplation of dreaded possibilities that fall beyond our own control or anybody's accountability.

The importance of threat to existential meaning in the elicitation of this relational theme of anxiety points to certain personality variables likely to contribute to a readiness to become anxious. An action that is a threat to one person because of a vulnerable ego identity need not be a threat to another more secure in this regard. This does not mean that only those with vulnerable egos get anxious—the tendency is probably universal—but rather that the personality trait is an important contributing factor, especially when the threat is mild. This emphasis allows us to account for differences in vulnerability to anxiety as a result of personality traits and specific features of the film. The issue is then identifying those antecedents of environment and personality that lead to specific generalizable reactions. When attempting to understand aesthetic emotional experience, the task is one of identifying the conditions that encourage imaginative contemplation of events both real and fantastic. Will these conditions stimulate thoughts of an existential threat and contemplation of dread beyond control?

According to Lazarus (1991), the only special concepts needed to explain aesthetic emotions are the principles that allow us to identify vicariously with observed behavior. We react emotionally to the portrayal of emotional realities that exist in our own lives. The more a portrayal touches a reality with relevance to problems in our lives, the more we respond as though the problems were real. Therefore, the principles that allow us to identify vicariously are critical to understanding aesthetic emotional response to film horror. Although different approaches have been taken in attempts to explain emotional reactions to horror, research on processes of identification has concentrated on certain personality traits and their relationship to content features typically found in graphic horror.

EMPATHY AND EMOTIONAL REACTIONS TO FILM

Models of cognitive processing suggest that individuals with a tendency to become imaginatively involved in another's experience have unusually strong reactions when observing emotionally charged events. Whether it is because of an increased ability to understand the situation that others are experiencing, or a sense as if the situation were being experienced oneself, these individuals should react with intensity to events that are being witnessed. If events are happy, this involvement should lead to joy; if tragic, it should lead to great sorrow. Hoffman (1978) suggested that this type of vicarious experience can be understood through the concept of empathy.

Empathy is an important factor in discussion of emotional reactions to any observed event. Individual differences on various dimensions of empathy have been shown to influence emotional responses in a variety of distressing contexts (Coke, Batson, & McDavis, 1978; Hoffman, 1977; Stotland, Mathews, Sherman, Hansson, & Richardson, 1978). In the case of graphic horror, film's capacity to portray human emotions vividly can be critical in the elicitation of these reactions (Zillmann, 1991). The belief that empathic processes can govern reactions to observed expression should lead us to expect specific patterns of aesthetic emotional reaction in individuals exposed to these films. Thus, empathy can be viewed as an antecedent of personality and considered in combination with environmental film cues in the model presented by Lazarus.

Dimensions of Empathy

The response to film exposure expected to result from empathic processes will differ according to the manner in which empathy is defined. Almost all definitions of empathy are limited to reactions concordant with observed emotions (cf. Zillmann, 1991). However, many definitions of empathy as a multidimensional construct include characteristics that may further limit their application to reactions associated only with the observation of negative emotions.

There are nearly as many definitions of empathy as there are individuals attempting to study it. In a simple sense, empathy refers to the reactions of one individual to the observed experiences of another (Davis, 1983). In the past decade, there has been an increased tendency to think of empathy as a multidimensional construct (cf. Davis, 1980; Richendoller & Weaver, 1994; Stiff, Dillard, Somera, Kim, & Sleight, 1988). The underlying rationale to this approach is that empathy can best be understood as a set of constructs, clearly distinct from each other, but related in that they all deal with the processes by which one individual reacts to the observed experiences of another.

Although there is still much debate over the dimensions that might be included, there is considerable agreement on the role of cognitive and affective dimensions of empathy (e.g., Davis, Hull, Young, & Warren, 1987; Strayer, 1987; Stiff et al., 1988; Tamborini & Mettler, 1990). Strayer (1987) noted that empathy conceptualized in affective terms is concerned with the concordant emotional reactions experienced by observers. In contrast, cognitive characterizations of empathy are based on the understanding of another's psychological state or feelings. Because understanding is determined by cognitive operations, if affect is evoked it is a result of these cognitive processes. According to Strayer (1987), the recent trend has been to treat empathy as a multidimensional construct by including aspects of affect and cognition as separate but interacting variables.

Cognitive Dimensions of Empathy. Many definitions of empathy suggest processes by which we cognitively place ourselves in another person's situation. Almost all these definitions deal with some aspect of imaginative process. The two dimensions of empathy most often investigated along these lines are *perspective taking* and *fictional involvement.* Perspective taking is one of the most widely discussed dimensions of empathy. It reflects the ability of an individual to see things from the viewpoint of another or to imagine what it would be like in their situation (Coke et al., 1978; Davis, 1980, 1983; Deutsch & Madle, 1975; Dymond, 1949; Feshbach, 1975; Krebs, 1975; Mead, 1934; Piaget, 1932). Fictional involvement refers to the transposition of oneself by imagination into the feelings and actions of fictitious characters. This dimension is derived from the work of Stotland et al. (1978) who suggested that the imaginative self-involvement of the observer is a basic element in the process of empathy. Both these dimensions of imaginative involvement deal with the ability of an individual to place himself or herself in the position of another person, either fictional or nonfictional, and suggest that this is an important consideration for understanding emotional experience.

A different but related cognitive dimension of empathy was suggested by Stotland et al. (1978). What we might call *wandering imagination* is the tendency to fantasize and daydream about fictional situations in an undirected manner. Although this does not deal specifically with the ability to place oneself in another's situation, this would appear to have direct bearing on our understanding of anxiety as an aesthetic emotional reaction expected from exposure to graphic horror. It seems logical that individuals who more freely allowed their imagination to wander, or who more easily imagined themselves in the situations of fictional characters would be more likely to contemplate their own uncertain existence, or threats to it such as those found in the situations and events in a graphic horror film.

Affective Dimensions of Empathy. As with cognitive characteristics, various definitions have identified several affective dimensions of empathy. Many of the definitions that fall in this category deal with some aspect of emotional sensitivity. Most common among these are empathic concern and personal distress. *Empathic concern* is a widely researched dimension of empathy. Although different researchers have given it labels such as *humanistic orientation* (Stiff, 1984), *sympathetic arousal* (Hoffman, 1977), *altruistic motivation* (Coke et al., 1978), and *sympathy* (Bennett, 1979), empathic concern deals with a form of sensitivity to the misfortune of others and feelings of compassion for their plight at seeing their pain, ill-treatment, loneliness, crying, and helplessness. *Personal distress* deals with the extent to which one is prone to feel aversion and discomfort in response to another's emotional problems (Davis, 1983). It is distinct from empathic concern in its self-oriented focus on the suffering one experiences when observing another's pain, instead of an other-oriented concern for the plight of the unfortunate victim.

Emotional contagion is somewhat different in that it does not necessarily suggest a concern for another person's plight, but instead refers to the adoption of the *same* emotions as those of the observed person (Mehrabian & Epstein, 1972; Stiff et al., 1988). Contagion occurs when one person experiences an emotional response parallel to the emotion observed or anticipated. Distinct in this dimension of empathy is the possibility of resulting positive affect. Most research on empathy has focused on reaction to negative events; however, it is apparent that empathic responses associated with contagion might be expected to result in positive emotional reactions to the observation of another's happiness. Although some recent work has questioned the application of such empathic responses to the witness of positive emotional experiences (Tamborini & Mettler, 1990), little question exists about its role in responding to unpleasant stimuli. As with cognitive dimensions of empathy, affective dimensions would appear to play an important role in our understanding of the emotional reactions associated with graphic horror. An individual who is sensitive to the misfortunes of others or who becomes distressed when others experience anguish might be expected to react more strongly to the pain and suffering displayed in horrifying films. From this, it appears that both affective and cognitive dimensions are useful in attempts to explicate emotional processes. Research integrating affective and cognitive dimensions has defined empathy as a multidimensional process. As we will see, this process is vital in determining emotional reactions that follow from the observed or anticipated emotional experiences of others.

Models of Empathy and Emotional Reactions

In addition to research focusing on its structural components (e.g., Davis, 1980), several researchers have focused on uncovering the causal determinants of empathic behavior, and offer support for their underlying rationales (Batson, Duncan, Ackerman, Buckley, & Birch, 1981; Cialdini et al., 1987; Coke et al., 1978; Hoffman, 1977; Stiff, Dillard, Somera, Kim, & Sleight, 1987). Recent investigations of empathy consistent with a multidimensional perspective have demonstrated strong patterns among several cognitive (perspective taking and fictional involvement) and affective (empathic concern and emotional contagion) dimensions. Based on these patterns, several models have attempted to explain the process of empathy and the manner in which it can determine reactions to the observation of another's emotional state. There is substantial agreement among researchers in this area that cognitive mechanisms initiate processes that induce internal emotional reactions (Coke et al., 1978; Feshbach, 1975; Stiff et al., 1988), and several studies support this claim.

In research on altruism, fictional involvement and perspective taking were found to be strong predictors of communicative responsiveness (Miller, Stiff, & Ellis, 1988; Stiff et al., 1988; Tamborini, Salomonson, & Bahk, 1993). Although perspective taking and fictional involvement are unique constructs, they are conceptually related—the target of the action differs, but both cognitive components are believed to stimulate affective response by their capacity to induce imaginative involvement with another's condition. This interpretation is supported by studies showing that empathic concern and emotional contagion are predicted by fictional involvement and perspective taking (Miller et al., 1988; Stiff et al., 1988; Tamborini, Salomonson, & Bahk, 1993).

In research dealing directly with media, most studies investigating the role of empathy have focused largely on negatively charged films such as tragedy and graphic horror (e.g., Tamborini, Bahk, & Salomonson, 1993; Tamborini & Mulcrone, 1987; Tamborini, Stiff, & Heidel, 1990). Davis et al. (1987) looked at two dimensions of empathy (perspective taking and empathic concern) and found them to be strong predictors of mood state following exposure to sad and angering films. In a study comparing reactions to positively and negatively charged films, Tamborini and Mettler (1990) produced a model showing that both cognitive dimensions (perspective taking and fictional involvement) and affective dimensions (empathic concern and emotional contagion) were useful in predicting concordant emotional reactions to a horror film, but were unrelated to reactions following comedy. Finally, in research on responses to graphic horror, Tamborini et al. (1990) demonstrated that wandering imagination and fictional involvement preceded emotional contagion and humanistic orientation (i.e., empathic concern) in predicting both coping responses and emotional reactions following exposure.

Beyond the general implications of these investigations for understanding the determinants of empathic responses to film, the study by Tamborini et al. (1990) is of particular interest for its demonstration that emotional contagion produced coping behaviors. This observation is consistent with cognitive-motivational-relational theory predictions, and suggests several alternative outcomes to viewing graphic horror depending on appraisal processes. Initially, coping might quickly alleviate an existing state of anxiety and simply extinguish the experience of emotion. Beyond this, it could impact appraisal of subsequent environmental conditions and resulting emotional experience. For example, a form of denial suggesting "this film is stupid, and it offends my intelligence" might impact subsequent appraisal of goal relevance, produce a new relational meaning, and lead to a core relational theme associated with the experience of mild anger. Denial in the form of "it is only a movie, and no longer this great concern" might lead to great relief. Denial in the form of "this doesn't frighten me, I am master of my fears" might lead to pride. Denial mixed with mild ridicule in the form of "this is silly and no real threat" might turn relief into amusement.

In combination with the earlier discussion of personality, research on the role of coping in the process of emotional experience provides insight on the value of cognitive-motivational-relational theory in explaining the determinants of responses to horror. These responses can be viewed as a function of processes related to appraisal outcomes. Various appraisals would be expected depending on antecedents of personality and learned associations with different environmental cues. This chapter proposes a model that is consistent with the growing body of research on these processes, and extends it to include issues concerning aesthetic emotional reactions to graphic horror film.

COGNITIVE-MOTIVATIONAL-RELATIONAL THEORY AND REACTIONS TO GRAPHIC HORROR

Lazarus (1991) viewed empathy as a process that determines one's ability to share another's emotions. According to this view, empathy's role in emotional reactions to horror can be described by a multivariate system of antecedent and mediating processes interdependently associated with immediate and long-term responses. The general model for empathy and film would suggest that personality factors (dimensions of empathy) in interaction with situational factors (film content) lead to an evaluation of the situation, and eventually result in an appraisal outcome (threat, insult, danger). The appraisal outcome is a mediating process that determines all that follows, including coping (e.g., denial, avoidance) and emotional response states (anxiety, relief, amusement). Lazarus viewed this outcome as a key element in the emotional system. It is the most immediate cause of initial response, and a dominant factor in subsequent behavior.

Specific outcomes from viewing graphic horror can be expected to result from the interaction of different personality and environmental antecedents. To begin with, antecedent personality characteristics can interact with each other to initiate evaluation of the situation. For example, perspective taking leads to different construal when accompanied by an empathic concern for another person's suffering than when accompanied by an emotionally contagious reaction to another's pain. When accompanied by concern we might expect feelings of compassion and an attempt to help others in need, but when accompanied by contagion we expect feelings of apprehension and attempts to avoid others' distress.

Similarly, environmental context interacting with personality is critical in determining relational meaning. For example, perspective taking can impact the specific goals at stake in different film environments. In a film graphically depicting the mutilation of victims by a demon like Jason in *Friday the 13th*, perspective taking might lead to appraisal of the film as insulting nonsense, and mild forms of anger should follow. However, conditions change when the same violent deaths are seen in a newscast as the work of a serial killer. Instead of insult and anger we expect compassion or apprehension as result of concern or contagion.

At the same time, even within the environment created by the demonic killer, different responses would be expected depending on the manner in which personality variables interact to initiate appraisal. If low levels of fictional involvement lead to an appraisal that the situation has no goal relevance, emotional experience of any type would immediately be halted. With involved viewers, however, attributes of film characters and events would interact with traits like concern and contagion to determine the specific goal relevance at stake. Based on initial appraisal, coping processes would be enacted to deal with the specific threat to ego. The results of this coping process feed back to the system and initiate adaptive reappraisal designed to change the relational meaning for the person's well-being. For example, if a contagious fear is appraised as a threat to self-esteem, to deny the threat's reality by telling yourself "it's only a movie" might lead to pride.

A MODEL OF EMPATHY AND EMOTIONAL REACTIONS TO HORROR

The antecedent factors of the empathic process and film environment distinguish the model presented in this chapter. The model presents a more detailed account of the manner in which these antecedent and mediating processes both produce and respond to the immediate and long-term effects (see Fig. 7.2). Empathic processes and film content represent the *antecedent conditions* of personality and environment. The interaction of these factors creates an *initial relational meaning* suggesting either no relevant threat, existential threat to others, or uncertain existential threat to self. The construed initial meaning provokes a *coping and reappraisal process* governed by cognitive and action coping strategies designed to deal with specific threats. The outcome of this process feeds back through the system to generate new relational meanings. These reappraised relational meanings produce the ensuing *emotional response state*, and determine all *subsequent behavior*.

The model is a simple depiction of what is surely a complex process impacted at several stages by a variety of physiological, sociological, and other psychological variables.   Although the model allows these to enter as antecedents or feedback from subsequent outcomes, it is not intended to limit their impact to these areas. Instead, the model's purpose is to focus attention on the process of empathy and its relation to experiences resulting from exposure to graphic film horror. The manner in which dimensions of empathy interact to determine relational meanings plays an important part in this process. Their specific relationship with the film is critical in the regulation of emotions..

Antecedent Conditions

The representation of empathy provided in Fig. 7.2 is consistent with research defining empathy as a process (Stiff et al., 1988; Tamborini, Salomonson, & Bahk, 1993). It suggests that the process of empathic response is initiated by wandering imagination.   Although perspective taking can play a part in empathic response, its role in aesthetic emotion is limited by the fictional nature of film horror. Wandering imagination is a proclivity for undirected fantasizing and daydreaming that is likely to lead one to imagine the experiences of others. When others in the environment are characters in a film, wandering imagination should enhance fictional involvement—the tendency to imagine the feelings of fictional characters.

This cognitive deliberation of a character's painful experience is presumed to stimulate empathic concern, and eventually emotional contagion. Cognitive deliberation allows greater understanding of the character's situation, and this understanding is expected to result in a form of sensitivity for the plight of the character that is indicative of empathic concern. To the extent that sensitivity stimulates recall of sensations and episodes corresponding with those of the character, concern will lead to emotional contagion and the experience of similar affect—an apprehensive feeling under these conditions.

Initial Relational Meaning

An empathic sensitivity or contagious apprehension can play a crucial role in initial relational meanings. If minimal levels of pertinent empathic traits lead to neither of these conditions, then the initial relational meaning will suggest no relevant threat, and no emotional experience will result.   In contrast, if empathic processes enhance a sensitivity to the plight of unknown people, then the initial relational meaning will suggest an existential threat to others. Under these conditions compassion is likely in the empathetically concerned viewer who has no real target to blame for such suffering. However, a more likely scenario is the situation in which empathic processes lead not to concern for unknown others, but to feelings of apprehension or a dread of uncertain danger.

The initial relational meaning in this situation suggests a state of uncertain existential threat to self, and once again there is no target for blame.

Coping and Appraisal Processes

The initial relational meanings of existential threat constrain the potential usefulness of action and cognitive coping strategies. The uncertainty of the danger makes us very vulnerable to these threats, and escape becomes more difficult to achieve. Without a concrete danger, typical action strategies are limited by the fact that behavioral efforts to change the person-environment relationship have no blameworthy target to attack. However, action coping may be useful in one particular case—situations in which the specific threat is uncertain, but one can anticipate its materialization with some precision.

Anticipation of uncertain threat can stimulate defensive coping strategies to either actively avoid (e.g., close your eyes) or cognitively deny the danger that is headed your way. Individuals extremely sensitive to the unpleasant images in horror often realize from previous exposure that certain scenes are too upsetting to view. Short of total abstention from exposure to films of this nature, they can employ different coping strategies to interfere with the onset of negative affect. By learning to accurately predict the occurrence of events that are horrifying, viewers can initiate strategies to prevent the potential harm. It is not difficult to explain how viewers learn to predict the onslaught of frightening events in film. In fact, it is common for horror films to provide clear cues to aid in this prediction. The warning of an impending shark attack provided by a reoccurring musical theme in *Jaws* is a classic example of film techniques that provide this type of cue.

Although action coping strategies may be useful for anticipated danger, the conditions of existential threat that leave no target for blame make cognitive coping mechanisms a potentially more useful strategy. Cognitive coping is a manner of thinking designed to change the person-environment relationship. As shown in Fig. 7.2, the outcome of this activity provides feedback that can alter the initial relational meaning. The reappraisal that follows modifies the emotional response state and impacts all subsequent experience. For example, if the event is appraised as an existential threat to one's well-being, denying the threat as "only a movie" might lead to relief. In a similar manner, if this event is ridiculed as a "silly threat," cynicism can turn relief into amusement. The coping behaviors of denial and ridicule generate new relational meanings and change the person-environment relationship to enhance the person's well-being. When well learned, such cognitive coping strategies can automatically initiate defensive reappraisal and short-circuit negative relational meaning. In this manner, coping and reappraisal processes can influence the quality and intensity of the ensuing emotional experience.

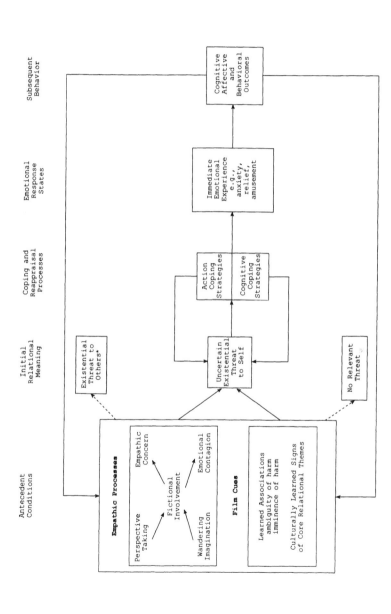

Antecedent Conditions   Initial Relational Meaning   Coping and Reappraisal Processes   Emotional Response States   Subsequent Behavior

Empathic Processes

Perspective Taking   Empathic Concern

Fictional Involvement

Wandering Imagination   Emotional Contagion

Film Cues

Learned Associations ambiguity of harm imminence of harm

Culturally Learned Signs of Core Relational Themes

Existential Threat to Others*

Uncertain Existential Threat to Self

No Relevant Threat

Action Coping Strategies

Cognitive Coping Strategies

Immediate Emotional Experience e.g., anxiety, relief, amusement

Cognitive Affective and Behavioral Outcomes

FIG. 7.2. Model of empathy and emotional reactions to horror. If relational meaning of existential threat to others results in compassion (being moved by another's suffering and wanting to help), there is no further need for coping processes to change the experience, and reappraisal is unlikely. The display of compassion is culturally valued and compassion is considered a positive quality.

Emotional Experience

The emotional experience resulting from reappraisal can be characterized by a pattern of impulse tendencies, physiological changes, and subjective evaluations. The impulse tendency is an innate readiness to respond to the particular goal at stake. Physiological change includes activity throughout the body such as brain functions, autonomic behaviors, hormonal patterns, and molar physical responses. Selective evaluations are the labels we attach to an experience and often refer to as affect (cf. Drever, 1952; Lazarus, 1991). Although diversity in emotional experiences is likely to result from differences in learned responses to film cues and empathic processes, some similarities are likely to exist in these emotional experience patterns due to common viewer backgrounds. The experiences of anxiety, relief, and amusement serve as examples of emotional response states likely to occur in different viewers following exposure to horror.

Anxiety

The effectiveness of coping strategies in dealing with horror are likely to be limited in film viewing situations. Action strategies designed to avoid horrifying scenes may be thwarted by failure to anticipate, or hindered by poor application. Even cognitive coping may have limited utility for individuals with personalities not prone to denial and cynicism. Under these conditions, coping processes are not likely to change the quality of the emotional experience, and may only limit its intensity. The uncertain nature of the existential danger increases our vulnerability to threat in these films. The experience that results from exposure to these threats might be characterized by certain features. The impulse to flee should be somewhat undirected in the absence of a concrete danger. Physiological change might take several different forms including increased arousal, muscle tension, or a sinking feeling in the stomach. The subjective evaluation should be a diffused sense of apprehension resulting from ambiguity in our understanding of existential threat. In all, the emotional response state would be one of *anxiety*, and could range anywhere from mild to acute.

Relief

On the other hand, coping and reappraisal processes might be more effective for individuals with different personality traits. Should these traits prompt successful cognitive strategies of denial, the quality of the emotional experience is likely to be changed. Apprehension from initial relational meanings of uncertain threat should be alleviated through reappraisal. The need to get away should dissipate, perhaps leaving no impulse tendency. At the same time, physiological changes should be marked by decreased arousal and muscle relaxation. In conjunction with this, the subjective evaluation that unpleasantries have taken a turn for the better differentiates this emotional response state as *relief*. Once again, the experience may be powerful or weak, depending on the individual differences.

Amusement

In a similar manner, more advanced cognitive strategies might offer greater potential benefit for a third kind of viewer. For individuals with personality traits that evoke strategies going beyond denial and prompt ridicule of the threat, the quality of the emotional experience can be altered once again and give rise to a preferable state. The initial process of coping and reappraisal once more leads to a sense of change for the better. However, in this case a tendency to approach and reach out replaces the original avoidance impulse. The experience might be associated with physiological manifestations like smiling, laughing, and related behavioral indicators. Moreover, subjective evaluation including a detached sense of mastery and a pleasant feeling of well-being identify this emotional response state of *amusement*. Depending on film cues and empathic processes the experience will vary in intensity. The state could be as mild as the faint sense of pleasure we associate with a derisive snicker, or as strong as the gleeful experience of joy that comes with a hardy last laugh.

Subsequent Experience

The immediate emotional response plays an important role in the determination of all subsequent experience. Some form of anxiety, a feeling of relief, a faint pleasure or unrestrained joy—these and other response states change the person-environment relationship to influence thoughts, feelings, and actions with both short-term and long-term implications.

Cognitive Outcomes

Extant research shows emotional states' effects on short-term cognitive functions like information processing strategies, storage mechanisms, and social judgements (cf. Forgas, 1991), and long-term impacts on learning (cf. Bower, 1992) and memory processes (cf. Blaney, 1986) are also heavily documented. For example, Sparks (chap. 8, this volume) suggests that experiences of anxiety such as those resulting from horror are related to individual differences in information-processing modes that have short-term implications. These differences can either inhibit the processing of external information in order to help focus attention or facilitate monitoring of the external environment for access to novel information. In a similar manner, long-term effects can be seen in research on mood congruent memory. Several investigations suggest negative emotional states can enhance the recall of past distressing events (cf. Tobias, Kihlstrom, & Schacter, 1992).

Affective Outcomes

The short-term influence on affect is true by definition, but the long-term development of habitual affective states may have greater consequence. If amount of consideration is an indicator of importance, the volumes on phobias and stress attest to the critical nature of these issues (e.g., Denny, 1991; Spielberger & Sarason, 1986), but research on subjective well-being has serious implications as well (cf. Diener, 1984; Strack, Argyle, & Schwarz, 1991). Particularly relevant to the discussion in this chapter is the claim by recent scholars that the comparative frequency with which one experiences momentary states of happiness or distress is related to lasting conditions of depression and well-being (Costa & McCrae, 1980; Diener, Sandvik, & Pavot, 1989; Lewinsohn & Amenson, 1978). If this is the case, the emotional response states that result from processes like those suggested here take on greater weight.

Behavioral Outcomes

The significance of emotional experience becomes even more meaningful when understood in relation to behavior. Not only can response state govern action and social interaction in the short term, but it may have considerable consequences for long-term somatic health. The impact on action can include stimulation of various affect impulses that inhibit or facilitate behavior. For example, it has long been known that fear and anxiety interfere with sexual functions (cf. Izzard, 1977), and several investigations show that performance of subsequent behavior can be intensified by the transfer of excitation from emotionally arousing media (cf. Zillmann, 1991). Social interaction effects can range from the short-term impact of media-induced affect on both prosocial and antisocial behavior (cf. Salomonson & Tamborini, 1994; Tan, 1985) to the long-term impairment of social skills that results from stress and anxiety (cf. Denny, 1991; Spielberger, 1966). Somatic health's association with research on stress and anxiety shows the seriousness with which it is considered. Although evidence that emotions have an impact on somatic health appears to suffer from theoretical and methodological limitations, the possibility remains that illness can result from prolonged or marked psychological disturbances

(Lazarus, 1991). Although it may be unlikely that exposure to graphic horror is the cause of most prolonged disturbances, marked disturbances from graphic horror may be problematic in childhood development, and the learning of coping strategies during early exposure to threatening materials can play an important role in adolescent development (cf. Cantor, 1994).

According to the model, all aspects of subsequent experiences feed back to the model's antecedent conditions and influence future interactions of empathy and film content. The harms and benefits associated with these subsequent experiences are the basis for future modifications of empathic processes, stimulus conditioning, and mechanisms for coping with negative relational meanings that result from the interaction of these antecedent conditions. To the extent that this feedback strengthens empathic processes leading to involvement with fictional media, the intensity of response to graphic horror films can be expected to increase. At the same time, in large part, the hedonic quality of these responses will be governed by resulting changes in conditioned stimuli and coping mechanisms.

Issues concerning the extent to which any specific appraisal depends on environmental realities or personality factors remain to be resolved. There are so many realities in film as in life, not just one possible evaluative outcome, that it would restrict our understanding of the emotional processes to think that personality factors associated with imaginative involvement would limit viewers to only one possible experience. Instead, from all experiences made possible in environments created by film, empathic processes can determine which realities are relevant; thus, a shark is a fish, but it can also be your dinner at a restaurant, or you can be its dinner in movies.

REFERENCES

Batson, C. D., Duncan, B. D., Ackerman, P., Buckley, T., & Birch, K. (1981). Is empathic emotion a source of altruistic motivation? *Journal of Personality and Social Psychology, 40,* 290-302.

Becker, E. (1973). *The denial of death.* New York: The Free Press.

Bell, C. (1914). *Art.* London: Chatto & Windus.

Bennett, M. J. (1979). Overcoming the golden rule: Sympathy and empathy. In D. Nimmo (Ed.), *Communication Yearbook 3* (pp. 407-422). New Brunswick, NJ: Transaction.

Binkley, T. (1977). Piece: Contra aesthetics. *Journal of Aesthetics and Art Criticism, 35,* 265-277.

Blaney, P. (1986). Affect and memory: A review. *Psychological Bulletin, 99,* 229-246.

Bower, G. (1992). How might emotions affect learning? In S. A. Christianson (Ed.), *Handbook of emotion and memory* (pp 3-31). Hillsdale, NJ: Lawrence Erlbaum Associates.

Cantor, J. (1994). Fright reactions to mass media. In J. Bryant & D. Zillmann (Eds.), *Media effects: Advances in theory and research* (pp. 213-246). Hillsdale, NJ: Lawrence Erlbaum Associates.

Cialdini, R. B., Schaller, M., Houlihan, D., Arps, K., Fultz, J., & Beaman, A. L. (1987). Empathy-based helping: Is it selflessly or selfishly motivated? *Journal of Personality and Social Psychology, 52,* 749-758.

Coke, J. S., Batson, C. D., & McDavis, K. (1978). Empathic mediation of helping: A two-stage model. *Journal of Personality and Social Psychology, 39,* 752-766.

Costa, P. T., & McCrae, R. R. (1980). Influence of extraversion and neuroticism on subjective well-being: Happy and unhappy people. *Journal of Personality and Social Psychology, 38,* 668-678.

Danto, A. (1964). The art world. *Journal of Philosophy, 61,* 571-584.

Danto, A. (1981). *The transfiguration of the commonplace.* Cambridge, MA: Harvard University Press.

Davis, M. H. (1980). Multidimensional approach to individual difference in empathy. *JSAS Catalog of Selected Documents in Psychology, 10,* 75.

Davis, M. H. (1983). Measuring individual differences in empathy: Evidence for a multidimensional approach. *Journal of Personality and Social Psychology, 44,* 113-126.

Davis, M. H., Hull, J. G., Young, R. D., & Warren, G. G. (1987). Emotional reactions to dramatic film stimuli: The influence of cognitive and emotional empathy. *Journal of Personality Psychology and Social Psychology, 52,* 126-133.

Denny, M. R. (1991). *Fear, avoidance, and phobias.* Hillsdale, NJ: Lawrence Erlbaum Associates.

Deutsch, F., & Madle, R. A. (1975). Empathy: Historic and current conceptualizations, measurements, and a cognitive theoretical approach. *Human Development, 18,* 267-287.

Diener, E. (1984). Subjective well-being. *Psychological Bulletin, 95,* 542-575.

Diener, E., Sandvik, E., & Pavot, W. (1989). Happiness is the frequency, not intensity, of positive versus negative affect. In F. Strack, M. Argyle, & N. Schwarz (Eds.), *The social psychology of subjective well-being* (pp. 119-139). Oxford, UK: Pergamon.

Drever, J. (1952). *A dictionary of psychology.* London: Penguin.

Dymond, R. (1949). A scale for the measurement of empathic ability. *Journal of Consulting Psychology, 13,* 127-133.

Feshbach, N. D. (1975). Empathy in children: Some theoretical and empirical considerations. *Counseling Psychologist, 5,* 26-29.

Forgas, J. P. (1991). *Emotion & social judgements.* Oxford, UK: Pergamon.

Frijda, N. H. (1989). Aesthetic emotions and reality. *American Psychologist, 44,* 1546-1547.

Fry, R. (1920). *Vision and design.* London: Chatto & Windus.

Gombrich, E. H. (1962). *Art and illusion.* London: Phaidon Press.

Hoffman, M. L. (1977). Sex differences in empathy and related behaviors. *Psychological Bulletin, 84,* 712-722.

Hoffman, M. L. (1978). Empathy, its development and prosocial implications. In C. B. Keasey (Ed.), *Nebraska Symposium on Motivation* (Vol. 25, pp. 169-218). Lincoln: University of Nebraska Press.

Izard, C. E. (1977). *Human emotions.* New York: Plenum.

Krebs, D. (1975). Empathy and altruism. *Journal of Personality Psychology and Social Psychology, 32,* 1134-1146.

Lazarus, R. S. (1991). *Emotion and adaptation.* New York: Oxford University Press.

Lazarus, R. S., & Folkman, S. (1984). *Stress, appraisal, and coping.* New York: Springer.

Lewinsohn, P. M., & Amenson, C. S. (1978). Some relations between pleasant and unpleasant events and depression. *Journal of Abnormal Psychology, 87,* 644-654.

Mead, G. H. (1934). *Mind, self, and society.* Chicago: University of Chicago Press.

Mehrabian, A., & Epstein, N. (1972). A measure of emotional empathy. *Journal of Personality, 40*(4), 525-543.

Miller, K. I., Stiff, J. B., & Ellis, B. H. (1988). Communication and empathy as precursors to burnout among human service workers. *Communication Monographs, 55*(3), 250-265.

Piaget, J. (1932). *The moral development of the child.* New York: Harcourt, Brace, & World.

Radford, C. (1975). How can we be moved by the fate of Anna Karenina? *Proceedings of the Aristotelian Society, 49,* 67-93.

Richendoller, N. R., & Weaver, J. B., III (1994). Exploring the links between personality and empathic response style. *Personality and Individual Differences, 17,* 303-311.

Rorty, A. (1978). Explaining emotions. *Journal of Philosophy, 75,* 139-161.

Salomonson, K. E., & Tamborini, R. (1994, November). *Stable and situational determinants of comforting: A model of empathy, film genre, and mood state.* Paper presented at the Annual Conference of the Speech Communication Association, New Orleans, LA.

Spielberger, C. D. (1966). *Anxiety and behavior.* New York: Academic Press.

Spielberger, C. D., & Sarason, I. G. (1986). *Stress and anxiety* (Vol. 10). Washington, DC: Hemisphere.

Stiff, J. B. (1984). *Communicative and emotional empathy.* Unpublished manuscript, Department of Communication, Michigan State University, East Lansing.

Stiff, J. B., Dillard, J. P., Somera, B., Kim, H., & Sleight, C. (1987, November). *Empathy, communication, and prosocial behavior.* Paper presented at the annual meeting of the Speech Communication Association, Boston.

Stiff, J. B., Dillard, J. P., Somera, L., Kim, H., & Sleight, C. (1988). Empathy, communication, and prosocial behavior. *Communication Monographs, 55,* 198-213.

Stotland, E., Mathews, K. E., Jr., Sherman, S. E., Hansson, R. O., & Richardson, B. Z. (1978). *Empathy, fantasy, and helping.* Beverly Hills, CA: Sage.

Strack, F., Argyle, M., & Schwarz, N. (1991). *Subjective well-being.* Oxford, UK: Pergamon.

Strayer, J. (1987). Affective and cognitive perspectives on empathy. In N. Eisenberg & J. Strayer (Eds.), *Empathy and its development* (pp. 41-63). Hillsdale, NJ: Lawrence Erlbaum Associates.

Tamborini, R., Bahk, C., & Salomonson, K. (1993, May). *The moderating impact of film exposure on the relationship between empathy and comforting.* Paper presented at the annual conference of the International Communication Association, Washington, DC.

Tamborini, R. & Mettler, J. (1990, November). *Emotional reactions to film: A model of empathic processes.* Paper presented at the annual conference of the Speech Communication Association, Chicago.

Tamborini, R., & Mulcrone, J. (1987, November). *The enjoyment of graphic horror featuring female victimization.* Paper presented at the annual conference of the Speech Communication Association, Boston.

Tamborini, R., Salomonson, K., & Bahk, C. (1993). The relationship of empathy to comforting behavior following film exposure. *Communication Research, 20,* 723-738.

Tamborini, R., Stiff, J., & Heidel, C. (1990). Reacting to graphic horror: A model of empathy and emotional behavior. *Communication Research, 17,* 616-640.

Tan, A. S. (1985). *Mass communication theories and research.* New York: Wiley.

Tobias, B. A., Kihlstrom, J. F., & Schacter, D. L. (1992). Emotion and implicit memory. In S. A. Christianson (Ed.), *Handbook of emotion and memory* (pp. 67-92). Hillsdale, NJ: Lawrence Erlbaum Associates.

Walters, K. S. (1989). The law of apparent reality and aesthetic emotions. *American Psychologist, 44,* 1545-1546.

Zillmann, D. (1991). Empathy: Affect from bearing witness to the emotions of others. In J. Bryant & D. Zillmann (Eds.), *Responding to the screen: Reception and reaction processes* (pp. 135-167). Hillsdale, NJ: Lawrence Erlbaum Associates.

Chapter 8

An Activation-Arousal Analysis of Reactions to Horror

Glenn G. Sparks
Purdue University

The last 20 years of research in psychology and communication have produced a burgeoning literature on human emotions. This increase in research activity has provided fertile soil for those scholars studying the emotional responses that occur in the general context of mass-mediated messages and, more specifically, in the context of frightening, horrific, and suspenseful entertainment. However, the studies on reactions to horror often reflect a diverse array of theoretical approaches to emotion processes. Moreover, the underlying theoretical assumptions about emotion are specified only occasionally in this recent literature.

This state of affairs is not surprising given that the general study of emotion could still be characterized by theoretical chaos (see Mandler, 1984; Strongman, 1987). Strongman's (1987) recent text provides overviews of over 30 different theories. The similarities and differences between alternative approaches are sometimes subtle and unclear. Given the wide array of theoretical options within the emotion literature, researchers working on issues related to emotional responses to mass-mediated messages would be well advised to become more deliberate about articulating their theoretical assumptions. Such articulation will foster comparison among approaches and stimulate specific questions for further research.

With these priorities in mind, the first section of this chapter attempts to sketch a general theoretical approach to the study of emotions. I call this general approach the innate or dispositional view, although there are other related terms that frequently arise in characterizing this perspective, including personality, genetic, temperamental, or individual difference stances. After consideration of the evidence in favor of the dispositional approach, the chapter briefly reviews Tucker and Williamson's (1984) activation-arousal framework as a specific example of a dispositional perspective on emotion. Finally, the chapter turns to the application of this approach to the study of emotional reactions to media horror. The fact that emotional reactions to horror are discussed later in the chapter, rather than earlier, should not obscure the fact that it is precisely these reactions that are the focus of interest. The chapter proceeds on the conviction that understanding these particular reactions will be enhanced only to the degree that the general systems producing them can be comprehended.

THE DISPOSITIONAL APPROACH TO EMOTION

The study of individual difference factors has played an increasingly important role in theorizing about emotional responses to media horror (see Tamborini, chap. 7, this volume; Zuckerman, chap. 9, this volume). One general type of individual difference factor in the study of emotion arises from the observation that a significant portion of human emotional response involves the working of components that appear to be innate or "hard-wired" at birth. The dispositional view of emotion begins with this fundamental observation and additionally notes that the particular configuration of the emotional apparatus across individuals is likely to vary considerably. In order to properly characterize the dispositional approach to emotion, support for each of these two observations is reviewed in the following.

The Hard-Wired Components of Emotions

Gainotti (1989) identified four general components of emotions that can properly be classified as "hard-wired" in the organism at birth. First, a preprogrammed central motor mechanism appears to exert control over a basic set of expressive motor functions. In support of this type of mechanism, research by Ekman and his associates (e.g., Ekman, Friesen, & Ancoli, 1980; Ekman, Levenson, & Friesen, 1983) and by Izard (1971, 1977; 1991) reveals that particular emotional experiences appear to be characterized by corresponding configurations of the facial musculature. These configurations seem to hold across diverse cultural groups. Second, there appears to be a basic set of specific external cues that are capable of eliciting particular expressive motor functions during the first days of life. For example, evidence from research conducted by Field, Woodson, Greenberg, and Cohen (1982) reveals that only days after birth, infants display a biased sensitivity in their facial expressiveness to interpersonal emotional displays from adults. Third, the central nervous system (particularly the brain) is characterized by an increased level of arousal during an emotional response. This observation is well established and was one main reason for the formulation of activation theory (Lindsley, 1951). More recent research on emotion embraces the assumption that an elaborate neural network underlies human emotional responses. Heath (1986) described the main structures and processes comprising the "neural substrate" of emotion and argued that there are particular neural events that correspond to and govern specific emotional experiences. Finally, the autonomic nervous system (controlling the glands and organs of the body; see Andreassi, 1989) is characterized by some level of activation during an emotional response. The evidence in favor of this proposition is overwhelming. The importance of autonomic arousal in emotion has long been recognized. James (1890) believed that perceptions of autonomic arousal produced emotional experience directly. Although this position has been debated and modified extensively, the central role of autonomic arousal in the experience of emotion would not be challenged by most current emotion theorists.[1]

Individual Variability in the Emotional System

The fact that there is substantial variability across individuals in the emotional system can hardly be disputed. The source of such variability is more controversial. Buss (1990) argued that "roughly half of the observed variance in personality traits, traditionally conceived, has been shown to be due to genetic differences among individuals" (p. 4). This statement is based on a variety of studies with twins and adopted children and, for the most part, would appear to be uncontroversial among those scholars working on the biological bases for behavior.

Consistent with this view, Thompson (1988) recently noted in his discussion of emotions that, "biological variability is the rule rather than the exception" (p. 330). Of particular importance for this discussion, he also noted in connection with the argument that biological variability has important implications for our understanding of emotion, that, "biological variability may predispose individuals to develop different psychiatric disorders" (p. 332). Although Thompson considered the possibility that such variability arises from environmental factors, his discussion strongly implies that genetic factors are key ingredients in the process.

In summary, there is considerable support for the two central propositions that underlie the dispositional approach to emotion. There are a number of basic mechanisms involved in emotional responses that are hard-wired and

---

[1]It should be noted, however, that the global construct of arousal has come under recent attack (Cacioppo, Petty, & Tassinary, 1989; Neiss, 1988, 1990). In a recent exchange of views (Burgoon & Le Poire, 1992; Greene & Sparks, 1992; Sparks & Greene, 1992), Greene and Sparks (1992) observed that it was time to consider moving beyond the traditional diffuse and global conceptions of arousal and toward a view that emphasized specific response systems and their role in behavior. Although such a view would certainly lead to a fundamental reconceptualization of arousal, it would not question the essential relationship between physiological responses and emotional experiences.

there are significant individual differences in the particular configuration of these mechanisms. Applying these observations to emotion-based traits would lead to the conclusion that the particular configuration of the hard-wired components of emotion accounts for a large share of the variance in emotional responses seen across individuals. Clearly, there are additional origins for such variance that are more social and cognitive in nature. Although it may not be possible to unequivocally interpret all of the following evidence for hard-wired differences in emotional mechanisms, much of the evidence is generally interpreted as supportive of this view. The evidence to be reviewed here falls into two general categories: (a) differences in physiological responding, and (b) early differences in temperament.

Differences in Physiological Responding. Sternbach (1966) and Andreassi (1989) both outlined the historical development of the concept of individual response specificity. Its origins may be traced to the work of Malmo and Shagass (1949), who documented that certain psychiatric patients with a history of heart trouble responded to pain with increases in muscle tension. Lacey, Bateman, and Van Lehn (1953) conducted the first formal experimental test of this phenomenon when they documented variations in subjects' physiological responses on three different measures while being subjected to four alternative stressful events. That is, some subjects showed consistently higher responses in skin conductance across the four stressors. Others showed higher responses in heart rate. Research by Schnore (1959) also documented that individuals have different physiological response patterns when placed under conditions of high arousal.

There are several implications of this well-documented tendency toward individual response specificity. First, researchers who measure physiological responses as indicators of emotional responding to horror films might reduce the error variance in their physiological data by taking this tendency into account. If subjects could be classified as skin conductance responders or heart rate responders, and so on, prior to exposure to a given stimulus of interest, the probability of obtaining more meaningful physiological results should increase. Because the "variance accounted for" in physiological responses to horror films is usually very low (5-10%), this general analysis strategy would seem worthwhile.

For the present purpose, the more critical implication of individual response specificity is that this tendency appears to be consistent with the notion that there are hard-wired variations in the emotional response system. Andreassi (1989) did nothing more than present the empirical evidence in favor of this phenomenon. He avoided any discussion of the specific mechanisms that may produce it. It is possible, of course, that specific patterns of physiological responding are learned. However, this view seems suspect given that biofeedback (learning control over one's physiological responses) requires extensive training and does not always produce optimum results. At least one recent criticism (Furedy, 1987) suggests that the current evidence in favor of the effectiveness of biofeedback lacks sufficient rigor. Along these lines, Andreassi (1989) noted:

> The question of whether biofeedback training has a specific effect on a target physiological function has sparked a lively debate among psychologists. [The] opposing positions require resolution through research showing that biofeedback training leads to self-regulation and that this produces specific effects that are clinically beneficial. (pp. 364-65)

Without disparaging the potential value in biofeedback training, the evidence from this literature points to physiological responses that are difficult to control even when substantial effort is directed to this end. When this state of affairs is combined with findings that reveal that physiological channels may be ordered in response intensity within an individual across different types of stressors (Lacey et al., 1953), a more compelling case seems to exist for the position that attributes variations in physiological responding to hard-wired differences. To the extent that the experience of an emotion involves a physiological response, the conclusion of this argument is that emotional experiences are themselves the partial products of hard-wired factors that vary from individual to individual.

Early Differences in Temperament. Additional support for the role of innate factors in producing differences in emotional experience is evident from the recent literature on temperamental differences during infancy and early childhood (see Buck, 1984; Buss, 1989). This line of research appears to be a logical extension of several specific theories of emotion that include a strong genetic component in their explanatory frameworks. For example, Eysenck (1970) posited a basic genetic difference in individuals' tonic levels of physiological arousal. These differences, he argued, predispose individuals toward either extraversion (stimulus seeking) or introversion (stimulus avoiding). In addition, the genetic differences in arousal serve to predispose individuals toward more or less emotional stability. Thus, Eysenck viewed one's basic emotional temperament on the stability-instability dimension as being genetically predisposed.

The influential work of Bowlby (1969, 1973) also reflects a general commitment to genetic factors that predispose emotional experience. Bowlby believed that "attachment behaviors" were genetically programmed to unfold at various points in the child's development. According to this view, the unfolding genetic program interacts with a child's environment to contribute to the child's emotional well-being. For example, Bowlby contended that if a child was separated from a primary caretaker during one of the critical periods of development governed by the genetic program, then the child might have lifelong difficulty forming normal attachments with others. Ultimately, the child could develop psychiatric disorders. The research on Bowlby's theory has produced mixed evidence (see Baggett, 1967, and Yarrow & Goodwin, 1973 for evidence contrary to the theory), but there is enough data to suggest that the idea of genetically controlled critical periods in child development should be taken seriously.

More recent research on young children also appears to be consistent with the notion that hard-wired factors produce differences in emotional experience. Fox (1989) summarized the results of one study by concluding that "there are individual differences in infant emotional reactivity to novel and mildly stressful events. Moreover, these differences in behavior are associated with varying degrees of parasympathetic or vagal influence" (p. 370). Infants in Fox's study who had high levels of heart rate variability were more behaviorally reactive to both positive and negative stimuli. High heart rate variability was also related to the ability to regulate stress reactions after exposure to negative stimuli. This study is representative of Fox's work on the psychophysiological correlates of emotional reactivity and is related to other work on infant temperament that links emotional reactivity and regulation to responses of the autonomic nervous system (Gunnar, Mangelsdorf, Larson, & Hertsgaard, 1989; Rothbart & Derryberry, 1981).

Finally, the work of Kagan and his associates on inhibited and uninhibited children (Kagan, 1989; Kagan, Reznick, Clarke, Snidman, & Garcia-Coll, 1984; Kagan, Reznick & Snidman, 1987, 1988; Kagan, Reznick, Snidman, Gibbons, & Johnson, 1988) provides compelling evidence for a genetic basis to differences in emotional reactivity. Kagan (1989) summarized his research program by noting that:

> About 15% of Caucasian children in the second year of life are consistently shy and emotionally subdued in unfamiliar situations, whereas another 15% are consistently sociable and affectively spontaneous. A majority of the children in these two groups retain these profiles through their eighth year. In addition, the two groups differ in physiological qualities that imply differential thresholds in limbic sites, especially the amygdala and the hypothalamus, suggesting that the two temperamental groups are analogous to closely related strains of mammals. (p. 668)

Kagan's (1989) research has shown that inhibited children tend to have, "higher and more stable heart rates, larger pupil diameters, greater motor tension, and higher levels of morning cortisol" (p. 672).

To summarize, the dispositional view of emotion holds that emotional experiences are heavily influenced by genetic or hard-wired factors. The literature mentioned earlier supports the hard-wired basis for emotional experience and additionally presents considerable evidence in favor of genetic predispositions that govern emotional responding. With this evidence in mind, the chapter turns to a consideration of Tucker and Williamson's activation-arousal framework. Following an overview of this more specific formulation, I review several studies that have attempted to extend this approach to the study of emotional reactions to frightening media stimuli.

THE ACTIVATION-AROUSAL FRAMEWORK

Tucker and Williamson (1984) presented a theoretical framework for understanding issues of emotion and self-regulation of behavior that relies on a particular conceptualization of the underlying neural control system. Their perspective first recognizes the evidence in favor of hemispheric differences in the brain that appear to be related to emotional processing. The right hemisphere is apparently well suited for tasks of information integration that require "holistic" analysis typical of that involved in emotional experience (Safer & Leventhal, 1977). The left hemisphere, in contrast, has been described as "nonemotional" and appears to be better equipped for analytical skill and sequential information processing that is traditionally associated with more rational thought (Schwartz, Davidson, & Maer, 1975).

On acknowledging the principle of hemispheric specialization, Tucker and Williamson advanced the notion that there are particular neural systems responsible for regulating hemispheric functions. These neural systems are a higher order reflection of two separate neural pathways located in the spinal cord that were described by Pribram and McGuinness (1975). One of these pathways is characterized by an increase in the firing of neurons in response to stimulation. The second pathway is characterized by the opposite tendency; the firing of neurons decreases with repetitive input. Tucker and Williamson then elaborated on the higher order systems (the activation system and the arousal system) that they believed are extensive elaborations on these basic spinal cord responses. These systems were initially described by Pribram and McGuinness (1975).

Consistent with the general cognitive theories of emotion (see Lazarus, 1984), Tucker (1986) argued that emotional experiences are directly related to the brain's function in modulating stimulus input. The activation and arousal systems are, in this view, the primary regulating systems (see Lindsey, 1990) that are directly related to emotional experience. Tucker (1986) noted that the activation system is important in "establishing internal control in vigilance and avoidance behavior" (p. 293). This system acts to inhibit the flow of external information in order to help focus attention and restrict motor behavior. The activation system is associated with activity in the left brain hemisphere and is linked to the production of the neurochemical dopamine. Activity in the activation system is associated with withdrawal from the immediate environment and a tendency toward low levels of emotional responding to surrounding stimuli.

In contrast to the activation system, the arousal system is oriented to the external environment and directs attention to novel stimuli. This system directs attention toward a large array of stimulus inputs and allows for a more global or holistic assessment of the environment. Arousal system activity is associated with the right brain hemisphere and is linked to the production of the neurochemical norepinephrine. Activity in this system promotes intense emotional reactions to surrounding stimuli.

Although Tucker and Williamson held that the activation and arousal systems work in concert to produce behavior, they also noted that individuals differ according to the particular configuration of the two systems such that a bias toward one system or the other may typically be observed. Individuals with a bias toward activity in the activation system may tend toward blunted emotional responses, whereas individuals with a bias toward the arousal system may tend to experience more intense emotional reactions to environmental stimuli. The notion of a characteristic bias toward one of the two systems was seen by Tucker and Williamson as a major factor in one's behavioral tendencies across a wide variety of life situations. For example, regarding a bias toward the arousal system, these authors noted:

> The external control produced by a disproportionate influence of arousal is reflected in the hysteric's tendency to become caught up in novel situations, impulsively forming intense relationships and making radical changes in living circumstances. Arousal is sufficient to produce, but not maintain, the hysteric's infatuation with novel persons or situations, leading to short-lived, superficial relationships and repeated adaptive failures (Shapiro, 1965). Although it seems unlikely that the characteristics of one neurotransmitter system can be explanatory for a personality prototype, there are interesting parallels between the external control facilitated by the enabling effect of NE [norepinephrine] pathways (Bloom, 1979) and the external control required by the self-regulatory style of the extravert or hysteric. Lacking the internal control of activation, the person operates with an incomplete set of adaptive cybernetics and can only self-regulate through being aroused by the emotional stimulation of the current environmental context. (Tucker & Williamson, 1984, p. 208)

If, as Tucker and Williamson believed, the activation-arousal system is related to attentional processes and emotional responses and that there are hard-wired differences in the configuration of this system such that individuals display a characteristic bias toward one or the other systems, then it seems reasonable to inquire about the potential utility of this theoretical approach to the domain of research on responses to media horror, fright, suspense, and so on. In the following section then, I report on a series of studies that attempt to relate the activation-arousal framework to research questions about emotional responses to media horror.

COPING WITH MEDIA HORROR: PREFERENCES AND EMOTIONAL RESPONSES

One implication of the activation-arousal view is that the characteristic bias toward either of the two systems may be reflected in measures of individual differences that have already been established for other purposes. For example, Lindsey (1990) noted that Larson's measure of individual differences in affect intensity (AIM; Larson, Diener, & Emmons, 1986) may indirectly assess bias toward either activation or arousal system activity. Presumably, individuals who are high in affect intensity (i.e., tending to experience intense affect across a variety of situations and emotions) are those who are biased toward arousal system activity. Likewise, individuals who are low in affect intensity carry the bias toward the activation system.

Along these same lines, Miller developed a measure (Miller Behavioral Style Scale, MBSS) that is designed to assess individual differences in coping styles during the experience of stressful events. Miller and Mangan (1983) noted that this measure "distinguishes those who prefer to distract themselves from those who prefer to monitor for information under threat of electric shock, during exposure to cold-pressor pain, and during performance of a stressful cognitive task" (pp. 224-25). According to Miller, the research on the MBSS clearly shows support for the fact that "monitors" prefer high levels of information in the face of a stressful event. "Blunters," in contrast, prefer low amounts of information and choose to engage in distraction in the face of stress. Successful employment of this blunting strategy will lead to "blunted" or diminished levels of emotional responding.

Sparks and Spirek (1988) argued that there are two major reasons for drawing a parallel between the MBSS and the activation-arousal system as outlined by Tucker and Williamson. First, the information-processing modes that characterize activity in the activation and arousal systems appear to be very similar to the modes that are associated with the monitoring and blunting coping styles. Monitoring the environment for information under stress seems to be quite consistent with the activity of the arousal system, which orients to novel input and has an external attentional focus. The activation system's internal attentional focus is similarly consistent with blunting behavior, which strives to reduce external inputs and attempts to distract attention away from information about the stressor.

Second, the emotional intensity associated with an arousal system bias seems to be consistent with the heightened emotional reactions that are more likely to characterize the "monitoring" coping style. In contrast, the reduced emotional intensity associated with the activation system bias is very consistent with the blunted emotional responding of individuals who favor coping strategies that "blunt" external information.

Following this logic, if individual coping styles as measured by the MBSS could be shown to be related to behavior with respect to frightening media, then some initial foundation would exist for discussing such behavior in the context of behavioral dispositions (e.g., the activation and arousal systems). The studies reviewed in the following were designed according to this purpose. After reviewing these investigations, some assessment of the theoretical implications, caveats, and future directions of this line of research are discussed.

Preferences for Stressful Media

In an initial exploration of the utility of the MBSS for predicting behavior in the media domain, Sparks and Spirek (1988) were able to take advantage of a spontaneous technological disaster—the explosion of the space shuttle *Challenger*. In addition to the spectacular video footage of the rocket exploding in flight, subsequent news reports focused very heavily on the negative emotional impact of this event on school children and the family members of the seven astronauts who were killed (see Sparks, 1987, for a discussion of the impact of this event on children's emotional reactions). There was considerable attention devoted by the media to ways in which the nation could cope effectively with this tragic event.

Of course, the MBSS purports to assess the preferred way in which individuals attempt to cope with stressful events. Reasoning that the shuttle explosion and the news reports that followed would count as a stressful event for many people, Sparks and Spirek proposed that scores on the MBSS would be related to the ways in which people reported that they managed their own exposure to the media coverage of this event. In a survey of 81 respondents, three specific statements were presented regarding one's media preferences on exposure to news coverage of the shuttle explosion. For each statement, respondents indicated on 11-point scales the extent to which the statement accurately represented their own disposition toward the news coverage. The statements were:

1. Immediately after I learned about the shuttle explosion, I wanted to see the videotape replays of the astronauts' family members as they watched the launch sequence.

2. Immediately after I learned about the shuttle explosion, I wanted to see the astronauts' family members talking about their own reactions to the incident.
3. During the reporting of the shuttle explosion, I wanted to hear as much information as possible about the reactions of school children around the country who had watched the explosion live on television.

Each of these three statements express a desire for more information about the shuttle explosion and the events following the explosion and, consequently, represent strategies that would be quite consistent with monitoring rather than blunting. Sparks and Spirek expected that monitors would be more likely to endorse the statements as true for themselves than would blunters (scores on the MBSS were gathered 2 weeks following the administration of the statements about the shuttle explosion and were collected under the guise of a completely unrelated investigation). Although there was no difference between monitors and blunters in the tendency to endorse the third statement, significant differences did emerge on the first two statements that were consistent with expectation. Monitors were significantly more likely to endorse each of these statements than were blunters (t tests produced significance levels of $p < .03$ on the first statement and $p < .06$ on the second statement).

The extent to which these findings can be generalized to predict preferences for exposure to horror films is still very much an open question. The extensive news coverage of the shuttle explosion created an atmosphere that was nearly impossible for an individual to avoid. Thus, one might argue that the stressful nature of this event was felt, to a certain extent, by nearly everyone and would tend to elicit various coping behaviors that could be classified as either monitoring or blunting and would directly involve the desire to either seek or avoid additional media coverage. The same may not be the case with respect to preferences for horror films. That is, the decision to either expose oneself to a horror film or to avoid such exposure is not nearly as likely to be a function of any stress that the horror film has caused prior to exposure. Nevertheless, in cases where a film receives very wide media exposure through news stories and/or advertising (e.g., the publicity given to *Silence of the Lambs* in *Newsweek;* Plagens, Miller, Foote, & Yoffer, 1991), it might be the case that monitors would be more likely to attend the movie in order to seek more information that might help them reduce any tension created by the news coverage or media promotions. This, of course, is a highly speculative analysis and must await future testing before it gains any credibility. However, this analysis is somewhat reminiscent of past literature that suggested that apprehensive people may seek exposure to media that promises to relieve their apprehension (Wakshlag, Vial, & Tamborini, 1983). In terms of the view posited in this chapter, perhaps the respondents in Wakshlag et al. tended toward monitoring rather than blunting. Because the monitoring coping style may be slightly more prevalent in the general population, this possibility does not seem unreasonable.

Reactions to Media Horror

In addition to the possible links between the activation-arousal system and preferences for exposure to stressful media, there is additional evidence to suggest that this theoretical scheme may be useful in predicting and explaining emotional reactions that are experienced during exposure to media horror or suspense. In three separate investigations, evidence has emerged to support the notion that emotional reactions to media horror may be partially attributed to an interaction between one's coping style (monitor vs. blunter) and the level of information that one possesses prior to viewing the stimulus. If differences in coping style preferences are a reflection of biases toward either the activation or arousal system, then evidence that connects these preferences to emotional responses to horror is suggestive of a link between these responses and activity in the activation-arousal system.

Background Literature on Effects of Forewarning on Emotional Reactions to Horror

The emotional effects of providing prior information about a stressful event have been studied rather extensively (see Miller, 1980, 1981, for reviews of this literature). With respect to horror films, however, the literature in this area is much more limited. In an initial study that examined the effects of forewarning on emotional responses to horror, Cantor, Ziemke, and Sparks (1984) outlined two competing hypotheses that were subjected to experimental test. First, the "forewarned is forearmed" hypothesis suggested that respondents who had more information about an upcoming horror film would be less vulnerable to the intense negative emotions that such a film might induce during viewing (i.e., fear, upset, anxiety, etc.). According to this view, prior information would serve to prepare the viewer for upcoming horror. Coping strategies could be activated prior to viewing and made ready for implementation. This state of readiness could cause the viewer to feel more prepared to meet whatever horror came along and thus would have a calming effect. In support of this view, Leventhal, Brown, Shacham, and Engquist (1979) reported the results of an experiment in which participants were provided with information about either the distinctive features or sensory properties of upcoming cold pressor distress. These participants suffered less distress during exposure to the cold pressor stimulus than participants who had been told about their likely emotional and arousal responses to the stimulus.

A second view tested in the experiment by Cantor et al. (1984) was that forewarning viewers about an upcoming horror film would trigger anticipatory thoughts about the movie. Consistent with research by Zillmann (1971) and by Zillmann, Mody, and Cantor (1974), it was thought that this anticipatory thinking could produce arousal that would subsequently intensify any emotional reaction produced by the threatening stimulus. The results of the experiment supported this second position. Viewers who had received an explicit forewarning of upcoming events in a television movie about a vampire experienced greater emotional reactions during the movie than viewers who received no forewarning at all.

The Importance of Coping Style in Predicting Emotional Reactions to Horror Under Different Levels of Forewarning

Miller, Brody, and Summerton (1988) argued for the plausibility of expecting an interaction between coping style and level of available information prior to an upcoming stressful event:

> High monitors and low blunters may fare better with more voluminous information and greater attention to psychosocial factors, as this is consistent with their coping-style preferences. In contrast, low monitors and high blunters may fare better without information and reassurance, as this is consistent with their coping style preferences. (p. 143)

This argument translates to the horror film context very readily. Monitors should be expected to suffer less intense emotional reactions to horror under conditions of high prior information. That is, monitors should find it much more pleasant to view a horror film when they have a high level of information about the film beforehand. In contrast, blunters should be expected to indicate exactly the opposite tendency. They should be most comfortable when conditions are consistent with their coping style preference of low levels of information about the upcoming stressful film. Whereas monitors should experience less intense emotional reactions when they have high levels of information prior to the film, blunters should experience more intense emotional reactions in this condition and show a decreased response under conditions of low information.

Study 1. The first study to reveal evidence in favor of the foregoing logic was reported by Sparks and Spirek (1988). In this study, 23 monitors and 21 blunters viewed a short segment (11 minutes and 30 seconds) from the movie *Nightmare on Elm Street*. All participants in this study read a short paragraph prior to their viewing. This paragraph communicated very little information about the upcoming segment but only "provided some minimum context that was required in order to understand the depicted events" (p. 203). According to the earlier analysis, this viewing condition was one of low forewarning and should have been less pleasant for monitors than for blunters. Consequently, it should have been expected that monitors would find the film segment more unpleasant and would experience more intense emotional reactions than would blunters. Although no evidence emerged in favor of this hypothesis on self-report measures of emotional reactions taken immediately after viewing, there was supporting evidence on a measure of skin conductance taken continuously during the movie segment. Monitors experienced an average increase of about 16% in skin conductance by the end of the film segment, whereas blunters only experienced an average increase of about 4.5%. This difference was statistically significant.

Sparks and Spirek speculated that the self-report responses taken immediately after viewing could have been affected by experiences of profound relief at the realization that the film was over. This relief experience could have neutralized actual differences between emotion that may have been experienced during the film by monitors and blunters. Skin conductance responses, in contrast, were monitored during the viewing and may have been a better reflection of emotional responses as they occurred. Although the results of this study were suggestive, the findings remain of limited value because level of forewarning was not manipulated. This limitation gave rise to two subsequent investigations in which monitors and blunters viewed a horror film under conditions of either low or high forewarning.

Study 2. Consistent with this logic, Sparks (1989) designed an experiment to test the interaction between forewarning and preferred coping style on emotional reactions to a frightening movie. Monitors (n = 34) and blunters (n = 41) were randomly assigned to either a low or high forewarning condition prior to viewing a 20-minute film clip from the the movie *When A Stranger Calls*. Approximately equal numbers of males and females were included in each of the coping style groups and in each of the levels of forewarning. In the low forewarning condition, participants heard a four-sentence introduction to the film clip that provided very little information. In the high forewarning condition, participants heard a very detailed description of the events in the film that they were about to see. This description included 20 sentences of text. It was predicted that monitors would find the high forewarning condition to be preferred over the low forewarning condition. Consequently, they were expected to show increased negative emotional responses in the low forewarning condition. In contrast, blunters were expected to show the opposite tendency—manifesting greater negative emotional responses under conditions of high forewarning.

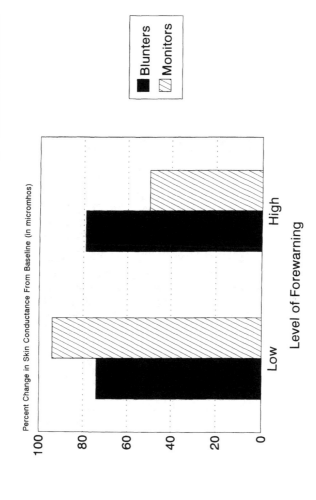

Fig. 8.1. Skin conductance responses for monitors and blunters.

Emotional responding was assessed in three different ways. First, participants responded to a series of self-report items immediately after the film was over. These items included the degree of fright, anxiety, and upset that had been experienced during the movie. An index of negative emotion was constructed from these three items and two others to serve as a measure of negative emotion experienced during the film (Cronbach's α = .85). A second measure of emotional responding to the movie consisted of a proportion of negative emotional thoughts divided by the total number of thoughts that participants listed as ones that they had while viewing the movie. Finally, skin conductance was used to assess physiological activity during the film. Average skin conductance levels for five different 15-second intervals were computed for each participant.

The results of this experiment revealed that there was evidence in favor of the predicted interaction between coping style and level of forewarning on each of the three measures of emotional response. Monitors were significantly more likely to report negative emotional reactions, list a greater proportion of negative thoughts, and experience increased skin conductance when they watched the film in the low forewarning condition. In contrast, blunters were more likely to manifest emotional reactions on each of these three measures when they watched the film in the high forewarning condition—although the differences in each case failed to meet conventional significance levels. Figure 8.1 displays the skin conductance reactions for monitors and blunters during a highly suspenseful chase sequence during the film clip. The interaction between preferred coping style and level of forewarning is quite apparent. Encouraged by these results, a third study was undertaken in an attempt to replicate these findings and possibly extend them to a different type of forewarning.

Study 3. Sparks and Ogles (1990) reported the results of another experiment that tested the interaction between level of forewarning and preferred coping style. The essential theoretical logic was identical to that employed in the earlier studies. However, in this study, the manipulation of forewarning differed according to the level of *emotional* information. Reasoning that movie ads often feature highly emotional descriptions that suggest intense emotional viewing experiences, Sparks and Ogles raised the following question: Will monitors prefer forewarnings that contain both emotional information and plot information over forewarnings that contain plot information alone?

In order to answer this question, 41 monitors and 31 blunters were randomly assigned to either the emotional or the nonemotional forewarning condition prior to viewing a 15-minute segment from the film *When A Stranger Calls*. The segment used in this study was different from the one used in Study 2. The text of the two forewarnings was identical except for the addition of emotional adjectives at critical points in the description. For example, a "killer" in the low emotional forewarning was described as a "deranged, psychopathic killer" in the high emotional version. The low emotional forewarning version described a "voice," whereas the high emotional forewarning described a "spine-tingling" voice. In the high emotional forewarning, there were 15 emotional additions to the description offered in the low emotional forewarning.

Emotional responses were assessed with a similar index of self-reported negative emotion and with skin conductance reactions during the movie. The only effect to emerge on the self-reports of emotion was that blunters expressed significantly less desire to see more of the movie if they were in the high emotional forewarning condition. On the measure of skin conductance, an interaction similar to the one reported in Study 2 emerged clearly. Monitors were significantly more aroused in the high emotional forewarning condition. Blunters showed the opposite tendency—experiencing more arousal in the low emotional forewarning condition. Taken together, these results provide additional evidence for the fact that preferred coping style mediates emotional reactions to horror under different levels of forewarning.

Limitations of the Research on Coping Styles

The conclusions drawn from these studies involving coping style should be tempered with the recognition of several key limitations. First, preference in coping style is not a manipulated variable; rather it constitutes an assigned variable based on differences that exist prior to participation in these laboratory studies. Consequently, it is not possible to unequivocally attribute the findings in these studies to the role of preferred coping style. There may be some other unmeasured variable that is related to both coping style and the emotional reactions that are observed in response to the horrific films. In favor of the causal role of coping style is the fact that the various findings were predicted by prior theoretical analysis and no likely third variable explanation for these results seems apparent. Nevertheless, the possibility of a plausible third variable explanation always exists. Because of this possibility, the findings reported above must be viewed as somewhat tentative.

A second limitation of this research concerns the extent to which the results can be taken as evidence in favor of the activation-arousal framework. The theoretical links between Miller's work on monitors and blunters and the neurophysiological systems of activation and arousal are based only on argument—not on any prior data. Moreover, neither Miller or Tucker and Williamson have ever connected these respective literatures. Thus, the entire nature of the theoretical link between the activation-arousal system and monitoring/blunting must be viewed cautiously. Even more important is the fact that monitoring and blunting tendencies might arise because of particular patterns of socialization and past experience. This possibility might be suggested in the finding that there is a greater tendency in the general population toward monitoring. Monitoring strategies may be more socially acceptable and reinforced in various ways during one's life (L. Trachtman, personal communication, 1991). This explanation for differences in preferred coping style would stand in contrast to one that argued that these differences were the product of hard-wired behavioral dispositions.

Ultimately, researchers working in the activation-arousal framework need to specify concrete links between the underlying neurophysiological systems and observable behaviors that can be observed and measured systematically. Unless these links can be established, the usefulness of the activation-arousal framework for studying emotional reactions to horror will remain limited.

SUMMARY AND CONCLUSIONS

This chapter has argued in favor of a dispositional view of emotion by pointing out that emotional experience is anchored in "hard-wired" mechanisms. Evidence for individual differences in physiological responding and in early temperament were offered as support for the dispositional view. The activation-arousal framework is one example of a dispositional view of emotion that could have potential for studies on reactions to media horror. Miller's work on preferred coping style was linked to the activation-arousal view and several studies indicate the utility of the coping style concept for understanding emotional responses to horror.

Despite the evidence presented, the major thrust of this chapter must be framed in "exploratory" terms. Although there is abundant evidence in favor of the dispositional view of emotional experience, the application of the activation-arousal view to the study of reactions to media horror has only begun. The recent evidence that suggests a relationship between preferred coping style and emotional responses to horror provides some sense of the kind of heuristic value such an approach may offer. Future research should concentrate on establishing more concrete links between the activation-arousal systems and specific emotional and behavioral responses. Such a move is critical if the activation-arousal view is to show any ultimate promise as a viable perspective on emotional responses to media horror.

REFERENCES

Andreassi, J. L. (1989). *Psychophysiology: Human behavior & physiological response* (2nd ed.). Hillsdale, NJ: Lawrence Erlbaum Associates.

Baggett, A. T. (1967). The effect of early loss of father upon the personality of boys and girls in late adolescents. *Dissertation Abstracts, 28*(1-b), 356-357.

Bloom, F. E. (1979). Chemical integrative processes in the central nervous system. In F. O. Schmitt & F. G. Worden (Eds.), *The neurosciences: Fourth study program* (pp. 51-58). Cambridge, MA: MIT Press.

Bowlby, J. (1969). *Attachment and loss. Vol. 1: Attachment.* New York: Basic Books.

Bowlby, J. (1973). *Attachment and loss. Vol. 2: Separation, anxiety and anger.* London: Hogarth.

Buck, R. (1984). *The communication of emotion.* New York: Guilford.

Burgoon, J. K., & Le Poire, B. A. (1992). A reply from the heart: Who are Sparks and Greene and why are they saying all these horrible things? *Human Communication Research, 18,* 472-482.

Buss, A. H. (1989). Personality as traits. *American Psychologist, 44,* 1378-1388.

Buss, D. M. (1990). Toward a biologically informed psychology of personality. *Journal of Personality, 58,* 1-16.

Cacioppo, J. T., Petty, R. E., & Tassinary, L. G. (1989). Social psychophysiology: A new look. In L. Berkowitz (Ed.), *Advances in experimental social psychology* (Vol. 22, pp. 39-91). San Diego, CA: Academic Press.

Cantor, J., Ziemke, D., & Sparks, G. G. (1984). Effect of forewarning on emotional responses to a horror film. *Journal of Broadcasting, 28,* 21-31.

Ekman, P., Friesen, W. V., & Ancoli, S. (1980). Facial signs of emotional experience. *Journal of Personality and Social Psychology, 39,* 1125-1134.

Ekman, P., Levenson, R. W., & Friesen, W. V. (1983). Autonomic nervous system activity distinguishing among emotions. *Science, 221,* 1208-1210.

Eysenck, H. J. (1970). A dimensional system of psychodiagnostics. In A. R. Mahrer (Ed.), *New approaches to personality classification* (pp. 169-207). New York: Columbia University Press.

Field, T. M., Woodson, R., Greenberg, R., & Cohen, D. (1982). Discrimination and imitation of facial expression by neonates. *Science, 218,* 179-181.

Fox, N. A. (1989). Psychophysiological correlates of emotional reactivity during the first year of life. *Developmental Psychology, 25,* 364-372.

Furedy, J. J. (1987). Specific versus placebo effects in biofeedback training: A critical lay perspective. *Biofeedback & Self-Regulation, 12,* 169-184.

Gainotti, G. (1989). Features of emotional behavior relevant to neurobiology and theories of emotions. In G. Gainotti & C. Caltagirone (Eds.), *Emotions and the dual brain* (pp. 9-27). Berlin: Springer-Verlag.

Greene, J. O., & Sparks, G. G. (1992). Intellectual scrutiny as an alternative to replies from the heart: Toward clarifying the nature of arousal and its relation to nonverbal behavior. *Human Communication Research, 18,* 483-488.

Gunnar, M. R., Mangelsdorf, S., Larson, M., & Hertsgaard, L. (1989). Attachment, temperament, and adrenocortical activity in infancy: A study of psychoendocrine regulation. *Developmental Psychology, 25,* 355-363.

Heath, R. G. (1986). The neural substrate for emotion. In R. Plutchik & H. Kellerman (Eds.), *Emotion: Theory, research, and experience* (pp. 3-35). Orlando, FL: Academic Press.

Izard, C. E. (1971). *The face of emotion.* New York: Appleton-Century-Crofts.

Izard, C. E. (1977). *Human emotions.* New York: Plenum.

Izard, C. E. (1991). *The psychology of emotions.* New York: Plenum.

James, W. (1890). *The principles of psychology* (Vol. 2). New York: Dover.

Kagan, J. (1989). Temperamental contributions to social behavior. *American Psychologist, 44,* 668-674.

Kagan, J., Reznick, J. S., Clarke, C., Snidman, N., & Garcia-Coll, C. (1984). Behavioral inhibition to the unfamiliar. *Child Development, 55,* 2212-2225.

Kagan, J., Reznick, J. S., & Snidman, N. (1987). The physiology and psychology of behavioral inhibition. *Child Development, 58,* 1459-1473.

Kagan, J., Reznick, J. S., & Snidman, N. (1988). Biological bases of childhood shyness. *Science, 240,* 167-171.

Kagan, J., Reznick, J. S., Snidman, N., Gibbons, J., & Johnson, M. O. (1988). Childhood derivatives of inhibition and lack of inhibition to the unfamiliar. *Child Development, 59,* 1580-1589.

Lacey, J. I., Bateman, D. E., & Van Lehn, R. (1953). Autonomic response specificity: An experimental study. *Psychosomatic Medicine, 15*, 8-21.

Larson, R. J., Diener, E., & Emmons, R. A. (1986). Affect intensity and reactions to daily life events. *Journal of Personality and Social Psychology, 51*, 803-814.

Lazarus, R. S. (1984). On the primacy of cognition. *American Psychologist, 39*, 124-129.

Leventhal, H., Brown, D., Shacham, S., & Engquist, G. (1979). Effects of preparatory information about sensations, threat of pain and attention in cold pressor distress. *Journal of Personality and Social Psychology, 37*, 688-714.

Lindsey, E. (1990). *Facilitative effects of others' nonverbal expressions of enjoyment.* Unpublished manuscript, Purdue University.

Lindsley, D. B. (1951). Emotion. In S. S. Stevens (Ed.), *Handbook of experimental psychology* (pp. 473-516). New York: Wiley.

Malmo, R. B., & Shagass, C. (1949). Physiologic study symptom mechanisms in psychiatric patients under stress. *Psychosomatic Medicine, 11*, 25-29.

Mandler, G. (1984). *Mind and body.* New York: Norton.

Miller, S. M. (1980). When is a little information a dangerous thing?: Coping with stressful life-events by monitoring vs. blunting. In S. Levine & H. Ursin (Eds.), *Coping and health* (pp. 145-169). New York: Plenum.

Miller, S. M. (1981). Predictability and human stress: Towards a clarification of evidence and theory. In L. Berkowitz (Ed.), *Advances in experimental social psychology* (Vol. 14, pp. 204-256). New York: Academic Press.

Miller, S. M., Brody, D. S., & Summerton, J. (1988). Styles of coping with threat: Implications for health. *Journal of Personal and Social Psychology, 54*, 142-148.

Miller, S. M., & Mangan, C. E. (1983). Interacting effects of information and coping style in adapting to gynecologic stress: Should the doctor tell all? *Journal of Personality and Social Psychology, 45*, 223-236.

Neiss, R. (1988). Reconceptualizing arousal: Psychobiological states in motor performance. *Psychological Bulletin, 103*, 345-366.

Neiss, R. (1990). Ending arousal's reign of error: A reply to Anderson. *Psychological Bulletin, 107*, 101-105.

Plagens, P., Miller, M., Foote, D., & Yoffe, E. (1991, April 1). Violence in our culture. *Newsweek*, pp. 46-52.

Pribram, K. H., & McGuinness, D. (1975). Arousal, activation, and effort in the control of attention. *Psychological Review, 82*, 116-149.

Rothbart, M. K., & Derryberry, D. (1981). Development of individual differences in temperament. In M. E. Lamb & A. L. Brown (Eds.), *Advances in developmental psychology* (Vol. 1, pp. 37-86). Hillsdale, NJ: Lawrence Erlbaum Associates.

Safer, M. A., & Leventhal, H. (1977). Ear differences in evaluating emotional tone of voice and verbal content. *Journal of Experimental Psychology: Human Perception and Performance, 3*, 75-82.

Schnore, M. M. (1959). Individual patterns of physiological activity as a function of task differences and degree of arousal. *Journal of Experimental Psychology, 58*, 117-128.

Schwartz, G. E., Davidson, R. J., & Maer, F. (1975). Right hemisphere lateralization for emotion in the human brain: Interactions with cognition. *Science, 190*, 286-288.

Shapiro, D. (1965). *Neurotic styles.* New York: Basic Books.

Sparks, G. G. (1987, February). Children and the space shuttle disaster. *Education Digest*, pp. 55-57.

Sparks, G. G. (1989). Understanding emotional reactions to a suspenseful movie: The interaction between forewarning and preferred coping style. *Communication Monographs, 56*, 325-340.

Sparks, G. G., & Greene, J. O. (1992). On the validity of nonverbal indicators as measures of physiological arousal: A response to Burgoon, Kelley, Newton, and Keeley-Dyreson. *Human Communication Research, 18*, 445-471.

Sparks, G. G., & Ogles, R. M. (1990, November). *The role of preferred coping style and emotional forewarning in predicting emotional reactions to a suspenseful film.* Paper presented at the annual meeting of the Speech Communication Association, Chicago.

Sparks, G. G., & Spirek, M. M. (1988). Individual differences in coping with stressful mass media: An activation-arousal view. *Human Communication Research, 15*, 195-216.

Sternbach, R. A. (1966). *Principles of psychophysiology.* New York: Academic Press.

Strongman, K. T. (1987). *The psychology of emotion.* Chichester, UK: Wiley.

Thompson, J. G. (1988). *The psychobiology of emotions.* New York: Plenum.

Tucker, D. M. (1986). Neural control of emotional communication. In P. D. Blanck, R. Buck, & R. Rosenthal (Eds.), *Nonverbal communication in the clinical context* (pp. 258-307). University Park: The Pennsylvania State University Press.

Tucker, D. M., & Williamson, P. A. (1984). Asymmetric neural control systems in human self-regulation. *Psychological Review, 91,* 185-215.

Wakshlag, J., Vial, V., & Tamborini, R. (1983). Selecting crime drama and apprehension about crime. *Human Communication Research, 10,* 227-242.

Yarrow, L. J., & Goodwin, M. S. (1973). The immediate impact of separation: Reactions of infants to a change in mother figures. In L. J. Stone, H. T. Smither, & L. B. Murphy (Eds.), *The competent infant* (pp. 1032-1040). New York: Basic Books.

Zillmann, D. (1971). Excitation transfer in communication-mediated aggressive behavior. *Journal of Experimental Social Psychology, 7,* 419-434.

Zillmann, D., Mody, B., & Cantor, J. (1974). Empathic perception of emotional displays in films as a function of hedonic and excitatory state prior to exposure. *Journal of Research in Personality, 8,* 335-349.

Chapter 9

Sensation Seeking and the Taste for Vicarious Horror

Marvin Zuckerman
University of Delaware

> *And much of Madness and more of Sin,*
> *and Horror the soul of the plot.*
> —Poe, *The Conquerer Worm* (1843)

The taste for morbid, frightening, and horror-invoking stimuli is nothing new, only the media have changed. Spectators at gladiatorial contests or public executions did not consider their recreation abnormal or perverted. No Roman wrote articles asking why people enjoy watching humans being eaten by wild animals. The monster myths related around the open camp-fire and the Grand Guignol theater have been transformed by modern technology to the film and television media. The media improve their techniques to bring more graphic violence to the screen. Older horror films are almost detached compared to the modern genre with Technicolor gore and special effects to image dismemberment and torture. Life imitates art and the nightly local television news programs largely bring us real murders, assaults, fires, and accidents (or their aftermaths) with detailed accounts by bystanders and victims.

Analyses of the people who unashamedly enjoy these spectacles, and there are millions of them, range from the sociobiological to the purely sociological. Psychoanalysts invoke instinctual sadism, repressed aggressive tendencies, or fear mastery. Sociologists point to the deterioration of urban society and the real terrors in the streets of our cities. The people who produce the media and reap the profits shrug their shoulders and say, "That's show biz."

Once we accept the fact that the phenomena has always been with us and that it is not necessarily a sign of psychopathology in the individual or the culture, we can answer a more meaningful question: What are the sources of individual differences in interest in morbid events and spectacles in normal personality variations? Many of the same questions have been applied to interests in explicit portrayals of sexual events in the media and the sources of individual differences in the taste for pornography (Zuckerman, 1976). There are some interesting relationships between the two types of interests, as we will see.

SENSATION SEEKING

The definition of a construct must sometimes be changed in order to accommodate new findings and I have made some changes in the definition of sensation seeking since the development of the first Sensation Seeking Scale (SSS-Form II; Zuckerman, Kolin, Price, & Zoob, 1964) as an operational measure of individual differences in the "Optimal Level of Stimulation" (Hebb, 1955). The definition was made more specific in my (Zuckerman, 1979a) book in terms of the qualities of sensation and experience that were attractive to sensation seekers and their risk-taking propensities in pursuit of such experiences. Further specifications and additions have been made more recently (Zuckerman, 1994) in view of the research between 1979 and 1991. The current definition of the trait is: Sensation seeking is a trait defined by the seeking of varied, novel, complex, and intense sensations and experiences, and the willingness to take physical, social, legal, and financial risks for the sake of such experience.

Originally (Zuckerman et al., 1964), the SSS consisted only of a General scale encompassing many kinds of sensations and experiences, but later factor analyses (Zuckerman, 1971; Zuckerman, Eysenck, & Eysenck, 1978) established the four subscales that have been used in Forms IV and V of the SSS used in most of the subsequent research along with the General scale in Form IV, and a total score in Form V. These factors within sensation seeking have been generally confirmed in adults in factor analyses done by others, even those using translated scales (at last count the SSS has been translated in 14 languages other than English). A description of the four SSS subscales is as follows:

- Thrill and Adventure Seeking (TAS) consists of items indicating a desire to engage in certain kinds of risky sports or activities involving speed, defiance of gravity, and exploration of novel environments (e.g. scuba diving), even if one has never engaged in these activities.
- Experience Seeking (ES) involves the desire to seek experience through the mind and senses and through an unconventional lifestyle shared with unconventional persons.
- Disinhibition (Dis) represents both desire and actual activities, seeking pleasure through partying, sex, gambling,

and social drinking.   It reflects a social-hedonistic philosophy.

- Boredom Susceptibility (BS) indicates an aversion to boredom produced by sameness or routine whether in work or in personal relationships and a restlessness when experience is constant.

Form V of the SSS contains the same number of items for each of the four subscales and a total score based on the sum of the four scores.   Internal reliabilities are good for TAS and Dis, fair for ES, and only borderline for BS. Retest reliabilities are high for all scales. Hundreds of validity studies have shown the relevance of the trait in relation to risk taking in sports and vocations; social, sexual, and marital behavior and relationships; use and abuse of tobacco, alcohol, and a variety of illegal drugs, food preferences and eating habits; preferences in art, media forms, music, fantasy and humor; and psychopathology of particular kinds such as antisocial personality disorder, substance abuse, manic-depressive, and schizophrenic disorders (Zuckerman, 1979b, 1983, 1994).   Research on the biological correlates of sensation seeking (Zuckerman, 1984; Zuckerman, Buchsbaum, & Murphy, 1980) has ranged from genetic studies (Fulker, Eysenck, & Zuckerman, 1980) to biochemistry (Zuckerman, 1979a, 1983, 1984) and psychophysiology (Zuckerman, 1990). Tentative psychobiological models for the trait have been proposed (Zuckerman, 1979a, 1994).

GENERAL CURIOSITY ABOUT MORBID AND SEXUAL EVENTS

Zuckerman and Litle (1986) devised scales to measure Curiosity about Morbid Events (CAME) and Curiosity about Sexual Events (CASE). The CAME scale describes enjoyment of violence in films or television, including horror movies, interest in the violent details in news accounts of murders and other crimes, and a hypothetical interest in watching autopsies and operations or spectacles like bullfights or gladiatorial contests. Negatively scored items indicate an aversion to such stimuli or events. The CASE scale reflects attitudes toward pornography or any explicit portrayals of sex in literature, films, or witnessing live sexual events.

Internal reliabilities were high for both CAME (.82) and CASE (.88) scales. The two scales were significantly correlated for men ($r = .39$) and women ($r = .24$). Men scored significantly higher than women on both CAME ($t = 8.11$, $p < .0001$) and CASE ($t = 6.98$, $p < .0001$). Clearly, there are large differences between young male and female college students in their tastes for media portrayals of both morbid and sexual events. As has been generally found in many other studies, men also scored significantly higher than women on SSS Total, TAS, Dis, and BS scales with no difference on the ES scale.

With only one exception (BS vs. CAME in males), all of the SSS scales correlated significantly with the CAME scale for both sexes. The highest correlations were with Dis for men ($r = .50$) and the Total score for women ($r = .36$). Multiple regressions show that Dis and TAS alone accounted for most of the variance in the relationship between the SSS and CAME. Total, Dis, ES, and BS scales also correlated significantly with the CASE scale for both sexes, but TAS did not correlate with CASE in either sex. Dis had the highest correlation with CASE for both men and women and accounted for most of the variance in the multiple regression on CASE.

The results indicate both a generalized relationship between sensation seeking and an interest in both morbid and sexual events and a somewhat stronger relationship with Disinhibition. A generalized social inhibition may account for an aversion to such events and a generalized disinhibition may be related to an appetite for these kinds of vicarious experience. TAS was not correlated with curiosity about morbid events and it was not related at all to curiosity about sexual events. CAME events represent vicariously experienced physical threats and those who are afraid of physical harm in real life may be made anxious by portrayals of such threats. Viewing or reading about sexual events, however, might not elicit anxiety in those cautious about physical risk taking unless they portrayed violent sexual activity like rape.

ART AND PICTURE PREFERENCES

Tobacyk, Myers, and Bailey (1981) investigated art preferences in relation to sensation seeking. They found both structural and content factors among the paintings that correlated with sensation seeking. The structural correlate was a greater preference for abstract painting and the content one was a preference for paintings with aggressive content. High sensation seekers tended to prefer either abstract paintings or those portraying violence. Zuckerman, Ulrich, and McLaughlin (1993) related degrees of liking for nature paintings with sensation seeking and also found a greater liking for expressionist paintings among high sensation seekers. Although people were not prominent in these paintings, some of them were rated as high in tension because they portrayed violent nature scenes like storms. High sensation seekers liked the high-tension pictures more than the low sensation seekers, but there was no difference in preferences for the low-tension paintings.

Zaleski (1984) used pictures that had been rated for their emotionally arousing characteristics. Positively arousing pictures included scenes of celebration and "mild love making" (not explicit sexual acts); negatively arousing pictures contained morbid scenes of torture, hanging, and corpses. A nonarousing, neutral category of pictures was also used. Polish university students were asked to pick out the pictures they liked the most, ignoring their artistic qualities. The low sensation seekers preferred the positively arousing pictures the most and the negatively arousing ones the least; the high sensation seekers preferred both positively and negatively arousing pictures to nonarousing ones. There was also an influence of sex in interaction with high sensation seeking; high sensation seeking men actually preferred the negatively arousing pictures to the positively arousing ones. But for high sensation seekers of both sexes the arousal value of the pictures was more salient than the positivity or negativity of the content in their preferences. These findings are readily interpretable in terms of the earlier theory of sensation seeking as based on the optimal level of arousal (Zuckerman, 1974). According to this theory, sensation seekers' activities and preferences are based on their desire to increase arousal, even if negative feelings like fear or disgust are components of that arousal. This theory would explain why the tastes for both sexual and violent stimuli are positively correlated and sensation seeking correlates with both. Both kinds of stimulation are arousing compared to milder themes.

MEDIA PREFERENCES

Brown, Ruder, Ruder, & Young (1974) and Scheirman and Rowland (1985) found that sensation seeking was related to attendance of movies containing explicit sexual activity (X-rated) but not related to going to films with more general themes. The low sensation seekers preferred musicals, comedies, and nonexplicit dramas. Rowland, Fouts, and Heatherton (1989) found that high sensation seekers among college students tended to watch less television than lows, but the low sensation seekers tended to avoid programs with sexual, "offensive," or frightening material.

Schierman and Rowland (1985) observed the viewing behavior of subjects given a choice of segments from five movies including one with violent action (*48 Hours*), a horror movie (*Halloween*), a comedy, a romance, and a drama. The high sensation seekers tended to switch back and forth more between the different movies, perhaps reflecting their need for change and boredom susceptibility. The high sensation seekers did spend a relatively greater portion of their viewing time on the violent action movie, whereas the lows spent more time watching the nonviolent, nonerotic comedy. Interestingly, there was no difference in time spent watching *Halloween*. None of the groups spent much time watching this movie. However, this result does not negate the findings to be discussed next on specific tastes for the genre of horror movies, because the experiment offered a forced choice between types of movies and it is conceivable that high sensation seekers like both realistically violent movies and the horror ones. It is also possible that more of the high sensation seekers had already seen *Halloween* than the violent action movie and therefore chose the more novel one. Another factor is that the clips of the movies only showed the opening 20 minutes of each film. The violent action movie literally started out "with a bang," depicting four shootings, some female nudity, and much profanity in the 20-minute segment. Most horror movies start slowly before the mayhem commences.

HORROR FILMS

Zuckerman and Litle (1986) asked subjects how often they had "gone to the gory kind of horror movies like *Halloween* or *The Texas Chainsaw Massacre*" (p. 56). Another question asked how often they had gone to X-rated movies. Attendance for the two types of films correlated significantly for men ($r = .27$) but not for women ($r = .11$). Men reported significantly more attendance at both horror and sex films than women. The CAME and CASE scales both correlated significantly with attendance for both types of films among men. The correlations were more specific for women; CAME correlated with horror film attendance and CASE with sex film attendance. Interests in horror and sex films seem to be more closely related in men than in women.

The Total, TAS, and Dis scales correlated significantly with reported viewing of horror films and the BS scale also correlated with such viewing in women. The highest correlation of horror film attendance in both sexes was with the Dis scale, and the Dis scale accounted for the most variance in the multiple regressions. Viewing of sex films correlated significantly with SSS Total, TAS, Dis, and BS scores in men and with Total, ES, and Dis scores in women. The correlations between film attendance and SS scales tended to be lower than those between the SSS and the broader CAME and CASE scales.

A study by Edwards (1984; data reported in Tamborini & Stiff, 1987, and Tamborini, Stiff, & Zillmann, 1987) showed interest in horror films correlated significantly with all of the SSS scales, with the Dis scale having the strongest relationship ($r = .54$). Actual attendance at horror films correlated significantly with Dis and TAS scales in both men and women, although as in the Zuckerman and Litle study, the correlations were lower for the specific variable of horror film attendance than for the more generalized measure of interest.

Tamborini and Stiff (1987) studied subjects from an audience that had just left a movie theater after seeing the film *Halloween II*. This would be a rather restricted sample because it would not include many of those who have no interest in horror films of this type. Subjects were asked why they liked or disliked horror films in general and their reaction to this particular film was assessed. They were also given the SSS. Using a LISREL analysis they attempted to test a model for the path relationships between gender, age, frequency of horror film attendance, sensation seeking, like for fright and preferences for destruction, humor, and a "just end" (monster permanently destroyed, hero saved) in the film. Sensation seeking was related to gender and age, as expected, and showed a significant correlation with liking for fright, but it was not significantly correlated with liking for destructiveness, humor, or just end in horror films; frequency of attendance at horror films; or specific liking of the film *Halloween II*. The path model showed that age and gender influenced frequency of horror movie attendance through their influence on sensation seeking and relative preference for destruction and just endings; males liked horror films because of the destructiveness, whereas females liked them more on the basis of the presence of a just ending. Along with these two reasons for liking the films, sensation seeking predicted the liking for fright and excitement in horror films and the latter variable most directly predicted frequency of attendance of horror movies. Sensation seeking was not a particularly strong predictor of a like for fright compared to the preferences for destruction and just endings in horror movies. However given the correlation between sensation seeking and interest in horror found in other studies from unselected populations, it was possible that the selective nature of this sample reduced the range of sensation seeking. The mean scores of the *Halloween II* audience subjects were about those that would be expected in a normal male population of their age, but half of their sample was female, so that the mean scores of the total group, used in the analyses, may have been a bit higher than normal.

Tamborini et al. (1987) used undergraduate volunteers for a study designed to look more specifically at the influences of gender in interaction with several personality traits, including sensation seeking, in predicting preferences for graphic horror in films. Subscales of the SSS, the Bem (1974) Androgeny scale, and the Christie and Geis (1970) Machiavellianism (Mach V) scale were used as predictors, along with film viewing history variables of exposure and enjoyment of films in different categories. Subjects were given descriptions of 13 films containing varying degrees of graphic violence and asked to rank them in terms of which ones they would like to see. Six of the films had two versions, one in which the victim was a male and the other in which the victim was female. Finally, the subjects viewed a portion of one of the films in which the victim of an assault was female and asked how much they disliked or liked that film.

Across all conditions, percentages of past film exposures to horror correlated positively and a history of exposure to light entertainment correlated negatively with preferences for graphic horror films in the experiment. Past enjoyment of violent drama films also predicted graphic horror preferences for both men and women in the experiment, but for men the correlation was positive and for women it was negative. Enjoyment of pornography in films predicted preference for graphic horror in films for men but not in women. As in other studies, there was more generalization from sex to violence in film preferences for men than in those for women.

Deceit, a subscale of the Mach scale, correlated with preference for graphic horror in both men and women. Dis, ES, and BS scales from the SSS predicted horror film preference in the total group and in men, but only Dis correlated with horror film preference in women. The authors minimized the prediction of the SSS Dis because its beta weight in the multiple R was not significant; only Deceit and past exposure to horror films contributed significantly to the multiple regression. However, the personality and previous exposure variables should not have been included in the same regression analysis. It is not surprising that a history of viewing violent films is related to current preferences for graphic horror. People tend to be consistent in their preferences and the heavy contribution of this variable to the prediction equation is expected. Sensation seeking may have related to graphic violence through its influence on the past exposure to horror.

An analysis of the film choices on which there were alternate male and female victim versions showed some interesting gender contrasts. For male subjects there was a positive correlation between the SSS BS scale and preference for graphic horror with both male and female victims, but for female subjects the BS scale correlated positively with preference for graphic violence when the victim was male and negatively when the victim was female. Among males, Dis and enjoyment of pornography both correlated with preference for graphic horror when the victim was female, but neither correlated with graphic horror when the victim was male. The correlation between enjoyment of pornography and graphic horror preference was quite high ($r = .73$), and together with the BS and Deceit scales it accounted for most of the variance in graphic violence with female victims.

PSYCHOPHYSIOLOGY AND THE OPTIMAL LEVEL OF AROUSAL

Sensation seeking theory was originally founded on an optimal level of arousal theory (Zuckerman, 1969). The theory suggested that high and low sensation seekers differed in optimal levels of stimulation and arousal. High sensation seekers felt and functioned best at higher levels of stimulation and arousal than low sensation seekers, other things being equal. The arousal referred to was cortical arousal. However, subsequent research suggested that although high sensation seekers had high optimal levels of stimulation (or need for variety, novelty, and intensity), cortical arousal was not the site of this need for stimulation. Instead the findings suggested that arousal of subcortical limbic systems (the catecholaminergic ones) related to positive arousal was the source of reward for high levels of stimulation (Zuckerman, 1979a, 1984).

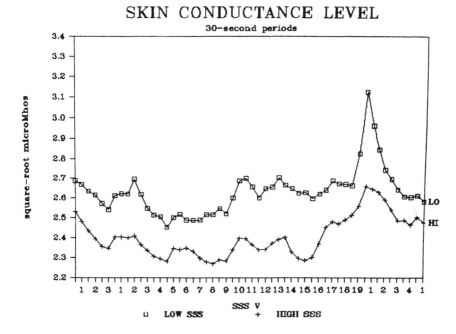

FIG. 9.1. Skin conductance levels of high and low sensation seekers to a 20-minute horror film. A decapitation scene is indicated by an arrow at Period 19. SSS = Sensation Seeking Scale. From Litle (1986). Previously published in Zuckerman (1991). Copyright 1991, Hemisphere. Reprinted with permission.

The findings on preferences in the media would seem to fit the original model for sensation seeking rather than the new one, for sensation seekers are attracted to stimuli that are arousing regardless of whether they stimulate negative or positive affect systems. Sensation seekers prefer being frightened or shocked to being bored.

Sensation seekers seem to have strong orienting responses (ORs), as assessed by skin conductance but more consistently by heart rate decelerations to novel stimuli of moderate intensity (Zuckerman, 1990). I have suggested that the OR reflects a need for information about novel stimuli in the environment (curiosity) and is associated with approach behavior, whereas defensive reflexes (stronger in low sensation seekers) reflect tendencies to mentally avoid novel stimulation. Anxiety weakens rather than augments the OR (Neary & Zuckerman, 1976). The OR tends to habituate quickly in high sensation seekers when the stimulus is repeated.

Smith, Davidson, Smith, Goldstein, and Perlstein (1989) used words classified as low, medium, or high intensity of sexual and aggressive content.

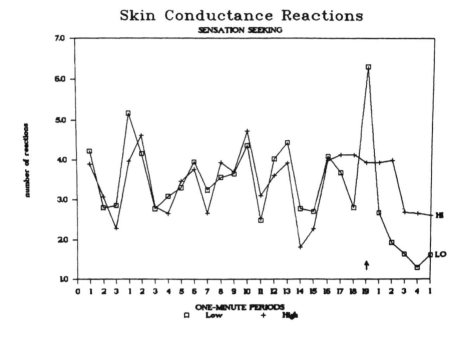

FIG. 9.2. Spontaneous skin conductance reactions of high and low sensation seekers to a
20-minute horror movie. A decapitation scene is indicated by an arrow at Period 19. From
Litle (1986). Previously published in Zuckerman (1991). Copyright 1991, Hemisphere.
Reprinted with permission.

Both high and low sensation seekers had stronger initial skin conductance
responses (SCRs) to high-intensity than to medium- and low-intensity words,
but the high sensation seekers gave stronger SCR-ORs to the aggressive and
sexual words than low sensation seekers, whereas differences between them
were minimal for the low-intensity words. If we accept the OR as a sign of
interest and attention, then high sensation seekers are more set to respond to
emotionally arousing stimuli, like sexual and aggressive ones, than lows.
Could such a propensity have some relationship to their liking for horror
movies?

Litle (1986) recorded skin conductance levels (SCLs) and SCRs while
subjects were watching a 20-minute segment of the horror film *Friday the
Thirteenth*. Figure 9.1 shows the SCR levels through the film segment and Fig.
9.2 shows the rate of SCRs for high and low sensation seekers. High sensation
seekers started at a somewhat lower (but not significantly so) level of SCL than
the low sensation seekers and the difference was maintained throughout the
film with both levels fluctuating with the action portrayed at various points in
the film. However, at 19 minutes into the film, the last intended victim chops

off the murderer's head with an ax and the head goes flying with blood spurting in all directions. At this point (indicated by the arrow) the SCL of the low sensation seekers showed a greater increase than that of the high sensation seekers.

The SCRs shown in Fig. 9.2 are even more sensitive to the events in the film and represent rates of electrodermal phasic responses to the stimuli during each moment. Each of the peaks occurs during violent episodes such as attacks and sudden discoveries of dead bodies. High and low sensation seekers showed similar initial levels and responded equally to all the scenes up to the climactic decapitation (Period 19). At this point the low sensation seekers SCRs shot up whereas the high sensation seekers showed little change in SCR activity. Perhaps by this time the high sensation seekers had habituated to the violence.

Assigning a value to the optimal level of arousal is difficult without confirming psychological data. The optimal level of arousal is the one at which an individual feels best. It would have been useful to have moment-by-moment self-ratings of positive versus negative feelings to compare with the psychophysiological data, but such recording might have distracted the subjects from involvement in the action of the film. Suppose the optimal level of arousal on SCRs (Fig. 9.2) for low sensation seekers was between 2 and 3 SCRs per minute, whereas the optimal level for the high sensation seekers was between 3 and 4 SCRs. This would mean that the high sensation seekers were at their optimal levels of arousal during most of the film, whereas the low sensation seekers were above their optimal levels for most of the film. One would expect that their psychological reactions during the climactic decapitation were extremely unpleasant because they were so far above their optimal levels.

Another possibility is that arousal is reacted to in a different way by high and low sensation seekers. The high sensation seeker might react to brief arousal spurts, even to points above the optimal level, as fun, whereas the low sensation seeker might react to any increase above the optimal level as unpleasant. Perhaps the psychological reaction precedes and causes the physiological reaction rather than vice versa. However, from what is known about the processing of emotion-laden information, emotional tone is probably added to stimuli before they are fully decoded by association with encoded memories at higher levels of the nervous system (LeDoux, 1987).

The low sensation seeker may be anxiety aversive. Given an equal appraisal of risk in a situation, the high sensation seeker tends to anticipate stronger positive than negative affective
reactions, whereas the low sensation seeker anticipates becoming anxious in the situation (Zuckerman, 1979b). There is clearly no real physical risk in watching a horror film, but there is a risk of getting upset, disgusted, or frightened by the graphic horror. When the low sensation seeker feels aroused

he or she may feel this as confirmation of their worst expectations, whereas the high sensation seeker may regard the same level of arousal more positively. Having one's negative emotions aroused by a film may be a very different experience for a high and a low sensation seeker.

SUMMARY AND CONCLUSIONS

Sensation seekers seek novel and arousing experiences in life and their tastes for violence and sexuality in art and the media may simply reflect this general theme of the trait. Correlations of the trait with actual attendance at horror films are significant but weaker than relationships with the general kinds of interest in these themes and they tend to be mediated by a liking for fright and excitement. In general, sensation seekers find real-life experiences more rewarding than vicarious experiences so they tend to watch television less than lows, particularly on weekends. Horror films can lose their shock value quickly and we have seen that high sensation seekers show signs of habituation of arousal within the course of a single film. Sensation seekers probably find alternate frightening activities in real life without the need to seek them in vicarious experiences. On the other hand the low sensation seekers who do expose themselves to vicarious horror in films (perhaps due to peer influence) may come to enjoy the medium after they have habituated down to their optimal levels of arousal.

Many have suggested that there is a sadistic element in the male enjoyment of pornography as well as the enjoyment of horror films. Certainly there appears to be more of a relationship between the tastes for morbid and sexual events in men than in women. The relationship between the disinhibitory type of sensation seeking and preference for graphic horror depended on the female being a victim in the film, although with boredom susceptibility the sex of the victim made no difference (Tamborini et al., 1987). For the high sensation seeker, a desire to view graphic violence may be a general way of coping with boredom and an expression of unconventional and socially disapproved sexual fantasies.

As with other kinds of phenomenal expression, we must be cautious about interpreting a preference in terms of a single trait or any disposition at all. There are many social facilitating factors that bring young people into these films. It's fun to get frightened with someone you like so you can cling together in the worst scenes. For some the films are sources of amusement, but if one wants amusement, comedies are probably a better bet.

It is interesting that those who want to ban pornography on the assumption that it encourages violence against women are rarely heard urging the censorship of horror films, in which the violence against both genders is much more graphic. If we assume that latent aggressive impulses are the only trait that might account for the taste for vicarious horror, one should be alarmed at the possible consequences of viewing such films because they might disinhibit violent tendencies. However, if sensation seeking is a prominent motive and fright arousal from vicarious threat is the main source of reward, then such films are probably innocuous.

REFERENCES

Bem, S. L. (1974). The measurement of psychological androgyny. *Journal of Consulting and Clinical Psychology, 42*, 155-162.

Brown, L. T., Ruder, V. G., Ruder, J. H., & Young, S. D. (1974). Stimulation seeking and the Change Seeker Index. *Journal of Consulting and Clinical Psychology, 42*, 311.

Christie, R., & Geis, F. C. (1970). *Studies in Machiavellianism.* New York: Academic Press.

Edwards, E. (1984). *The relationship between sensation seeking and horror movie interest and attendance.* Unpublished doctoral dissertation, University of Tennessee, Knoxville.

Fulker, D. J., Eysenck, S. B. G., & Zuckerman, M. (1980). The genetics of sensation seeking. *Journal of Personality Research, 14*, 261-281.

Hebb, D. O. (1955). Drives and the C. N. S. (conceptual nervous system). *Psychological Review, 62*, 243-254.

LeDoux, J. E. (1987). Emotion. In F. Plum (Ed.), *Handbook of physiology, Vol. 5, Higher functions of the brain* (pp. 419-460). Bethesda, MD: American Physiological Society.

Litle, P. A. (1986). *Effects of a stressful movie and music on mood and physiological arousal in relation to sensation seeking.* Unpublished doctoral dissertation, University of Delaware, Newark.

Neary, R. S., & Zuckerman, M. (1976). Sensation seeking, trait and state anxiety, and the electrodermal orienting reflex. *Psychophysiology, 13*, 205-211.

Rowland, G., Fouts, G., & Heatherton, T. (1989). Television viewing and sensation seeking: Uses, preferences and attitudes. *Personality and Individual Differences, 10*, 1003-1006.

Schierman, M. J., & Rowland, G. L. (1985). Sensation seeking and selection of entertainment. *Personality and Individual Differences, 6*, 599-603.

Smith, B. D., Davidson, R. A., Smith, D. L., Goldstein, H., & Perlstein, W. (1989). Effects of strong stimulation on electrodermal activation and memory task performance. *Personality and Individual Differences, 10*, 671-679.

Tamborini, R., & Stiff, J. (1987). Predictors of horror film attendance and appeal: An analysis of the audience for frightening films. *Communication Research, 14*, 415-436.

Tamborini, R., Stiff, J., & Zillmann, D. (1987). Preference for graphic horror featuring male versus female victimization. *Human Communication Research, 13*, 529-552.

Tobacyk, J. J., Myers, H., & Bailey, L. (1981). Field-dependence, sensation seeking and preference for paintings. *Journal of Personality Assessment, 45*, 270-277.

Zaleski, Z. (1984). Sensation seeking and preference for emotional visual stimuli. *Personality and Individual Differences, 5*, 607-608.

Zuckerman, M. (1969). Theoretical formulations. In J. P. Zubek (Ed.), *Sensory deprivation: Fifteen years of research* (pp. 407-432). New York: Appleton-Century.

Zuckerman, M. (1971). Dimensions of sensation seeking. *Journal of Consulting and Clinical Psychology, 36*, 45-52.

Zuckerman, M. (1974). The sensation seeking motive. In B. A. Maher (Ed.), *Progress in experimental personality research* (Vol. 7, pp. 79-148). New York: Academic Press.

Zuckerman, M. (1976). Research on pornography. In W. W. Oaks, G. A. Melchiode, & I. Ficher (Eds.), *Sex and the life cycle* (pp. 147-161). New York: Grune & Stratton.

Zuckerman, M. (1979a). *Sensation seeking: Beyond the optimal level of arousal.* Hillsdale, NJ: Lawrence Erlbaum Associates.

Zuckerman, M. (1979b). Sensation seeking and risk taking. In C. E. Izard (Ed.), *Emotions in personality and psychopathology* (pp. 163-197). New York: Plenum.

Zuckerman, M. (1983). A biological theory of sensation seeking. In M. Zuckerman (Ed.), *Biological bases of sensation seeking, impulsivity, and anxiety* (pp. 37-76). Hillsdale: NJ: Lawrence Erlbaum Associates.

Zuckerman, M. (1984). Sensation seeking: A comparative approach to a human trait. *Behavioral and Brain Sciences, 7,* 413-471.

Zuckerman, M. (1990). The psychophysiology of sensation seeking. *Journal of Personality, 58,* 313-345.

Zuckerman, M. (1991). One person's stress is another persons's pleasure. In C. D. Spielberger, I. Sarason, S. Kulcsar, & G. L. Van Heck (Eds.), *Stress and emotion* (Vol. 14, pp. 31-45). Washington, DC: Hemisphere.

Zuckerman, M. (1994). *Behavioral expressions and psychobiological bases of sensation seeking.* New York: Cambridge University Press.

Zuckerman, M., Buchsbaum, M. S., & Murphy, D. L. (1980). Sensation seeking and its biological correlates. *Psychological Bulletin, 88,* 187-214.

Zuckerman, M., Eysenck, S. B. G., & Eysenck, H. J. (1978). Sensation seeking in England and America: Cross-cultural, age, and sex comparisons. *Journal of Consulting and Clinical Psychology, 46,* 139-149.

Zuckerman, M., Kolin, E. A., Price, L., & Zoob, I. (1964). Development of a sensation seeking scale. *Journal of Consulting Psychology, 28,* 477-482.

Zuckerman, M., & Litle, P. (1986). Personality and curiosity about morbid and sexual events. *Personality and Individual Differences, 7,* 49-56.

Zuckerman, M., Ulrich, R. S., & McLaughlin, J. (1993). Sensation seeking and reactions to nature paintings. *Personality and Individual Differences, 15,* 563-576.

Chapter 10

A Uses and Gratifications Analysis of Horror Film Preference

Patricia A. Lawrence
University of Texas at El Paso
Philip C. Palmgreen
University of Kentucky

This chapter endorses the self-report method traditionally employed by uses and gratifications scholars as a means toward better understanding why some individuals are enticed by horror films. It reviews selected studies that have used self-reports, and it then presents a reanalysis of data from an earlier study by the chapter authors. In both the literature review and the data analysis, psychological needs for affective and generalized arousal play significant roles in predicting horror film preference. Specific film content—nudity, graphic sex scenes, obscene language, and violence—emerges as an important avoidance motive and two gratifications sought—identifying with film characters and using audience reactions to facilitate enjoyment—are significantly related to liking of horror films.

LITERATURE REVIEW

Horror films can be highly frightening and disturbing for many individuals. These films differ markedly from other film genres because they typically feature a predator-prey relationship, are quite serious in their overall portrayal of their characters, and either display or suggest violence or violent death (Edwards, 1984). Yet, even though many moviegoers avoid horror films, others are enticed by them. Why?

This chapter suggests that this perplexing question can be approached fruitfully within the broad framework of uses and gratifications (U & G) theory and research. U & G is a theoretical perspective that focuses on mass media audiences and their motives for media exposure and consumption (Blumler & Katz, 1974; Rosengren, Wenner, & Palmgreen, 1985). Research in this tradition takes the social and psychological needs of individuals as a starting point, and examines audience members' consumption of media content as a means of seeking and obtaining gratifications or need fulfillment from mass media use.

Relatively few studies have used self-report methodology, typically employed in U & G investigations, to explore or explain gratifications sought from horror film consumption. However, several experimental studies have treated the gratifications derived from horror films as a central concept in explaining the genre's attraction. These have included positive affect or enjoyment, "safe" fright, arousal, witnessing graphic destruction, the experience of power, and experiencing a satisfying plot resolution in which horrific protagonists are punished (Hoffner, 1990; Hoffner & Cantor, 1991; Sparks & Cantor, 1986; Tamborini, Stiff, & Zillmann, 1987; Zillmann, Weaver, Mundorf, & Aust, 1986).

Others have used self-report measures to explore gratifications derived from horror films but without specifically referring to the U & G tradition (e.g., Sparks, 1986; Tamborini & Stiff, 1987). Because all these investigations deal with motives for (gratifications derived from) media consumption, they may be said to be consistent with the central tenets of a U & G theoretical framework. Even the methods employed in those studies are compatible with the adoption of a broader repertoire of methodological approaches to U & G research urged by scholars in recent years (Blumler, Gurevitch, & Katz, 1985; Lull, 1985; Zillmann, 1985).

This chapter, however, does not review the findings of those experimental studies; that literature is discussed in detail in other chapters of this volume. Instead, it concentrates on the few studies that have adopted a traditional self-report approach of gratifications sought from horror films. These investigations suggest that, although movie consumption in general is guided by a variety of motives, the consumption of horror films is strongly influenced by audience members' needs for psychological arousal or activation. That speculation is explored here by first reviewing selected literature on gratifications sought from movies in general, the relationship between arousal needs, particularly sensation-seeking, and moviegoing motives (with an emphasis on horror film preferences), and then discussing the results of a study by the chapter authors.

MOVIE MOTIVES

Studies in the U & G tradition, using self-report, have found that a wide variety of motives, or gratifications sought, guide audience consumption of theatrical films in general (Lawrence & Palmgreen, 1991; Palmgreen, Cook, Harvill, & Helm, 1988; Palmgreen & Lawrence, 1991). These include entertainment or diversion, general learning, mood control or enhancement, personal identity, social and communication utility, audience involvement, communication avoidance, and medium characteristics. The study by Palmgreen and Lawrence (1991) found that avoidance motives also influence theatrical film consumption. For example, individuals avoid going to the movies due to physical and social environmental constraints or specific film content. The Lawrence and Palmgreen (1991) investigation revealed that arousal needs underlie many of the motives for going to the movies. However, the relationship between arousal needs and avoidance motives was not examined.

AROUSAL NEEDS

Arousal theories of human behavior have long assumed that individuals continually strive to maintain an optimal level of psychological arousal or activation at which they are the most comfortable (Hebb, 1955). Lawrence (1990) suggested that individual needs for psychological arousal fall into three interdependent types—generalized (need to be alert), affective (need to feel good), and cognitive (need for information). Several communication studies have demonstrated that arousal-based needs play a major role in attention to and selection of mass media messages (Donohew, 1981; Donohew, Helm, Lawrence, & Schatzer, 1990; Donohew, Palmgreen, & Duncan, 1980; Donohew, Palmgreen, & Rayburn, 1987; Helregel & Weaver, 1989; Lawrence & Palmgreen, 1991; Zillmann, 1982, 1988; Zillmann & Bryant, 1985; Zillmann, Hezel, & Medoff, 1980).

Measures of Arousal Needs

Needs for different kinds of psychological arousal not only vary among individuals but also can be measured with the Sensation Seeking Scale (Zuckerman, Kolin, Price, & Zoob, 1964; Zuckerman, chap. 9, this volume) and the Novelty Seeking Scale (Pearson, 1971). The Sensation Seeking Scale is based on the premise that arousal needs may be gratified through thrill and adventure seeking, such as taking part in physically risky activities; experience seeking, including experimenting with unusual art forms, music, drugs, and associating with unconventional people; disinhibition, such as participating in wild parties and alcohol consumption and having a variety of sex partners; and boredom susceptibility, including avoiding boring people and routine situations. The SSS taps all four of these tendencies, which deal primarily with generalized and affective arousal but not with needs for cognitive activation.

Pearson's scale measures predispositions to seek novelty through external sensation, such as engaging in unusual and physically exciting actions; internal sensation, including losing one's self in daydreams and fantasies, and enjoying intense or strange feelings; internal cognition, such as thinking about and trying to analyze ideas and human behaviors; and external cognition, including finding out how machines work, figuring out how to solve problems, and learning facts about how to do or construct things.

Individuals who consistently score high on the Zuckerman and Pearson scales tend to be continually on the lookout for unusual or exciting events, people, and situations. They often act impulsively, have short attention spans, are physically hyperactive, and engage in somewhat uncontrollable pleasure-seeking behaviors. Those with low scores tend to shy away from the unusual, preferring that which is familiar, nonthreatening, and not apt to stimulate them beyond their optimal level of arousal. In either case, individuals are assumed to be sensitive to their internal needs and to actively select external stimuli that can gratify them.

AROUSAL NEEDS AND MOVIE MOTIVES

By employing both the Zuckerman and Pearson scales, Lawrence and Palmgreen (1991) found that needs for generalized, affective, and cognitive arousal had significant effects on several motives for attending theatrical movies. In that study, 312 males and females, aged 18 to 82, were surveyed to assess their arousal needs, their motives for going to the movies, and the relationship between the two. A factor analysis of 53 gratifications sought (from moviegoing) items produced nine movie motives, and six factors emerged from an analysis of 32 arousal needs items.[1] Hierarchical regression models then revealed that needs to engage in risk taking, for internal sensation, and for internal cognitive novelty explained significant amounts of the variance in six of the movie motives, and that the impact of arousal needs on movie motives differed as a function of age.

Young (ages 18-22; $n = 140$) adult moviegoers' primary motives for going to movies—to learn about people, places, and other cultures; to be entertained; to control or enhance their mood; to identify with film characters; and to use other audience members' reactions to increase their enjoyment of a film—were

---

[1]The 53 gratifications sought items were drawn from essays written by undergraduate communication students and employed in Palmgreen et al. (1988). The 32 arousal needs items were derived by factor analyzing the 40-item Zuckerman and the 80-item Pearson scales separately and then selecting the strongest loading items from each factor, in an effort to reduce respondent fatigue (Lawrence, 1990). The Zuckerman scale was thus reduced to 12 items (three from each subscale), and the Pearson scale was reduced to 20 items (five from each subscale). With the exception of Zuckerman's experience-seeking subscale, which had a Cronbach α of .58, the reliability coefficients ranged from .67 to .87.

guided primarily by needs for risk taking, internal cognition, and internal sensation. In sharp contrast, more mature (ages 23 and older; $n = 119$) adult moviegoers' principal motives for attending theatrical films—general learning, entertainment, mood control, personal identity, and personal involvement—were accounted for predominantly by the affective need for internal sensation.

Even though such findings provide empirical support that needs-based motives guide theatrical film consumption in general, Austin (1983, 1986, 1989) argued that the motives for attending movies in general and for selecting a specific type of movie may differ. Thus there remains a need to re-examine the Lawrence and Palmgreen (1991) data to detect any relationship between arousal needs, movie motives, and preference for specific movie types. There is some research that indicates that such a relationship does exist, especially for horror film use.

AROUSAL NEEDS AND HORROR FILMS

Tamborini and Stiff (1987) conducted a study of horror film consumption that combined self-report measures of motives and sensation seeking. Respondents were 155 individuals who attended a showing of *Halloween II* at a Midwestern theater. Structural equation analysis indicated that the effect of horror films is influenced by a desire to experience the satisfying plot resolutions often provided in such films, a desire to see graphic destruction, and sensation seeking as measured by Zuckerman's Sensation Seeking Scale. Sensation seeking was not a strong predictor of horror film appeal, but this may have been due to the fact that the sample was limited to horror fans, which probably reduced the variance in both the sensation seeking and the horror film consumption measures.

Tamborini, Stiff, and Zillmann (1987) also conducted an experiment in which respondents completed scales measuring past film viewing, sensation seeking, Machiavellianism, and androgyny, and then ranked their preference for 13 film descriptions that differed in the degree of graphic violence and also manipulated male versus female victimization. Three subscales of the sensation seeking scale (disinhibition, experience seeking, and boredom susceptibility) displayed significant moderate simple correlations with a preference for graphic horror scale, although the deceit dimension of the Machiavellianism measure was a stronger predictor. Regression analyses, on the other hand, did not reveal any significant effects of the Sensation Seeking Scale (SSS) dimensions on preference for graphic horror. However, even though they were not reported, intercorrelations among the SSS subscales, and perhaps between these and a horror film exposure measure (included as an independent variable), may have introduced multicollinearity problems. In any event, boredom susceptibility emerged as a strong predictor of preference for graphic horror scores in analyses with subgroups of the total sample created by crossing respondent gender and victim gender.

In a related survey of 220 adolescents, ages 13 to 16, Johnston and Dumerauf (1990) found that 95% of the teenage respondents reported that they viewed slasher movies. The study identified three motives among this young group for viewing slasher films—rebellion against authority, thrill-seeking arousal, and sadistic gore gratification. These motives were explained by different personality traits—sensation-seeking tendencies, capacity for empathy, and capacity for fear. Young people who use slasher films for all three gratifications also have high scores on the thrill and adventure-seeking (TAS) dimension of Zuckerman's Sensation Seeking Scale. In fact, this need was the best predictor for the thrill-seeking motive (liking to have fun and be scared or freaked out by slasher films). Low empathy scores best predicted the other two motives—gore gratification (liking to see blood and guts) and rebellion (viewing to make parents angry and to feel more mature or brave). The authors postulated that adolescents who are able to distance themselves emotionally from the victims in slasher films derive different affective gratifications during viewing than those who are not. They suggested that the TAS trait underlying the thrill-seeking motive enables young viewers to tolerate intense emotions.

Finally, Edwards (1991) hypothesized that individuals' needs for sensation may manifest themselves in gratification seeking from horror films. Using Zuckerman's SSS, Edwards surveyed 40 males and 52 females, ages 16 to 65, to assess the relationship between sensation-seeking scores and interest in, and frequency of viewing, horror films on television and in theaters. She found positive and statistically significant correlations between all four dimensions of the SSS and interest in horror films (from .35 to .58) and in frequency of viewing horror films (from .19 to .36). Total sensation-seeking scores and subscale scores also correlated significantly with a preoccupation with death (from .12 to .33), an interest in the occult—belief in spirits (from .25 to .43) and belief in alien life (.15 to .40).

Other findings were that individuals who attend horror films at moderate to high frequency rates believe that the most important functions of a movie are to "help people forget worries" and "to be thought provoking." Less important functions for this group are "to provide excitement," "to occupy time," and "to provide a social outing." Furthermore, a substantial number of those who frequently attend horror movies also tend to watch more movies in general, and they prefer to watch movies alone, according to her study. Edwards concluded that sensation-seeking tendencies do explain why some people, especially those with high needs for disinhibition, are interested in the macabre. She suggested that, because high disinhibition seekers are willing to seek out new and exciting experiences, even those that are frightening or illegal, perhaps watching horror films allows these individuals to safely explore almost any social taboo.

The preceding studies reveal a variety of motives for liking and attending horror films. They also strongly suggest that needs for psychological arousal underlie some motives for both horror film appeal and consumption. The study reported here extends those analyses by re-examining the data from the Lawrence and Palmgreen (1991) study and investigating the impact of not only arousal needs and gratifications sought but also of avoidance motives on horror film preference.[2] As such, it uses a large and diverse sample of moviegoers in an attempt to reveal a comprehensive uses and gratifications analysis of horror film preference.

METHODOLOGY

Self-report data were collected from 159 undergraduate communication students at a large university, 119 employees of a demographically diverse business organization, and 34 senior citizens. Three behavioral indicators of moviegoing were obtained: frequency of attendance, of going to movies alone, and of impulsive moviegoing. Respondents indicated how often they go to movies at a movie theater by marking one of six foils ranging from *hardly ever* (1) to *once a week* (6). They responded to the questions "How often do you go to a movie by yourself?" and "How often do you go on the spur of the moment?" on scales from *not often at all* (1) to *very often* (7).

Various psychographic variables—movie dependency, motives for going to the movies, liking for various movie types, arousal needs, and motives for avoiding theatrical films—were measured using 7-point Likert scales. The survey respondents indicated the strength of their agreement, from *strongly disagree* (1) to *strongly agree* (7), on five statements designed to measure movie dependency. They also indicated how much they agreed with each of 53 reasons (gratifications sought) that others have given for going to movies on scales ranging from *strongly disagree* (1) to *strongly agree* (7). Preferences for movie types were measured by asking respondents to indicate their liking for each of 11 types of movies on scales from *I don't like at all* (1) to *I like very much* (7).

Sensation-seeking needs were assessed by asking respondents to indicate how much each of 12 statements (drawn from the Zuckerman scale) sounded

---

[2]The earlier study was focused on theatrical film consumption only and did not investigate exposure to horror films on VCRs or rental movies. Future studies should, of course, take into account the consumption of home viewing of horror films, and we acknowledge this limitation on the study presented here.

like them, from *this does not sound like me at all* (1) to *this sounds exactly like me* (7). To measure novelty-seeking needs, subjects were instructed to indicate how much they like to engage in each of 20 activities (drawn from the Pearson scale), from *I definitely do not or would not like to do* (1) to *I definitely do like or would like to do* (7).[3]

Finally, respondents were presented with 24 reasons that might cause them to avoid going to see a movie at a theater and asked to indicate how important each reason would be, by itself, to cause them to avoid theatrical movies in the future, on a scale from *not important at all to me* (1) to *extremely important* (7).

Analysis

All the statistical tests were conducted using SPSSx. The movie dependency scale, based on the concept by Rubin and Windahl (1986), was identical to that used in Palmgreen and Lawrence's (1991) study, which found that gratifications sought are important predictors of dependency on theatrical movies. The alpha coefficient for the scale here was .86, and it correlated significantly ($p < .001$) with frequency of attendance for the total sample ($r = .53$) as well as for horror film fans only ($r = .60$).

The same factor scales employed in the earlier study (Lawrence & Palmgreen, 1991) for moviegoing motives and arousal needs were used in the statistical analyses here.[4] The 24 avoidance items were factor analyzed, and the avoidance scales were tested for their predictive value on liking for horror films.

After liking for the 11 types of films was assessed, the full sample ($n = 312$) was split at the mean score (3.45) for liking of horror films. Using two-tailed t tests, comparisons of means were made between horror film fans ($n = 146$) and nonfans ($n = 166$) on liking for all 11 types of movies, age, the moviegoing behaviors—frequency of attendance, the tendency to go to movies alone, and impulsive consumption (going to movies on the spur of the moment), movie dependency, arousal needs, moviegoing motives, and movie

---

[3]The sensation-seeking and the novelty-seeking scales were each converted from forced choice to Likert scales because prior studies had shown that respondents sometimes are unable to make forced choices and leave some of the scale items unanswered. Wording of the Pearson items was not changed, and the Zuckerman items were phrased either positively or negatively at random. The conversion not only provided more refined interval measures of the various arousal needs but also reduced the intercorrelations among the four subscales of each scale (Lawrence, 1990).

[4]In that study, the Zuckerman and Pearson items were factor analyzed together, yielding six factors (listed in Table 10.2). The factor analysis of the gratifications sought items resulted in nine factors (listed in Table 10.2). In both instances, maximum likelihood extraction with orthogonal rotation was employed, and the factor criteria were a minimum eigenvalue of 1.0 and at least two items loading at > .40 per factor.

avoidance motives. Comparisons between means for male and female fans were examined by conducting t tests on the behavioral and psychographic variables already listed.

Chi-square tests on crosstabulations of high versus low liking of horror films by age (three groups—18-22, $n = 151$; 23-44, $n = 91$; and 45-82, $n = 70$) and sex (189 females and 123 males), were conducted to test the likelihood that age or sex significantly differentiates fans from nonfans and also from each other.

The earlier Lawrence and Palmgreen (1991) analysis had already shown that scores on six arousal needs subscales correlate significantly with scores on from three to all nine movie motives. In this study, Pearson-zero order correlation coefficients were examined to assess the relationship between arousal needs and avoidance motives and also to test the predictive value of age, the three behavioral indicators, movie dependency, the six arousal needs, the nine movie motives, and the three avoidance motives on horror film preference.

Because it was found that, for the total sample, age correlated strongly and negatively ($r = -.53$; $p < .001$) with liking of horror films, partial correlations, controlling for age, were conducted to retest the predictive value of all 22 independent variables on horror film preference.

A hierarchical regression model was then formulated, with age as a control variable, to determine the amount of total variance accounted for, in horror film preference, by blocks of the three avoidance motives, the six arousal needs, and the nine moviegoing motives (gratifications sought).

RESULTS

Three avoidance motives emerged from the factor analysis of the 24 avoidance items and accounted for 39.6% of the total variance.[5] Factor 1 was labeled Viewing Constraints and included the following items: crying babies, other people talking too much or blocking their view of the film, theaters that are too hot or too cold, uncomfortable seats, and inappropriate crowd reactions. Factor 2, Specific Content, included: nude scenes, explicit or graphic sex scenes, obscene language, and violence. The third factor was labeled Previewing Constraints and included items such as movie ticket prices, fighting traffic to get to the movies, high prices of popcorn, candy, and soda pop at the movies, having to pay babysitters, and large crowds at the movies.

---

[5] A maximum likelihood extraction with varimax rotation was employed, with factor criteria of a minimum eigenvalue of 1.0 and at least two items loading at > .40. The intercorrelation matrix passed the tests for sampling and psychometric adequacy. The Kaiser-Meyer-Olkin measure was .85, indicating that an adequate number of items was present; and the Bartlett test of sphericity was 2793.26 ($p < .001$), allowing rejection of the null hypothesis of independence for the 24 avoidance items.

Reliability tests of the three factor-labeled avoidance scales yielded Cronbach alphas of .83 for Viewing Constraints, .86 for Specific Film Content, and .77 for Previewing Constraints.

Simple correlations between arousal needs and avoidance motives revealed that all but the cognitive arousal needs were strongly ($p < .001$) and negatively related to the Specific Content factor (Table 10.1), suggesting that individuals with high needs for generalized and affective arousal not only have a high tolerance for the kind of content offered by horror films but also may be enticed by it. In addition, although the coefficients were lower, needs for risktaking, internal sensation, and for disinhibition correlated significantly and negatively with the Viewing Constraints avoidance motive. It may be that even these kinds of negative constraints for many individuals provide some gratification for other individuals with high needs for stimulation. No meaningful relationships were observed between any of the arousal needs measures and the third avoidance motive, Previewing Constraints.

TABLE 10.1
Intercorrelations Among Arousal Needs Scores and Movie
Avoidance Motives for Total Sample ($N = 312$)

Arousal Need	Avoidance Motive		
	Viewing Constraints	Specific Content	Previewing Constraints
Risk taking	-0.18**	-0.40***	-0.05
External cognitive	0.03	-0.06	-0.06
Internal cognitive	0.03	-0.01	-0.02
Internal sensation	-0.14**	-0.33***	-0.02
Disinhibition	-0.11*	-0.34***	0.05
Boredom susceptibility	-0.08	-0.19***	0.01

*$p < .05$. **$p < .01$. ***$p < .001$.

An examination of movie type preferences, by the full sample ($n = 312$), revealed that horror films are among the least liked by moviegoers in general, with a mean of 3.45 out of a possible 7 points (Table 10.2). However, this genre ranked fourth in preference for horror film fans ($M = 5.63$), preceded only by comedy, action/adventure, and suspense/mystery films—all of which have a strong potential to gratify various needs for arousal or excitation. For nonfans, the mean ($M = 1.54$) on liking of horror films was quite low and ranked last among that group's movie type preferences. T tests revealed significant differences between fans and nonfans on 9 of the 11 movie types, with fans showing distinct preferences for films containing exciting content over ones highlighting historical events, social issues, or musical themes.

TABLE 10.2
Comparison of Means on Movie-Type Preferences Between Horror Film Fans and Nonfans

Movie Type	Full Sample $n = 312$ Mean/Rank	Fans $n = 146$ Mean/Rank	Nonfans $n = 166$ Mean/Rank	t value
Action/Adventure	5.673/ 2	5.884/ 2	5.488/ 2	2.48*
Romance	5.272/ 4	5.103/ 5	5.422/ 3	-1.64
Comedy	6.292/ 1	6.432/ 1	6.169/ 1	2.07*
Science-Fiction	4.125/ 5	4.486/ 6	3.807/ 8	2.91**
Horror	3.452/10	5.630/ 4	1.536/11	36.61***
Animated fantasy	3.558/ 9	3.671/ 8	3.458/ 9	1.02
Suspense/Mystery	5.5 /3	5.753/3	5.277/ 4	2.71**
Musicals	4.090/ 6	3.377/10	4.717/ 6	-5.82***
Erotic films	3.423/11	4.103/ 7	2.825/10	5.39***
Historical	4.0 / 7	3.144/11	4.753/ 5	-8.05***
Social issues	3.933/ 8	3.580/ 9	4.235/ 7	-2.93**

*$p < .05$. **$p < .01$. ***$p < .001$.

Chi-square tests on crosstabulated frequencies of high versus low liking for horror films by age and sex ($n = 312$) revealed that high liking occurs more often among younger (18-22 year old) male and female moviegoers than among the two older male and female groups ($\chi^2 = 73.33$; $p < .001$) and also more often among males than among females in general ($\chi^2 = 12.04$; $p < .001$). Yet, even though horror film fans tend to be young males, within the group of fans only ($n = 146$), approximately equal numbers of males and females occurred within each age group ($\chi^2 = 0.776$; $p = 0.678$). This suggests that horror film preference can be attributed to specific characteristics shared by some members of both sexes, across age groups, rather than to sex or age alone.

A comparison of horror film fans to nonfans, on age and on 22 other measures, revealed several behavioral and psychographic differences between these two groups of moviegoers (see Table 10.3). For example, horror film fans attend movies more often than nonfans, are less likely to go to movies alone, and are more impulsive in terms of going to movies on the spur of the moment. However, neither group is highly dependent on movies and no significant difference was found on this measure.

Other differences were that horror film fans are much less motivated than nonfans to avoid going to movies due to Viewing Constraints or Specific Content such as that typically found in horror movies. Previewing Constraints were not strong avoidance motives for either fans or nonfans.

TABLE 10.3
Comparison of Means on Movie Going Profile Factors Between Horror Film Fans and Nonfans

	Fans (n = 146)	Nonfans (n = 166)	
	Mean	Mean	t value
Age	24.1	40.9	-9.70***
Moviegoing behavior			
Frequency of attendance	3.27	2.80	3.16**
Goes alone	1.14	1.81	-4.34***
Impulsive consumption	5.01	3.94	5.14***
Movie dependency	2.92	3.07	-0.95
Avoidance motive			
Viewing constraints	4.17	4.59	-2.98**
Specific film content	2.52	3.79	-7.00***
Previewing constraints	3.35	3.30	0.40
Arousal need			
Risk taking	4.95	3.79	6.35***
External cognitive	2.90	2.95	-0.27
Internal cognitive	4.66	4.92	-1.67
Internal sensation	4.24	3.45	4.87***
Disinhibition	4.08	2.89	6.41***
Boredom susceptibility	3.85	3.09	4.54***
Motive for going to movies			
General learning	3.72	4.27	-3.28**
Entertainment	5.64	5.39	1.92
Mood control/enhancement	4.02	3.79	1.31
Personal identity	4.19	3.39	4.58***
Communication utility	3.69	3.49	1.42
Medium characteristics	3.70	3.67	0.14
Social utility	4.94	4.34	3.29**
Audience involvement	2.90	2.33	3.79***
Communication avoidance	2.49	2.11	2.42*

*$p < .05$. **$p < .01$. ***$p < .001$.

Horror film fans had significantly higher scores than nonfans on four of the six arousal needs scales—need to engage in risk taking, need for internal sensation, need for disinhibition, and boredom susceptibility. Their needs for both internal and external cognitive novelty were about the same as those for the nonfans.

Finally, fans are more motivated than nonfans to go to the movies to identify with the characters in the film, use other audience members' reactions to facilitate their own enjoyment of theatrical films, have something to do socially, and to use moviegoing to avoid talking to other people for a while. They are less motivated than nonfans to use movies to learn things about other people, places, cultures, and lifestyles.

TABLE 10.4
Comparison of Means on Movie-Type Preference Scales Between Female and Male Horror Film Fans

Movie Type	Females $n = 73$ Mean/Rank	Males $n = 73$ Mean/Rank	t value
Action/Adventure	5.548/ 4	6.219/ 2	-3.22**
Romance	6.000/ 2	4.206/ 7	7.18***
Comedy	6.384/ 1	6.479/ 1	-0.63
Science-Fiction	3.726/ 7	5.247/ 5	-5.12***
Horror	5.425/ 5	5.836/ 3	-2.11*
Animated fantasy	3.575/ 8	3.767/ 8	-0.69
Suspense/Mystery	5.753/ 3	5.753/ 4	0.00
Musicals	3.836/ 6	2.918/11	2.84**
Erotic films	3.288/10	4.918/ 6	-4.97***
Historical	2.685/11	3.603/10	-3.31**
Social issues	3.562/ 9	3.616/ 9	-0.17

*$p < .05$. **$p < .01$. ***$p < .001$.

Some sex differences were found within the group of fans. For example, within the five most liked types of movies for both sexes, females ranked horror films fifth, whereas males ranked them third (Table 10.4). Female fans also indicated a lower liking than did male fans for erotic, action/adventure, science-fiction, and historical films, but they had a higher liking for romance movies and musicals.

A comparison of male and female horror film fans, on the same profile indicators examined in Table 10.4 between fans and nonfans, revealed statistically significant differences on only 5 of the 23 measures. Females had significantly ($p < .001$) higher scores on impulsivity—the tendency to go to movies on the spur of the moment—than did males ($M = 5.48$ to $M = 4.53$). They also were more motivated than males ($M = 3.17$ to $M = 2.39$; $p < .01$) to avoid going to movies due to specific film content, suggesting that females are more offended by graphic nudity, sex, and violence. Finally, they had lower mean scores than males on three types of arousal needs—risk taking (4.51 vs. 5.39; $p < .01$), external cognitive (2.41 vs. 3.39; $p < .001$), and boredom susceptibility (3.61 vs. 4.10; $p < .05$).

Controlling for Age

Pearson zero-order correlations between horror film preference and the 22 independent variables suggested that all three behavioral indicators, two of the three avoidance motives, five of the six arousal needs, and eight of the nine moviegoing motives were significantly related to liking of horror films (Table

TABLE 10.5
Zero-Order and Partial Correlation Coefficients (Controlling for Age) Between
Horror Film Preference and Other Variables of Interest ($n = 312$)

	Zero-Order Coefficients	Partial Coefficients
Moviegoing behavior		
Frequency of attendance	0.21***	0.03
Goes alone	0.23***	-0.05
Impulsive consumption	0.32***	0.13**
Movie dependency	-0.03	-0.08
Avoidance motive		
Viewing constraints	-0.18**	-0.07
Specific film content	-0.39***	-0.22***
Previewing constraints	0.06	-0.00
Arousal need		
Risk taking	0.40***	0.22***
External cognitive	-0.03	0.01
Internal cognitive	-0.11*	-0.10*
Internal sensation	0.30***	0.12*
Disinhibition	0.37**	0.22***
Boredom susceptibility	0.30***	0.22***
Motive for going to movies		
General learning	-0.12*	-0.09*
Entertainment	0.15*	-0.04
Mood control/enhancement	0.11*	-0.08
Personal identity	0.32***	0.11*
Communication utility	0.13*	0.01
Medium characteristics	0.05	-0.05
Social utility	0.21***	-0.05
Audience involvement	0.28***	0.13*
Communication avoidance	0.17**	0.02

*$p < .05.$ **$p < .01.$ ***$p < .001.$

10.5).   When age was held constant, however, only 10 of the partial
correlations were statistically significant.   Horror film preference remained
significantly and positively related to impulsive movie consumption, four of
the six arousal needs (risk-taking, internal sensation, disinhibition, and
boredom susceptibility), and the personal identity and audience involvement
moviegoing motives. In addition, significant negative relationships remained
between horror film preference and avoiding movies due to specific content,
the need for internal cognitive activation, and using moviegoing for general
learning.

The hierarchical regression equation accounted for 44.3% of the total
variance in the horror film preference measure (Table 10.6).   The model
clearly demonstrated that, after age was entered as a control variable,
avoidance motives, arousal needs, and gratifications sought from moviegoing

all were significant predictors of horror film preference. The block of avoidance motives accounted for an additional 3.7% ($p < .01$) of the variance. Although this variable may also offer a common-sense explanation for horror film preference, the regression equation provided evidence that, even after avoidances were entered in the model, arousal needs and gratifications sought still were relatively strong predictors of horror film preference. Arousal needs accounted for an additional 6.9% ($p < .001$) of the variance in the liking measure and gratifications sought from moviegoing accounted for an additional 5.7% ($p < .001$).

TABLE 10.6

Hierarchical Regression: Avoidance Motives, Arousal Needs, and Gratifications Sought as Predictors of Horror Film Preference ($N = 312$)

Variables Entered	Multiple R	R^2	R^2 Change
Age	0.526	0.276	0.276***
Avoidance motives	0.560	0.314	0.037**
Arousal needs	0.619	0.383	0.069***
Gratifications sought	0.663	0.443	0.057***

** $p < .01$. *** $p < .001$.

DISCUSSION

The findings here both support and extend those of previous research on the psychological antecedents of liking for horror films. At the same time, they provide evidence of the utility of a needs-based uses and gratifications approach to horror film consumption questions. The most important finding is that the arousal needs of individuals clearly underlie liking of horror films. Five needs for psychological arousal or stimulation significantly correlate with horror film preference, even after controlling for age, for this large and diverse sample of moviegoers. Moreover, the four arousal measures that are positively associated with such a preference—risk taking, disinhibition, internal sensation, and boredom susceptibility—reflect personal needs for generalized and affective arousal. On the other hand, the need for external cognitive novelty is unrelated to the preference measure, and the need for internal cognitive activation is weakly but negatively related to liking for horror. Thus, individuals who are enticed by horror films have higher than average needs for emotional and social stimulation—both of which can be gratified through consumption of horror films, especially within the context of a theatrical environment.

This conclusion is supported by the related findings that the preference for horror films also is positively correlated to the personal identity and the audience involvement motives for film consumption in general. By identifying with film characters and their problems and using the reactions of other audience members to enhance their own enjoyment of films, horror film fans can easily gratify their needs to experience intense and strange feelings, avoid or alleviate boredom, and engage in uninhibited, socially stimulated behaviors.

That the measures of arousal needs, gratifications sought, and avoidance motives did not account for a greater amount of variance in the preference measure may be traced to the fact that their original referent was general movie consumption, not horror films per se. As hinted at by some studies, reviewed previously, motives for seeking and avoiding horror films could be expected to relate in a stronger fashion to measures of horror consumption.

One question remaining for future uses and gratifications investigations is how specific motives for seeking or avoiding horror films are related to the kinds of arousal needs that were explored here, and how such needs and motives jointly may help to explain horror film consumption. Other studies might probe the relationship between gratifications sought from horror films in general, gratifications obtained from specific horror films, and how the relationship between the two may help explain satisfaction with the horror film experience. Still others, which follow the expectancy-value approach to uses and gratifications (Palmgreen & Rayburn, 1985), might explore how audience expectations of horror films change over time and influence horror audience members' motives and satisfaction levels. These kinds of investigations may help illuminate not only the horror film audience members' needs, motives, and expectations but also the industry's trend toward a continuing escalation in the graphic intensity of horror film content.

REFERENCES

Austin, B. A. (1983). Researching the film audience: Purposes, procedures, and problems. *Journal of the University Film and Video Association 35*(3), 34-43.
Austin, B. (1986). Motivations for movie attendance. *Communication Quarterly, 34*(2), 115-126.
Austin, B. (1989). *Immediate seating: A look at movie audiences.* Belmont, CA: Wadsworth.
Blumler, J., Gurevitch, M., & Katz, E. (1985). Reaching out: A future for gratifications research. In K. E. Rosengren, L. A. Wenner, & P. Palmgreen (Eds.), *Media gratifications research: Current perspectives* (pp. 255-273). Beverly Hills, CA: Sage.
Blumler, J., & Katz, E. (1974). *The uses of mass communications: Current perspectives on gratifications research.* Beverly Hills, CA: Sage.
Donohew, L. (1981). Arousal and affective responses to writing styles. *Journal of Applied Communication Research, 9*(2), 109-119.
Donohew, L., Helm, D., Lawrence, P., & Schatzer, M. (1990). Sensation-seeking, marijuana use, and responses to prevention messages. In R. R. Watson (Ed.), *Prevention and treatment of drug and alcohol abuse* (pp. 73-93). Clifton, NJ: Humana Press.
Donohew, L., Palmgreen, P., & Duncan, J. (1980). An activation model of information exposure. *Communication Monographs, 47,* 295-303.
Donohew, L., Palmgreen, P., & Rayburn, J. (1987). Social and psychological origins of media use: A

lifestyle analysis. *Journal of Broadcasting & Electronic Media, 31*, 255-278.

Edwards, E. (1984). *The relationship between sensation-seeking and horror movie interest and attendance.* Unpublished doctoral dissertation, University of Tennessee, Knoxville.

Edwards, E. (1991). The ecstasy of horrible expectations: Morbid curiosity, sensation-seeking, and interest in horror movies. In B. Austin (Ed.), *Current research in film: Audience, economics, and law* (Vol. 5, pp. 19-38). Norwood, NJ: Ablex.

Helregel, B., & Weaver, J. (1989). Mood-management during pregnancy through selective exposure to television. *Journal of Broadcasting & Electronic Media, 33*, 15-33.

Hoffner, C. (1990, June). *Adolescents' preference for coping with frightening mass media: The role of dispositional empathy.* Paper presented at the meeting of the International Communication Association, Dublin, Ireland.

Hoffner, C., & Cantor, J. (1991). Factors affecting children's enjoyment of a frightening film sequence. *Communication Monographs, 58*, 41-62.

Hebb, D. O. (1955). Drives and the C.N.S. (conceptual nervous system). *Psychological Review, 62*, 243-254.

Johnston, D., & Dumerauf, J. (1990, November). *Why is Freddie a hero? Adolescents' uses and gratifications for watching slasher films.* Paper presented at the meeting of the Speech Communication Association, Chicago.

Lawrence, P. (1990). *Arousal needs and gratifications sought from theatrical movies.* Unpublished doctoral dissertation, University of Kentucky, Lexington.

Lawrence, P., & Palmgreen, P. (1991, May). *Arousal needs and gratifications sought from theatrical films.* Paper presented at the meeting of the International Communication Association, Chicago.

Lull, J. (1985). The naturalistic study of media use and youth culture. In K. E. Rosengren, L. A. Wenner, & P. Palmgreen (Eds.), *Media gratifications research: Current perspectives* (pp. 209-224). Beverly Hills, CA: Sage.

Palmgreen, P., Cook, P., Harvill, J., & Helm, D. (1988). The motivational framework of movie going: Uses and avoidances of theatrical films. In B. Austin (Ed.), *Current research in film: Audiences, economics, and law* (Vol. 4, pp. 1-23). Norwood, NJ: Ablex.

Palmgreen, P., & Lawrence, P. (1991). Avoidances, gratifications, and consumption of theatrical films: The rest of the story. In B. Austin (Ed.), *Current research in film: Audience, economics, and law* (Vol. 5, pp. 39-55). Norwood, NJ: Ablex.

Palmgreen, P., & Rayburn, J. (1985). An expectancy-value approach to media gratifications. In K. E. Rosengren, L. A. Wenner, & P. Palmgreen (Eds.), *Media gratifications research: Current perspectives* (pp. 61-72). Beverly Hills, CA: Sage.

Pearson, P. (1971). Differential relationships of four forms of novelty experiencing. *Journal of Consulting and Clinical Psychology, 37*, 323-330.

Rosengren, K., Wenner, L., & Palmgreen, P. (1985). *Media gratifications research: Current perspectives.* Beverly Hills, CA: Sage.

Rubin, A., & Windahl, S. (1986). The uses and dependency model of mass communication. *Critical Studies in Mass Communication, 3*, 184-199.

Sparks, G. (1986). Developing a scale to assess cognitive responses to frightening films. *Journal of Broadcasting & Electronic Media, 30*, 65-73.

Sparks, G., & Cantor, J. (1986). Developmental differences in fright responses to a television program depicting a character transformation. *Journal of Broadcasting & Electronic Media, 30*, 309-323.

Tamborini, R., & Stiff, J. (1987). Predictors of horror film attendance and appeal: An analysis of the audience for frightening films. *Communication Research, 14*, 415-436.

Tamborini, R., Stiff, J., & Zillmann, D. (1987). Preference for graphic horror featuring male versus female victimization. *Human Communication Research, 13*, 529-552.

Zillmann, D. (1982). Television viewing and arousal. In D. Pearl, L. Bouthilet, & J. Lazar (Eds.), *Television and behavior: Ten years of scientific progress and implications for the eighties* (DHHS Publication No. ADM 82-1196, Vol. 2, pp. 53-67). Washington, DC: U.S. Government Printing Office.

Zillmann, D. (1985). The experimental exploration of gratifications from media entertainment. In K. E. Rosengren, L. A. Wenner, & P. Palmgreen (Eds.), *Media gratifications research: Current perspectives* (pp. 225-239). Beverly Hills, CA: Sage.

Zillmann, D. (1988). Mood management through communication choices. *American Behavioral Scientist, 31*(3), 327-340.

Zillmann, D., & Bryant, J. (1985). Affect, mood and emotion as determinants of selective exposure. In D. Zillmann & J. Bryant (Eds.), *Selective exposure to communication* (pp. 157-180). Hillsdale, NJ: Lawrence Erlbaum Associates.

Zillmann, D., Hezel, R., & Medoff, N. (1980). The effect of affective states on selective exposure to televised entertainment fare. *Journal of Applied Social Psychology, 10*, 322-339.

Zillmann, D., Weaver, J., Mundorf, N., & Aust, C. (1986). Effects of and opposite-gender companion's affect to horror on distress, delight, and attraction. *Journal of Personality and Social Psychology, 51*, 586-594.

Zuckerman, M., Kolin, E., Price, L., & Zoob, I. (1964). Development of a sensation seeking scale. *Journal of Consulting Psychology, 28*, 477-482.

Chapter 11

Horror's Effect on Social Perceptions and Behaviors

Ron Tamborini and Kristen Salomonson
Michigan State University

Social research has a long history of investigations looking at the determinants of perception and behavior associated with various environmental features. When these investigations have considered the role of communication stimuli, they have often focused on violent and horrific content. Although there is reason to posit that this type of content has functional outcomes for the development and governance of a person's emotional well-being, its impact on outcomes pertaining to other individuals remains an issue of great concern. Critical research on aspects of person perception involve interpersonal attraction and perceptions of victims of violence. At the same time, research on social behavior has concentrated on aggression and social support. This chapter attempts to explore these issues as they relate to fictional horror.

SOCIAL JUDGMENTS

Extensive research on the determinants of social judgments has focused on both cognitive and affective operations related to perception. Research in this area has paid particular attention to the influence of affect and cognition on both the availability of information for use in decision making and the different processing strategies employed with information available. In conjunct these factors play a critical role in determining the outcome of social judgments. Understanding this role can provide greater insight to the impact of fictional horror on person perception.

Availability of Information

One of the most popular areas of study in affect and cognition focuses on mechanisms governing attention. The literature claims that environmental stimuli can activate the cognitive structures used in the formation of social judgments (Kaplan, 1991). This suggests that information contained in those cognitive structures can play an important role in governing social perception. As such, the impact of fictional horror on person perception can be seen as a direct function of its effect on the specific information made available during the decision-making process.

The activation of cognitive structures by affiliated stimuli governs mechanisms of attention, storage, and retrieval of information. These mechanisms determine which information is employed when formulating social judgments. Priming can be accomplished by the activation of cognitive representations or other related components in an associated network. These impact judgments by making available relevant cognitive representations about similar events, semantic categories, and other connected information (Forgas, 1991). In recent conceptions of priming, affect is a factor that may facilitate the activation of cognitive structures in the associative network (Isen, 1984; Kaplan, 1991). It is seen as influential both in priming structures to make available related information for use in decision making, or simply in its use as additional information for making judgments (Schwartz & Clore, 1988). Because mood states can be important in the activation of specific affective components, fictional horror's influence on mood and its associated network can have a strong impact on person perception. General patterns in reactions to the content of horror can lead us to expect a response set in line with related structures.

The impact of mood on activation of affective components is particularly relevant to attentional mechanisms. Attention becomes focused as activation of network components prompts vigilance to information consistent with the current state. In turn, social judgments are influenced by the greater availability of mood-consistent schema and cognitive categories (Clore & Parrot, 1991). Extensive evidence suggests that individuals in a pleasant affective state give more positive evaluations on almost all matters. This includes judgments of other people, satisfaction with their own lives, and regard for their own personal possessions (Fiedler, Pampe, & Scherf, 1986; Forgas & Bower, 1987; Forgas, Bower, & Krantz, 1984; Mayer, Mamberg, & Volanth, 1988).

Although the data are less clear in the case of negative moods (cf. Fiske & Taylor, 1991) similar outcomes might still be expected under these conditions. Several studies on social judgments suggest that person perceptions would be more disapproving for people in an unpleasant state. Research shows, for example, that frightened males judge others as more fearful and anxious (Feshbach & Singer, 1957), whereas depressed people judge others according to related negative traits (Erber, 1991). More directly, Gouaux (1971) demonstrated that mood induced by depressing films reduced judgments of interpersonal attraction. Together, these studies indicate that depression and fear seem to cloud person perception, and that this type of impact can be traced to film exposure. In concert with the abundance of research demonstrating fictional horror's impact on negative affective states, a strong case can be made for the expectation that horror will have a harsh impact on person perception.

Information-Processing Strategies

Support for this position can be found in literature investigating the impact of mood on information processing strategies. Beyond the role of availability in determining which network components are used in making decisions, both affect and cognition can influence the set used to process these activated representations. When considering the influence of fictional horror on person perception, affect can be seen to play a pivotal role in determining the processes governing the use of available information.

People in good moods have been found to use different strategies than those whose moods are neutral (Isen, 1984) or negative (Forgas, 1989). Forgas (1991) suggested that positive moods give us a sense that the environment is nonthreatening. As a result, processing strategies become based on simple heuristics rather than detailed consideration of substance. These *loose* processing strategies allow for more creativity in associations and interpretations of stimuli (Fiedler, 1988). With unpleasant moods, however, *tight* processing strategies bring concern over environmental deficiencies and negative elements. Judgments are made with close attention to valuative criteria, and risks are less likely to be taken.

The content and structure of fictional horror is unlikely to create positive affect. The frightening images, discordant music, confused camera effects, and impending doom all foster emotional distress. Although some individuals find horror amusing, evidence suggests that most find it distasteful and unappealing (Tamborini, 1987). As such, we might expect moods created by graphic horror to prompt concern with imperfection and failure to meet standards that would have bearing on person perception. It should be noted, however, that the impact of these heuristics is not so strong that it obscures all other influence. For example, factors like relational intimacy (Branscombe & Cohen, 1990) and criminal background (Forgas & Moylan, 1987) have been found to reduce mood's impact on social judgments. Nonetheless, even though they do not veil other critical factors, these heuristics appear to play a prominent role in perception.

This discussion suggests that in concert with each other information-processing strategies and availability play an important role in the formation of social judgments. Although the impact of fictional horror on the processing strategies employed is confined to different heuristic alternatives, the range of possible influences on information availability will depend on the specific content contained in the message and its impact on attentional mechanisms. Specification of the cognitive structures likely to be activated by features found in horror will delineate horror's impact on social judgments.

Structures Activated by Horror

Speculation concerning the content of modern horror films is sometimes inconsistent with evidence found in research (cf. Sapolsky & Molitor, chap. 3, this volume). As such, content analyses give us a better indication of certain features typically present and presumably able to activate cognitive structures. Not surprisingly, elements associated with violence are prominent in modern horror. A recent analysis of popular "slasher" films shows an average of over 40 beatings, shootings, and stabbings leading to major injury or death per film (Sapolsky & Molitor, chap. 3, this volume). In addition, elements related to issues of sexual violence have been studied extensively of late. As expected, examination shows several characteristics consistent with traditional gender-role stereotyped behavior. The first set of features concerns gender in relation to violence and victimization. Research indicates that males are more likely to be the aggressors, and to fight back when assaulted, whereas females seldom initiate aggression and often turn to flee from attack (Weaver, 1991). Men appear to die more often in these films, but women are shown expressing fear for much longer periods of time on screen (Sapolsky & Molitor, chap. 3, this volume). The second set of features includes the connection between violent behavior and sex. Although sexual activity is not particularly abundant in horror (Sapolsky & Molitor, chap. 3, this volume), results indicate that when scenes of a sexual nature appear in these films death follows immediately in one third of the occasions (Weaver, 1991). If the highly dramatic nature of horror makes its attributes prone to activate related cognitive structures (Berkowitz, 1993), person perception is likely to be connected to violence and gender images replete in the genre.

Interpersonal Attraction

Overall, the literature on social judgments leads us to expect a certain cognitive framework following exposure to horror. The frightening images should foster a negative affective state. A resulting *tight* processing strategy would follow, characterized by concern over environmental deficiencies and negative elements. In addition, specific content should prime features related to violence and gender, and should make information consistent with this content more accessible in the network structure. This framework can be used to understand the relationship between fictional horror and dimensions of person perception that focuses on interpersonal attraction and perceptions of female victims.

Environment's impact on judgments of person perception can be explained according to several social and psychological processes. Research on fictional horror suggests that the environment created by film exposure plays a strong role in determining interpersonal attraction. In a study investigating this issue, subjects viewed a horror film segment in the presence of an opposite-gender companion who displayed either mastery, indifference, or distress (Zillmann, Weaver, Mundorf, & Aust, 1986). Judgments of the companion's attractiveness and personality were observed. The study found only conditional support for the notion that males who displayed mastery were found to be more attractive. In addition, the opposite tendency for distressed females to be more appealing did not result. Separate from appeal, however, more positive traits were attributed to both males and female who showed mastery during exposure. In addition, among less appealing companions, those showing mastery were deemed more desirable working partners by both male and female subjects. The authors interpret these and other findings as consistent with a gender-role socialization model of affect.

Of concern here, however, is the role played by horror beyond that expected according to gender-role behavior's impact on interpersonal attraction. After all, the gender-role socialization model suggests that traditional behaviors are found attractive regardless of exposure to film. Nevertheless, an impact of film exposure on person perceptions can be discussed according to several rationales. First, frightening fiction might create a *tight* heuristic leading individuals to process more critically. Thus, behaviors that violate pertinent criteria should lead to less positive evaluations. In this case, evaluated deficiencies can be viewed in terms of gender roles, or in terms of typically valued behavior. Because the violation of gender-appropriate behaviors did not decrease the appeal of men or women in this study, this rationale is not supported by these findings. In contrast, the heightened positive evaluations for both males and females that resulted from demonstration of mastery are consistent with the notion that a *tight* heuristic focused attention on more generally valued characteristics. If this *tight* heuristics rationale is accurate, role violations should have a greater effect after exposure to horror than after more pleasing film forms. Replication employing positive film materials would greatly advance our ability to distinguish this process.

In addition to affect's influences on general processing strategies, content features found in fictional horror could prime specific behavioral attributes and focus attention on those characteristics during person perception. In this case, the film's gender representations could focus attention on gender-appropriate behavior and impact perceptions of attraction to favor actions consistent with primed gender-role structures. Although common features of horror might inform our predictions for overall exposure to the genre, the features of the film employed in the Zillmann et al. (1986) study are more useful for consideration of these specific findings. The film clip in this study showed a female being chased by Jason in *Friday the 13th: Part III*. The woman in the film not only survives an attack that killed all other male and female companions, but on separate occasions is shown stabbing Jason with a knife, knocking him out with a shovel, strangling him with a rope, and appearing to kill him with an axe as the clip ends. If the specific content here is expected to prime related categories, it seems unlikely that these would be associated with gender representations of powerless females. It is also noteworthy that no sexual content was likely to prime related structures. As such, the finding of Zillmann et al. showing more positive traits attributed to both male and female companions displaying mastery can be seen as consistent with interpretations suggesting that a prime focused attention on attributes of potent behavior.

Finally, the horror film viewing experience can be seen as an environmental attribute that carries with it many network components related to appropriate gender-role behavior. As such, the context itself could prime a behavioral scheme that would increase the attractiveness of companions who display behavior consistent with the activated opposite-gender companion structures.

The preceding information-processing and category-activation rationales are consistent with other research on this topic. Watching horror films is said to offer viewers a socially sanctioned opportunity to perform behaviors consistent with the traditional gender stereotypes (Mundorf, Weaver, & Zillmann, 1989). This exposure setting offers the chance to develop the skills needed to enact these gender-role behaviors (Zillmann et al., 1986). Modern cultural norms provide males with few situations where they can practice fear mastery behaviors, and females have few occasions to display distress or to seek male protection apart from viewing graphic horror presentations.

Perceptions of Victims

Attraction processes are not the only social judgments that have been studied in relation to horror. Exposure also seems to impact relevant cognitions concerning judgments of victims and punishment of criminal behavior. This research has investigated horror's impact on determinations of female sexual readiness, assignment of female victim blame, and punishment assessments for the perpetrators of such actions. The conflicting interpretations of findings in these investigations have made this one of the most controversial areas within the discipline.

Violence Against Women. Early work on this topic found that males exposed to a sexually violent "slasher" film increased their acceptance of beliefs that some violence against women is justified and that it may have positive consequences (Malamuth & Check, 1981). Related research demonstrated that repeated exposure to sexually violent horror led to changes in perceptions of aggression against women (Linz, Donnerstein, & Adams, 1989; Linz, Donnerstein, & Penrod, 1984). Repeated exposure resulted in aggressive film behaviors being perceived as more humorous, and less violent, offensive, and degrading to women. Exposure also led to increased enjoyment of the materials over the course of the study. These perceptions of film content featuring violence against women are consistent with research on selective exposure showing males prefer horror featuring the victimization of women, whereas women prefer the absence of such content (Tamborini, Stiff, & Zillmann, 1987). This pattern of results complements the idea that the violent images replete in horror activate cognitive structures akin to such content, and foster acceptance of such behavior as regularly occurring.

Judgments of Rape Victims. The research investigating perceptions of violence against women has led to examination of related issues. This work has focused on perceptions of rape victims and assailants who commit these crimes. The findings suggest that males who view slasher films have a tendency to prescribe lesser sentences to convicted perpetrators, and to attach greater blame to female victims. After repeated exposure, males become more likely to judge rape victims as worthless and to assess crime-related injuries as less serious (Donnerstein & Linz, 1984; Linz et al., 1984). Even film clips of sexually violent horror as brief as 10 to 12 minutes have been found to lower punitive judgments against convicted rapists (Weaver, 1987). In comparison to nonviolent erotica, males exposed to slasher films became less anxious and distressed, and were also less sympathetic toward rape victims in general (Linz, Donnerstein, & Penrod, 1988). Moreover, some of the findings for horror's impact on the perceptions of males have been observed in female viewers as well. Women exposed to horror also appear to report less concern and sympathy for victims of rape (Krafka, 1985). In addition, evidence that brief exposure to sexually violent horror can lower punitive judgments against convicted rapists has been observed in both females and males (Weaver, 1987).

Consistent with availability notions, these results have been explained in terms of film content priming schema relevant to the loss of respect for female sexual autonomy (Weaver, 1987). In support of this logic, although suggesting that other categories could explain the primed effects, research shows similar effects from brief exposure to photographs. Graphic pictures of a dead soldier and a lynching victim increased perceptions of rape-victim blame among both males and females (Wyer, Bodenhausen, & Gorman, 1985). This reveals the strong impact of even brief exposure to violent stimuli on social judgments concerning rape.

In general, interpretation of findings in this area has been an issue of considerable controversy. Arguments center both on processes of influence and specific "problematic" content. Some clear indications have been shown for short-lived priming effects, but lasting influence processes are harder to explicate. Debate persists concerning effects due to processes of learning, extinction, and desensitization. These matters become even more difficult to resolve when the specific content responsible for change is considered. Sharp distinctions have been made between effects of graphic violence, erotica, or unique combinations of the two (cf. Donnerstein & Linz, 1984; Weaver, 1991; Zillmann & Bryant, 1988). However, as most debate is centered on erotica's role in predicted outcomes, graphic horror's influence can be considered more freely.

Social Behavior

Although fictional horror's impact on social judgments is generally thought of in relation to person perception, its impact on determinants of social behavior involves specific conduct with prosocial and antisocial implications. Some of the cognitive and affective processes at work deal with attentional mechanisms similar to those believed to govern social perceptions. Other processes focus on related mechanisms that deal with learning and sensitization. In addition to this, some reflection has been given to arousal and its expected impact on the immediate experience. In all of these areas, the issues most researched deal with aggression and forms of social support.

Aggressive Behavior

In research on aggressive behavior, it is generally believed that exposure to violent images such as those typically found in horrid fiction is capable of producing certain short-term responses through activation of cognitive structures semantically related to hostile action. In the same way that by-products of priming can impact the development of social perceptions, activation of various cognitive structures may also influence displayed social behavior. Following exposure to materials with violent images or expressions, additional aggressive thoughts, scripts, and schema can be primed.

Priming Aggression. Based on a cognitive-neoassociationistic perspective, Jo and Berkowitz (1994) suggested that media can influence the perceptions of individuals so that "for a short time afterwards, their thoughts and actions are colored by what they have just seen, heard, and/or read" (p. 45). The position goes beyond most priming conceptions, however, to claim that exposure to media can do more than activate thoughts with semantically related meanings. These activated concepts can precipitate related feelings, memories, and even behaviors associated with the images presented (Berkowitz, 1993). The particular meanings primed by violent media increase the likelihood of hostile thoughts and aggressive behavior.

Evidence for priming's impact on aggression and related behaviors can be found in a variety of forms. Neuberg (1988) found that priming "competition" led to more competitive behavior during game playing. Wann and Branscombe (1990) showed that aggressive sports' primes led to a preference for aggressive activities. Carver, Ganellen, Froming, and Chambers (1983) found that subjects whose schemas were primed by an aggressive model displayed greater aggression in their subsequent behavior. In a related vein, a classic study by Berkowitz (1974) found that angered subjects were more likely to retaliate against the target of their anger if there was a gun lying on the table nearby. Additional research shows that conditions that are simply aversive can activate aggressive reactions. Studies show aggression resulting from aversive stimuli like uncomfortable temperatures (Baron, 1977; Griffitt, 1970), foul odors (Rotton, Frey, Barry, Milligan, & Fitzpatrick, 1979), smoke (Zillmann, Baron, & Tamborini, 1981), depressed moods (Finman & Berkowitz, 1989; Hynman & Grush, 1986), and objects associated with unpleasantness (Leyens & Fraczek, 1983).

Priming and Exposure to Horror. Although most work in this area has focused on other genres, it is hard to imagine that the violent portrayals so central to horror would not act as a powerful prime. This is particularly true if one takes the position that aggression can result simply from aversive antecedents like depressed moods and unpleasant stimulation. Regardless of whether the process is a "built in" association between negative affect and anger or aggression (Berkowitz, 1993), or mediated by appraisal of the situation and attributions of blame (cf. Clore, Ortony, Dienes, & Fujita, 1993), the content of horror creates conditions conducive for provoking these aggressive primes. For example, in cases where appraisal mechanisms are enacted and individuals have sophisticated standards, the content of modern horror is ripe with distressing images well-suited to distract from appraisal's intervention. On the other hand, if the process is "built in" as suggested, horror films should have strong activating potential. Their violent images "are easily recalled because of their visual, highly dramatic, and conceptually simple nature. When memories come to mind, their aggressive content could prime additional aggression-related thoughts, feelings, and motor reactions" (Berkowitz, 1993, p. 211).

Although media violence is not always expected to elicit aggressive behavior, certain conditions considered to increase this potential are typically found in graphic horror. Priming tendencies are heightened by a host of factors, including perception of the scene as aggressive, perception of the aggressive behavior as justified and rewarded, identification with the aggressor, and perceived reality of the media event (Jo & Berkowitz, 1994). Although the extent to which these features are found in fictional horror varies greatly across forms within the genre, features standard in horror are generally consistent with most of these facilitating conditions. The basic structure of horrid fiction follows a simple attack and counterattack storyline with heinous villains as the object of retaliation. This formula makes aggression very prominent in the perceptual frame, and presents reprisal as both morally justified and beneficial for survival. Identification with an aggressor is difficult to avoid because all major characters perform extremely violent acts. Although the supernatural character of some fictional horror is likely to work against the generation of aggressive action tendencies, nonsupernatural horror common in contemporary "slasher" films is likely to be perceived as more realistic.

Given these conditions, the content of fictional horror can be expected to increase the chances that hostile actions will follow from exposure to this genre. That such content can foster short-lived effects is well supported by available research. Meta-analysis of controlled laboratory studies (Andison, 1977) and experiments allowing "natural" aggression (Wood, Wong, & Chachere, 1991) convincingly demonstrate violent media's potential impact on short-term aggressive behaviors. At the same time, however, it needs to be stressed that this content does not routinely promote hostile conduct. Even when violent or aversive content primes aggressive action tendencies, mediating variables intervene in the process to determine the behavior enacted. Several authors suggest that appraisal processes at this point are the critical determinant of behavior (cf. Clore et al., 1993; Lazarus, 1991; Tamborini, chap. 7, this volume), and although aggression in some forms is a likely aftermath, other functional and more valued behaviors are also possible.

Arousal. In addition to the likelihood that violent primes will activate thoughts semantically related to hostile action tendencies, horror may induce other short-term responses relevant to the governance of aggressive conduct. Arousal is thought to play a major role in determining the strength of all behavior, regardless of its origins. Characteristics of violent images typically found in fictional horror hold qualities related to arousal's potential influence.

Arousal is thought to be a response-energizing mechanism that intensifies reactions without determining the direction of resulting experience. According to excitation transfer (Zillmann, 1982), residual arousal from previous encounters combines with arousal from subsequent events to determine the strength of a response at any given moment. In the case of media exposure, arousal from message content can combine with excitation from other environmental conditions. Whereas excitatory components determine the strength of the response, the direction of the experience is determined by dispositional considerations and appraisal of appropriate reactions.

Media's capability to promote affective reactions of great intensity is well-documented in the entertainment literature. Strong arousal has been shown to result from exposure to drama, humor, erotica, and a variety of other forms (cf. Zillmann, 1982).

Regardless of the source, arousal is expected to energize any subsequently enacted behavior. As such, arousing media should heighten the intensity of any existing inclinations to aggress. Of course, this does not mean that aggression is expected to result from exposure to arousing media. Elevated aggression is more likely in angered people, but excitation transfer will energize any type of motivated response. Transfer does not favor antisocial behavior over prosocial conduct even following exposure to violent media content. Whatever behavior is prompted by existing conditions should be intensified according to this model.

At the same time, if existing factors motivate hostile behaviors, violent media can be expected to perpetuate aggression due to its impact on affect-maintaining cognitions (Zillmann, 1979). Because affinity between violent materials and aggression is generally high in both its hedonic and behavioral characteristics, these materials have little potential to interrupt the contemplation of thoughts related to hostile acts. Different content, like comedy or other forms of engaging media dissimilar in behavior and tone, would have a greater potential to intervene in the rehearsal of animosity and curtail the existing hostile bent. Lacking this potential, violent content is likely to perpetuate thoughts, feelings, and behavior in line with the malicious intent.

Arousal From Exposure to Horror. When taking into account features of today's graphic horror, it is difficult to miss the excitatory capacity typical of the genre's content and form. Not only are the images arousing by their nature, but they are magnified by media's ability to focus our attention on details of violence often overlooked. The facial expressions of characters' pain in combination with circumstances producing their suffering have an enormous potential to arouse. With film's technical capability to present electrifying lifelike presentations of people caught in circumstances of preposterous violence, the impact of exposure to modern horrid fiction can be an exhilarating emotional experience.

For example, in most horror films, viewers are confronted with aversive stimuli like dark entrapments, demonic killers, and sharp knives. When shocking sound effects, threatening music, and fast-paced editing techniques are added, heightened excitation is likely to occur. As a result, most viewers will experience an intense affective reaction, regardless of its hedonic tone. Although appraisal can lead to different types of reactions, the normal outcome is heightened distress (cf. Tamborini, 1991). Given the earlier proposal that horror is conducive to provoking aggressive primes, the possibility that arousal will be transferred to hostile impulses cannot be overlooked. This is even more likely if one accepts the position that aversive antecedents like depressed moods and unpleasant stimulation can lead to aggressive actions (Berkowitz, 1993).

Learning From Fictional Horror. Issues surrounding media's long-term impact on aggressive behavior have received considerable attention. Although many processes have been suggested to account for its potential effects, the most well-researched deal with forms of social learning. Prolonged viewership of violence is generally believed to result in the modeling of related behaviors. Bandura (1977) asserted that the development of action patterns is based on behavior learned from environmental observation and the development of internal determinants that promote modeling. One of the best environmental sources for observational learning can be found in the images of media. When media portray acts of social hostility, learning and the development of internal determinants of aggressive behavior are likely to ensue. The outcome of this learning process is one that has been an issue of prolonged debate.

Various modeling effects have been observed in children based on studies framed within a rewards perspective (Bandura, 1977). These studies suggest that children are prone to model aggression when they have learned to associate it with reward, but they are likely to inhibit the same types of behaviors when they have learned to associate aggression with punishment. The expansive literature on the topic has been interpreted to suggest that media violence leads to real-life aggression (cf. Comstock, 1985). Geen (1994) asserted that, "the general conclusion of most . . . [is that] the observation of violence is often followed by increases in both physical and verbal aggression" (p. 152). The relevant issue for this discussion concerns certain conditions that facilitate aggression and their relationship to the experience of horror.

Factors Facilitating Aggression. The factors associated with priming's short-lived influence on the potential for hostility can also impact the development of internal regulators that govern aggressive behavior. These factors operate essentially the same across short-term and long-term processes, but certain conditions typically found in graphic horror are particularly relevant to discussion of these internal determinants.

The punishment of violence in media presentations is considered a critical factor in observational learning. When violence goes unpunished or is shown as justifiable increased viewer aggression can occur (Pearl, Bouthilet, & Lazar, 1982; Tan, 1981). As mentioned earlier, the formula for most horror makes reprisal against the evil perpetrator beneficial and morally justifiable. Of particular concern here, however, are other films within the genre in which perpetrator violence goes relatively unpunished. This outcome is now found in films that end with the perpetrator prevailing over the noble protagonist. In most "slasher" films like *Friday the 13th* this is simply a function of the fiend's indestructibility after undergoing great punishment. In cases like *Texas Chainsaw Massacre*, however, no punishment is ever inflicted on the villain. In fact, in two *Omen* films, not only does the demon not suffer, but his malevolence is greatly rewarded at the film's end. Such portrayals should be particularly detrimental to the development of internal inhibitors of aggression.

This type of ending has direct bearing on identification with the aggressor and its role in observational learning. When individuals imagine themselves as the perpetrator of gratuitous violence, this activates and strengthens related tendencies (Berkowitz, 1993). As suggested, horror fosters identification with aggressors because major characters all perform violent acts. Beyond this, however, many horror films make identification with suffering victims more difficult by focusing attention on the evil perpetrator. Excessive violence is often aimed at faceless characters whose only story purpose is to create a target for victimization. The structure makes victims almost seem deserving of the horrible treatment they receive. Once again, this content can be seen as leading to the reduction of internal inhibitors.

A final important element in determining the strength of internal regulators is the perceived reality of the event. In general, this factor should work strongly toward limiting fictional horror's influence on the development of internal regulators of aggression. Because most horrid fiction is preposterous in its nature, it should not be perceived as realistic. Research suggests that this realization should limit the likely impact of these portrayals on enactment of aggression (Berkowitz, 1984). At the same time, it should not be overlooked, that for immature populations, it is more likely that horror will not be distinguished as fiction (Hoffner & Cantor, 1990).

Desensitization and Media Violence. Closely related to learning processes governing the enactment of aggression is the process of desensitization to violence. Contrary to the feelings of aversion to violence and suffering that could increase the strength of internal regulators of aggression, evidence suggests that the images common in horror can lead to an emotional blunting or a desensitization to the violence displayed (Thomas, 1982; Thomas & Drabmen, 1977). Hence, viewers become indifferent to aggression. Berkowitz (1993) contended that this bored reaction from viewing violence in horror films (or elsewhere) will encourage aggressive behavior. This is supported by research showing greater aggression in subjects who reported being bored by violent presentations (Thomas, 1982). When individuals are no longer shocked at the presentations of killing, fighting, and gore, antagonistic thoughts activated by witnessing violence appear more likely to facilitate hostility.

Social Support

Modeling effects and activation of behaviors are not limited to aggressive action tendencies. They have been observed in a variety of prosocial contexts involving characteristics of altruism and self-control (cf. Liebert & Sprafkin, 1988). Although the research on altruism has generally not focused on exposure to fictional horror, recent work in this area has begun to explore the relationship of horrid fiction to social support. The findings generally suggest that insensitive portrayals can diminish the provision of aid. Whether through activation of related structures or the modeling of exhibited behaviors, reduced support appears to follow from exposure to fictional horror.

The results of myriad studies indicate that good moods lead individuals to help others (Dovidio, 1984). Possible explanations for these results include the focus-of-attention notion (Wood, Saltzberg, & Goldsmat, 1990), the separate-process view (Cunningham, Steinberg, & Grev, 1980), the improved-outlook explanation (Carlson, Charlin, & Miller, 1988), and the mood-maintenance hypothesis (Isen, 1987). With regard to negative moods, the situation is less clear. Some studies indicate that negative moods can induce help to reduce guilt (Carlson & Miller, 1987) or distract from one's own distress (Millar, Millar, & Tesser, 1988). However, when the helping focuses attention on the conditions producing one's own affect, the negative mood is enhanced and helping is less likely (Millar et al., 1988).

Social Support and Horror. A variety of different genres, including comedy, tragedy, and horror presentations have been employed as stimuli in studies of mood's impact on social support. Not surprisingly, fearfulness and anger are moods likely to result from exposure to fictional horror (Salomonson & Tamborini, 1994). Several studies have shown that in comparison to comedy and tragedy, exposure to horror reduces the comforting and verbal immediacy offered to distressed individuals (Borkgrevink & Tamborini, 1994; Tamborini, Bahk, & Salomonson, 1993; Tamborini, Salomonson, & Bahk, 1993a; Tamborini, Salomonson, & Bahk, 1993b). This pattern of results also holds when mood is manipulated by written horror presentations instead of film exposure (Tamborini, Salomonson, & Bahk, 1994).

Recent investigations on comforting have attempted to explain these differences in terms of environmental factors such as message sensitivity and the hedonic tone observed in different film genres. It is suggested that the sensitivity portrayed in a film may be more important than a genre's hedonic quality in determining a viewer's willingness to comfort somebody seen in distress (Tamborini, Bahk, & Salomonson, 1993; Tamborini, Salomonson, & Bahk, 1993a). Horror (which is seldom sensitive) and tragedy (when it is not) have been found to reduce forms of comforting. The logic provided suggests that the same might be expected with other forms of prosocial behavior.

Negative Hedonic Tone. Most work on the situational determinants of prosocial behavior has focused almost exclusively on messages of negative hedonic tone. In general researchers have not isolated separate types of negative emotions, despite the fact that they might be expected to cause different reactions. However, recent studies of emotional responses have examined the differences between sympathy and personal distress (cf. Eisenberg et al., 1991). Both sympathy and personal distress can induce prosocial behavior; however, the processes are thought to be very different. Sympathy-induced support is thought to result from an altruistic concern for another individual, and is expected to always produce helping responses. Personal distress, conversely, is a form of discomfort that fosters self-concern and prompts efforts to cope with aversive states. Support is unlikely to follow when aversion reduction can be easily accomplished by avoiding the distressed individual. As such, the ability of horror to incite sympathy and personal distress should determine its impact on social support. Although the violent images in horror can be expected to cause distress, the extent to which they arouse sympathy is in question.

Beyond the impact of violent portrayals on the production of increased distress, it is possible that the depersonalized images found in most horrific films are capable of producing self-concern and reduced aid (Tamborini & Salomonson, 1992). When violence is aimed at faceless characters who exist only for the purpose of victimization, these stories can be seen as teaching counterempathy (Zillmann, 1991). This has important implications for viewers who are not distressed by exposure to horror. To the extent that depersonalized images activate an insensitivity that is similar to the self-centered focus resulting from distressing materials, these images are capable of producing avoidance behavior that leads to reduced forms of support. A moment's thought makes it clear that the sensitivity of a stimulus can be independent from its distress-producing capacity. For example, although comedy can be insensitive and tragedy can be distressing, neither one is limited to those roles. At the same time, however, horror's position on these dimensions might be less free to vary.

Evidence suggests that social support can be influenced by both a message's sensitivity and hedonic tone (Tamborini et al., 1994). When sensitivity is lacking, comedy and tragedy have no advantage over horror in facilitating support. Under affective conditions of anxiety and discomfort typical during exposure to horror, the impact of portrayed sensitivity on assistance is negligible. Conversely, under different affective conditions resulting from tragedy or comedy, increased sensitivity is capable of enhancing the display of supportive responses. This strengthens the contention that although the unpleasantness contained in a message can lead to reduced assistance, messages combining unpleasantness with sensitivity are more likely to enhance social support. It may be that perception of sensitivity is impossible with the type of violence and bloodshed typical of fictional horror. In either case, diminished social support should be expected to result because sensitive portrayals are uncharacteristic in the genre.

194 TAMBORINI AND SALOMONSON

REFERENCES

Andison, F. S. (1977). TV violence and viewer aggression: A cumulation of study results. *Public Opinion Quarterly, 41*, 314-331.

Bandura, A. (1977). *Social learning theory.* Englewood Cliffs, NJ: Prentice-Hall.

Baron, R. A. (1977). *Human aggression.* New York: Plenum.

Berkowitz, L. (1974). Some determinants of impulsive aggression: Role of mediated associations with reinforcements for aggression. *Psychological Review, 81*, 165-176.

Berkowitz, L. (1984). Some effects of thoughts on anti- and prosocial influences of media events: A cognitive-neoassociation analysis. *Psychological Bulletin, 95*, 410-427.

Berkowitz, L. (1993). *Aggression: Its causes, consequences, and control.* Philadelphia: Temple University Press.

Borkgrevink, C. & Tamborini, R. (1994, November). *Empathy and the verbal immediacy of messages in face-to-face comforting.* Paper presented at the annual conference of the Speech Communication Association, New Orleans, LA.

Branscombe, N. R., & Cohen, B. M. (1990). Motivation and complexity levels as determinants of heuristic use in social judgement. In J. Forgas (Ed.), *Emotion and social judgement* (pp. 145-160). Oxford, UK: Pergamon.

Carlson, M., Charlin, V., & Miller, N. (1988). Positive mood and helping behavior: A test of six hypotheses. *Journal of Personality and Social Psychology, 55*, 211-229.

Carlson, M., & Miller, N. (1987). Explanation of the relation between negative mood and helping. *Psychological Bulletin, 102*, 91-108.

Carver, C., Ganellen, R., Froming W., & Chambers, W. (1983). Modeling: An analysis in terms of category accessibility. *Journal of Experimental Social Psychology, 19*, 403-421.

Clore, G., Ortony, A., & Dienes, B., & Fujita F. (1993). Where does anger dwell? In R. Wyer & T. Srull (Eds.), *Perspectives on anger and emotion* (pp. 57-89). Hillsdale, NJ: Lawrence Erlbaum Associates.

Clore, G., & Parrot, G. (1991). Moods and their vicissitudes: Thoughts and feelings as information. In J. Forgas (Ed.), *Emotion and social judgements* (pp. 107-125). Oxford, UK: Pergamon.

Comstock, G. (1985). Television and film violence. In S. J. Apter & A. P. Goldstein (Eds.), *Youth violence: Programs and prospects* (pp. 178-218). New York: Pergamon.

Cunningham, M. R., Steinberg, J., & Grev, R. (1980). Wanting to and having to help: Separate motivations for positive mood and guilt-induced helping. *Journal of Personality and Social Psychology, 38*, 181-192.

Donnerstein, E., & Linz, D. (1984, January). Sexual violence in the media: A warning. *Psychology Today*, 14-15.

Dovidio, J. F. (1984). Helping behavior and altruism: An empirical and conceptual overview. In L. Berkowitz (Ed.), *Advances in experimental social psychology* (Vol. 17, pp. 361-427). New York: Academic Press.

Eisenberg, N., Fabes, R. A., Schaller, M., Miller, P., Carlo, G., Poulin, R., Shea, C., & Shall, R. (1991). Personality and socialization correlates of vicarious emotional responding. *Journal of Personality and Social Psychology, 61*, 459-470.

Erber, R. (1991). Affective and semantic priming: Effects of mood on category accessibility and inference. *Journal of Experimental Social Psychology, 61*, 481-494.

Feshbach, S., & Singer, R. D. (1957). The effects of fear arousal and suppression of fear upon social perception. *Journal of Abnormal and Social Psychology, 55*, 283-288.

Fiedler, K. (1988). Emotional mood, cognitive style, and behavior regulation. In K. Fiedler & J. P. Forgas (Eds.), *Affect, cognition, and social behavior* (pp. 149-164). Toronto: Hogrefe.

Fiedler, K., Pampe, H., & Scherf, U. (1986). Mood and memory for tightly organized social information. *European Journal of Social Psychology, 16*, 149-164.

Finman, R., & Berkowitz, L. (1989). Some factors influencing the effect of depressed mood on anger and overt hostility toward another. *Journal of Research in Personality, 23*, 70-84.

Fiske, S., & Taylor, S. (1991). *Social cognition.* New York: McGraw Hill.

Forgas, J. P. (1989). Mood effects on decision-making strategies. *Australian Journal of Psychology, 41*, 197-214.

Forgas, J. P. (1991). Affect and social judgements: An introductory review. In J. P. Forgas (Ed.), *Emotion and Social Judgements* (pp. 3-31). Oxford, UK: Pergamon.

Forgas, J. P., & Bower, G. H. (1987). Mood effects on person perception judgements. *Journal of Personality and Social Psychology, 53*, 53-60.

Forgas, J. P., Bower, G. H., & Krantz, S. (1984). The influence of mood on perceptions of social interactions. *Journal of Experimental Social Psychology, 20*, 497-513.

Forgas, J. P., & Moylan, S. J. (1987). After the movies: Mood effects on social judgements. *Personality and Social Psychology Bulletin, 12*, 467-478.

Geen, R. G. (1994). Television and aggression: Recent developments in research and theory. In D. Zillmann, J. Bryant, & A. Huston (Eds.), *Media, children, and the family* (pp. 151-165). Hillsdale, NJ: Lawrence Erlbaum Associates.

Gouaux, C. (1971). Induced affective states and interpersonal attraction. *Journal of Personality and Social Psychology, 20*, 37-43.

Griffitt, W. (1970). Environmental effects on interpersonal behavior: Ambient effective temperature and attraction. *Journal of Personality and Social Psychology, 15*, 240-244.

Hoffner, C., & Cantor, J. (1990). Forewarning of threat and prior knowledge of outcomes: Effects on childrens' emotional responses to a film sequence. *Human Communication Research, 16*, 323-354.

Hynman, D. J., & Grush, J. E. (1986). Effects of impulsivity, depression, provocation, and time on aggressive behavior. *Journal of Research in Personality, 20*, 158-171.

Isen, A. M. (1984). Toward understanding the role of affect in cognition. In R. S. Wyer, Jr., & T. K. Srull (Eds.), *Handbook of social cognition* (Vol. 3, pp. 179-236). Hillsdale, NJ: Lawrence Erlbaum Associates.

Isen, A. M. (1987). Positive affect, cognitive processes, and social behavior. In L. Berkowitz (Ed.), *Advances in experimental social psychology* (Vol. 20, pp. 203-253). New York: Academic Press.

Jo, E., & Berkowitz, L. (1994). A priming effect analysis of media influences: An update. In J. Bryant & D. Zillmann (Eds.), *Media effects: Advances in theory and research* (pp. 43-61). Hillsdale, NJ: Lawrence Erlbaum Associates.

Kaplan, M. (1991). The joint effects of cognition and affect on social judgement. In J. Forgas (Ed.), *Emotion and social judgements* (pp. 73-83). Oxford, UK: Pergamon.

Krafka, C. L. (1985). Sexually explicit, sexually violent, and violent media: Effects of multiple naturalistic exposures and debriefing on female viewers (Doctoral dissertation, University of Wisconsin, Madison). *Dissertation Abstracts International, 47*, 2672B.

Lazarus, R. (1991). *Emotion and adaptation.* New York: Oxford University Press.

Leyens, J. P., & Fraczek, A. (1983). Aggression as an interpersonal phenomenon. In H. Tajfel (Ed.), *The social dimension* (Vol. 1, pp. 184-203). Cambridge, UK: Cambridge University Press.

Liebert, R. M., & Sprafkin, J. (1988). *The early window: Effects of television on children and youth* (3rd. ed.). New York: Pergamon.

Linz, D., Donnerstein, E., & Adams, S. M. (1989). Physiological desensitization and judgements about female victims of violence. *Human Communication Research, 15*, 509-522.

Linz, D., Donnerstein, E., & Penrod, S. (1984). The effects of multiple exposures to filmed violence against women. *Journal of Communication, 34*(3), 130-147.

Linz, D., Donnerstein, E., & Penrod, S. (1988). Effects of long-term exposure to violent and sexually degrading depictions of women. *Journal of Personality and Social Psychology, 55*, 758-768.

Malamuth, N. M., & Check, J. V. P. (1981). The effects of mass media exposure on acceptance of violence against women: A field experiment. *Journal of Research in Personality, 15*, 436-446.

Mayer, J. D., Mamberg, M. H., & Volanth, A. J. (1988). Cognitive domains of the mood system. *Journal of Personality, 56*, 453-486.

Millar, M. G., Millar, K. U., & Tesser, A. (1988). The effects of helping and focus of attention on mood states. *Personality and Social Psychology Bulletin, 14*, 536-543.

Mundorf, N., Weaver, J., & Zillmann, D. (1989). Effects of gender roles and self perceptions on affective reactions to horror films. *Sex Roles, 20*, 655-673.

Neuberg, S. L. (1988). Behavioral implications of information presented outside of communication awareness: The effect of subliminal presentation of trait information on behavior in the prisoner's dilemma game. *Social Cognition, 6,* 207-230.

Pearl, D., Bouthilet, L., & Lazar, J. (Eds.). (1982). *Television and behavior: Ten years of scientific progress and implications for the eighties* (Vol. 2). Washington, DC: U.S. Government Printing Office.

Rotton, J., Frey, J., Barry, T., Milligan, M., & Fitzpatrick, M. (1979). The air pollution experience and physical aggression. *Journal of Applied Social Psychology, 9,* 397-412.

Salomonson, K., & Tamborini, R. (1994, November). *Stable and situational determinants of comforting: A model of empathy, film genre, and mood state.* Paper presented at the annual conference of the Speech Communication Association, New Orleans, LA.

Schwartz, N., & Clore, G. L. (1988). How do I feel about it? The informative function of affective states. In K. Fiedler & J. P. Forgas (Eds.), *Affect, cognition, and social behavior* (pp. 44-62). Toronto: Hogrefe.

Tamborini, R. (1987). Emotional responses to horror: Appeal scores. Unpublished raw data.

Tamborini, R. (1991). Responding to horror: Determinants of exposure and appeal. In J. Bryant & D. Zillmann (Eds.), *Responding to the screen: Reception and reaction processes* (pp. 305-329). Hillsdale, NJ: Lawrence Erlbaum Associates.

Tamborini, R., Bahk, C., & Salomonson, K. (1993, May). *The moderating impact of film exposure on the relationship between empathy and comforting.* Paper presented to the annual conference of the International Communication Association, Washington, DC.

Tamborini, R., & Salomonson, K. (1992, November). *The relationship of empathy to comforting behavior following film exposure.* Paper presented at annual conference of the Speech Communication Association, Chicago.

Tamborini, R., Salomonson, K., & Bahk, C. (1993a). The relationship of empathy to comforting behavior following film exposure. *Communication Research, 20,* 723-738.

Tamborini, R., Salomonson, K., & Bahk, C. (1993b, November). *Situational determinants of comforting: The impact of messages differing in hedonic quality.* Paper presented at the annual conference of the Speech Communication Association, Miami, FL.

Tamborini, R., Salomonson, K., & Bahk, C. (1994, July). *The relationship of empathy, hedonic quality, and sensitivity to comforting behavior.* Paper presented at the annual conference of the International Communication Association, Sydney, Australia.

Tamborini, R., Stiff, J., & Zillmann, D. (1987). Preference for graphic horror featuring male versus female victimization: Individual differences associated with personality characteristics and past film viewing experiences. *Human Communication Research, 13,* 529-552.

Tan, A. S. (1981). *Mass communication theories and research.* Columbus, OH: Grid.

Thomas, M. H. (1982). Physiological arousal, exposure to a relatively lengthy aggressive film, and aggressive behavior. *Journal of Research in Personality, 16,* 72-81.

Thomas, M. H., & Drabmen, R. (1977, August). *Effects of television on expectations of others' aggression.* Paper presented at annual meeting of the American Psychological Association, San Francisco.

Wann, D. L., & Branscombe, N. R. (1990). Person perception when aggressive or nonaggressive sports are primed. *Aggressive Behavior, 16,* 27-32.

Weaver, J. B., III (1987). Effects of portrayals of female sexuality and violence against women on perceptions of women (Doctoral Dissertation, Indiana University). *Dissertation Abstracts International, 48,* 2482A.

Weaver, J. (1991). Are slasher horror films sexually violent? A content analysis. *Journal of Broadcasting and Electronic Media, 35,* 385-392.

Wood, J., Saltzberg, J., & Goldsmat, L. (1990). Does affect induce self-focused attention? *Journal of Personality and Social Psychology, 58,* 899-908.

Wood, W., Wong, F. Y., & Chachere, J. G. (1991). Effects of media violence on viewers' aggression in unconstrained social interaction. *Psychological Bulletin, 109,* 371-383.

Wyer, R. S., Jr., Bodenhausen, G. V., & Gorman, T. F. (1985). Cognitive mediators of reactions to rape. *Journal of Personality and Social Psychology, 48,* 324-348.

Zillmann, D. (1979). *Hostility and aggression.* Hillsdale, NJ: Lawrence Erlbaum Associates.

Zillmann, D. (1982). Television viewing and arousal. In D. Pearl, L. Bouthilet, & J. Lazar (Eds.), *Television and behavior: Ten years of scientific progress and implications for the eighties*

(DHHS Publication No. ADM 82-1196, Vol. 2, pp. 53-67). Washington, DC: U.S. Government Printing Office.

Zillmann, D. (1991). Empathy: Affect from bearing witness to the emotions of others. In J. Bryant & D. Zillmann (Eds.), *Responding to the screen: Reception and reaction processes* (pp. 135-169). Hillsdale, NJ: Lawrence Erlbaum Associates.

Zillmann, D., & Bryant, J. (1988). The effects of prolonged exposure to pornography on family values. *Journal of Family Issues, 9*, 518-544.

Zillmann, D., Weaver, J., Mundorf, N., & Aust, C. (1986). Effects of an opposite-gender companion's affect to horror on distress, delight, and attraction. *Journal of Personality and Social Psychology, 51*, 586-594.

Zillmann, D., Baron, R., & Tamborini, R. (1981). Social costs of smoking: Effects of tobacco smoke on hostile behavior. *Journal of Applied Psychology, 11*, 548-561.

Author Index

Subject Index

A

Activation-arousal
  framework for, 131–133
  implications of, 133–136
  in response to horror, 125–131, 136–137
Aggressive behavior
  factors facilitating, 192–193
  in response to horror, 188–190
  influence of priming on, 188–192
Arousal
  in response to horror, 163, 190–191
  need for
      horror film preferences, 165–167
      movie preferences, 163–165

C

Catharsis
  of fear and phobias, 26, 88
Cognitive-motivational-relational theory,
      104–106
  reactions to graphic horror, 113–114
Cognitive-neoassociationistic perspective, 188
Coping processes
  behavioral outcomes, 120–121
  coping styles, 137–142
  emotional outcomes, 118–120
  in response to horror, 116, 133–136

D

Developmental shifts
  concreteness of thought, 71
  perceptual to conceptual, 71–72
  perceptually dominated, 71

theories of cognitive development, 74

E

Economic history of film industry, 50–54
Emotional reactions
  aesthetic responses to horror, 103–105
  components of, 126–127
  differences in temperament, 129–131
  dispositional approach to, 126–131
  importance of coping style in, 137–141
  in response to horror, 108–109, 125–126
  individual differences in, 127–129
  model of, 111–113, 114–116
Empathy
  in response to horror, 108–109
  dimensions in, 109–111
  model of, 111–113, 114–116
Experience of relief, *see* Catharsis

F

Fairy tales, 15, 16, 82–83
Fright reactions
  blood sports, 20–23
  conditioning in, 65
  explanation of, 64–65
  expression of fear, 26, 28, 82–83, 85–88,
      90–91, 98–99
  fear inducing content
      dangers and injuries, 65–66
      distortions of natural forms, 66
      sense of endangerment, 66–69
  focus of attention notion, 194
  film induced, 64, 68, 107
  identification, 27, 192–193